Errata

References made to Spener 1997b in Chapter 11, pages 233 to 257, should have been made to U.S. Commission on Immigration Reform. 1997. *Migration Between Mexico and the United States.* Binational Study on Migration. Washington, D.C.: U.S. Commission on Immigration Reform.

THE U.S.-MEXICO BORDER

THE U.S.-MEXICO BORDER

Transcending Divisions, Contesting Identities

edited by
David Spener and Kathleen Staudt

LYNNE
RIENNER
PUBLISHERS

BOULDER
LONDON

Published in the United States of America in 1998 by
Lynne Rienner Publishers, Inc.
1800 30th Street, Boulder, Colorado 80301

and in the United Kingdom by
Lynne Rienner Publishers, Inc.
3 Henrietta Street, Covent Garden, London WC2E 8LU

Library of Congress Cataloging-in-Publication Data
The U.S.-Mexico border :   transcending divisions, contesting identities
  /   edited by David Spener and Kathleen Staudt.
       p.   cm.
     Includes bibliographical references and index.
     ISBN 1-55587-796-6 (hard cover :   alk. paper)
     1. Mexican-American Border Region.   2. United States—Relations—
Mexico.   3. Mexico—Relations—United States.   4. Mexican-American
Border Region—Economic conditions.   5. Mexican-American Border
Region—Politics and government.   6. Mexican-American Border Region—
Social conditions.   7. Mexican-American Border Region—Ethnic
relations.   I. Spener, David, 1961– .   II. Staudt, Kathleen A.
F787.U66   1998
303.48'273072—dc21   98-29810
                                                                          CIP

British Cataloguing in Publication Data
A Cataloguing in Publication record for this book
is available from the British Library.

Printed and bound in the United States of America

     5 4 3 2 1

Contents

Acknowledgments   vii

Part 1   Conceptualizing Borders

1   The View from the Frontier:
Theoretical Perspectives Undisciplined
Kathleen Staudt and David Spener   3

2   Nations and Borders:
Romantic Nationalism and the Project of Modernity
Víctor Zúñiga   35

**Part 2   Economic, Political, and
Social Organization on the Border**

3   Re-Presenting the Public Interest on the U.S.-Mexico Border
Michelle A. Saint-Germain   59

4   Small Business, Social Capital, and Economic Integration
on the Texas-Mexico Border
David Spener and Bryan R. Roberts   83

5   Visiting the Mother Country:
Border-Crossing as a Cultural Practice
Olivia Ruiz   105

6   Mexico Reflects on the United States: *Colonias,* Politics,
and Public Services in Fragmented Federalism
Kathleen Staudt, with Angélica Holguín and Magda Alarcón   121

Part 3   Bordered Identities

7   Globalizing Tenochtitlán? Feminist Geo-Politics:
     Mexico City as Borderland
     Julie A. Murphy Erfani   143

8   Border Signs: Graffiti, Contested Identities,
     and Everyday Resistance in Los Angeles
     Bradley J. Macdonald   169

9   The Competing Meanings of the Label "Chicano" in El Paso
     Pablo Vila   185

Part 4   Debordering and Rebordering

10   New Relationships Between Territory and State:
     The U.S.-Mexico Border in Perspective
     Mathias Albert and Lothar Brock   215

11   Conclusion: Rebordering
     David Spener and Kathleen Staudt   233

The Contributors   259
Index   261
About the Book   264

Acknowledgments

As always, many people behind the scenes make completion of a project of this kind possible. In addition to thanking the editors at Lynne Rienner Publishers—Bridget Julian and Lesli Brooks Athanasoulis—each of us has a number of individuals and institutions whose support we wish to acknowledge.

* * *

My border research and writing would not have been possible had it not been for the support of several institutions, including the Ford Foundation (Mexico City and New York offices), which financed much of my initial work in the region; the Population Research Center (PRC) of the University of Texas, where I worked as a graduate assistant and postdoctoral research scientist from 1992 to 1997; and the Tom and Mary Turner Faculty Fellowship from Trinity University, which provided financial support during the final phase of writing and editing. The Colegio de la Frontera Norte was a partner with the PRC in the research funded by the Ford Foundation and provided a base for research and meetings in Mexico as well as a wealth of data. I have been able to count on a group of friends and colleagues for indispensable orientation, advice, and hospitality while working in the field, including Angela Escajeda, Jorge Carrillo, Roland Chanove, Tim Dunn, Karl Eschbach, Alfredo Hualde, Jorge Mendoza, Fernando Pozos, Néstor Rodríguez, Sergio Tamayo, and Pablo Vila. In addition, I owe a substantial debt to Frank D. Bean and Bryan R. Roberts of the PRC, who not only have been my sociological mentors but also have given me unwavering support in my research on the border. I especially wish to thank Kathleen Staudt for inviting me to collaborate with her on this book, and also for the counsel and material help she provided during my many research trips to El Paso over the last six years. Finally, I wish to acknowledge the patience and perseverance of my family, whose love and support keep me going.   —*David Spener*

I would like to thank the National Science Foundation (HRD #9253027), which supported faculty and students in research on informal economies at the U.S.-Mexico border. In particular, I was blessed with colleagues like Alejandro Lugo, Cheryl Howard, and Gregory Rocha, who worked with me on the research. My good colleague and friend, Beatriz Vera, is a source of inspiration and support. Political science colleagues and librarians at the University of Texas at El Paso offer a congenial and supportive workplace. Members of my family, husband Robert Dane'el, son Mosi, and daughter Asha, provide deeper meaning for my life.

—Kathleen Staudt

Part 1

Conceptualizing Borders

1

The View from the Frontier:
Theoretical Perspectives Undisciplined

Kathleen Staudt and David Spener

As we straddle the border between Mexico and the United States at the dawn of a new millennium, we are reminded of Pierre Vilar's striking remark that "the history of the world is best observed from the frontier" (Sahlins 1989: xv). Until recently, the social sciences tended to approach this border as a puzzling anomaly in need of explanation, a space whose main attraction as an object of study has been its dramatic exceptionality— a space that was, on the one hand, neither Mexican nor "American" and, on the other, both Mexican and "American." In many senses, the border has been a truly "in-between" space where the routinized international relations of daily life have produced not an outward-looking cosmopolitanism but rather a curiously provincial culture aware of its own unique status as a crossroads. It is our contention, however, that the Mexico-U.S. border has become something more than a cultural curiosity.

Instead, in this chapter we argue that the border now represents a *global* crossroads in which the forces of world historical change inscribe themselves in stark relief in the lives and ways of life we encounter there. Where before the border may have been a useful outlier against which we might compare the central tendencies of the respective national spaces of Mexico and the United States, today the borderlands have become an important staging ground for economic, cultural, social, and political forces that transcend the nation-state and, in so doing, call into question its continued relevance as a unit of analysis. Paradoxically, as our doubts about the appropriateness of the nation-state as a unit of analysis grow, Vilar's comment remains trenchant, though perhaps not in the way he intended. If formerly the perspective we gained from the border was that of looking from the margins of history back toward the center, now the border stands at the center and offers us a front-row view of history's drama unfolding.[1]

This book is about the boundary between the United States and Mexico and the inhabitants of the social space defined by the existence of that political dividing line. It is typical for articles and books about the border and the borderlands to start off by defining the dimensions of their subject in statistical terms: The international boundary is nearly 2,000 miles long. In 1990, the combined population of Mexican *municipios* and U.S. counties that abut the border was 8.9 million, but if we construe the borderlands as comprising six Mexican and four U.S. border states, the borderlands population leaps to nearly 52 million persons (Martínez 1996: xviii). Other relevant statistics are typically offered: the number of maquiladora plants located in Mexican border cities and their contribution to Mexico's foreign earnings, the extremely high poverty rates of most of the U.S. border counties, the number of auto and pedestrian border crossings made annually, the value of goods passing back and forth between the two countries over the land border, the large proportion of Mexican immigrants and Mexican Americans in the populations of the U.S. border counties, the numbers of Mexican nationals apprehended by the U.S. Border Patrol annually—and the list goes on.

In this volume, we take a different approach. Rather than viewing the Mexico-U.S. border and the borderlands as a single, territorially specific space, we examine the border as an ongoing, dialectical process that generates multiple borderland spaces, some of which are not located very close to the official international boundary itself. This approach follows the lead of Roger Rouse (1991: 17), who argues that we are today witnessing "a proliferation of border zones" as "the international border is widening and, at the same time, miniature borders are erupting throughout the two countries." Rouse, for his part, draws upon the work of pioneering border scholar Americo Paredes, who recognizes that a border exists not only as a line on a map but also as "a sensitized area where two cultures or two political systems come face to face" (Paredes 1978: 68). Writing before the publication of Rouse's seminal article, Thomas Weaver noted that "border culture" occurred wherever people transacted and negotiated in its terms:

> Following this line of thought, we could conclude that when we speak of the boundaries of border culture and subculture we are referring to something akin to the complex outline of the leaves and branches of a tree, as it sways in the wind and changes with the season, and we try to define where its moving boundaries integrate and separate from the air and sky. (Weaver 1983: 250–251)

Accordingly, in our view the border operates not only in the vicinity of the international line itself, but any place in either country where Mexican and U.S. national systems confront one another: at the entrance to welfare offices in New York; at the *aduanas* (customs checkpoint) of the international airport in Mexico City; in the treatment of Mexican workers by U.S. factory owners in both Los Angeles and Aguascalientes; on the picket line of farmworkers in Watsonville, California; in a Mexican grocery store in Chicago or a dance hall in Austin, Texas; in the U.S. chamber of commerce offices in Guadalajara; or under the golden arches of McDonald's in Monterrey.[2]

In addition, we recognize that not only are border "zones" proliferating in the interior of both Mexico and the United States, but also that the dynamic characteristics of border space differ from place to place along the official border. Striking differences are evident among the various pairs of border cities. It becomes rapidly apparent to even the most casual observer that in spite of sharing the same border, Ciudad Juárez–El Paso, *ambos* (both) Nogales, and San Diego–Tijuana are three quite different sorts of places that exhibit contrasting forms of binational interaction and ways of life. Occasionally, we have found this aspect of border reality reflected in the remarks of Mexican informants who talk not of a singular border but of a plurality of borders—not *la frontera* but *las fronteras*—in order to distinguish, for instance, between *la frontera de Nogales* and *la frontera de Laredo*.

Analysts have struggled with the question of which of these *fronteras* is the one we should use as the basis for our borderwide generalizations. For James Clifford, "The quintessential borderland is El Paso/Juárez. Or is it Tijuana/San Diego?" (1994: 304; but see Smith and Tarallo on Texas and Arizona, not California, as "trend-setters" 1995: 674–675). We believe that this question misses the point and prefer the strategy advocated by Víctor Zúñiga (see Chapter 2, this volume): "On each border, and at diverse points along a single border, singular syntheses are produced that must be the object of particular observations. For this reason, a border and the diverse neuralgic points that compose it must be seen as a complex confluence of adjacencies." At the same time, we concur wholeheartedly with Robert Alvarez that as a spatial icon, the "Mexican-U.S. border [has become] the model of border studies and borderlands genre throughout the world" (1995: 451).

We both live in Texas (Staudt in El Paso and Spener in San Antonio), a state where adjacency to Mexico is a part of everyday reality. As a result, the border is important to us as a geographical construct with tangible social consequences. But borderlines exist in other dimensions of human experience aside from those based on national territory, and these borderlines form part of our intellectual agenda as well. These lines often take on a political character as they reflect the opposing interests and identities of workers and bosses, men and women, faculty and administrators. They also reflect the compartmentalization of our collective intellectual project, as institutionally imposed disciplinary boundaries limit the ability of political scientists, sociologists, anthropologists, economists, and geographers to articulate a mutually intelligible discourse. Borderlines pervade our public and private lives, as well as our teaching and academic research.

People react to lines, whether material or metaphorical, in a variety of ways: they contest them, accept them, draw new ones, or find ways to get around them. Nonetheless, the lines themselves create special kinds of spaces that often differ from the core, the mainstream, or the heartlands. Borders also imply margins—the ends, the beginnings, the bridges, the marginal divides, and the opportune frontiers. Homi Bhabha recognizes borders as "in-between places" (1994: 309) and in so doing has furthered a philosophical and literary discussion of borders in which the U.S.-Mexico border already played a prominent role, as manifested in the pioneering verse of Gloria Anzaldúa (1987). This collection embeds discussions of a number of symbolic frontiers, borders, and "marginals" in the "real" space of the U.S.-Mexico border. It does so in an attempt to develop the notion that the gap between materialist and metaphorical conceptions of borders is bridgeable and because we believe that this particular borderland allows us to observe certain symbolic discourses more clearly than in the heartland.

In order to bridge the metaphorical-material border gap, we must give our disciplined attention to rethinking boundaries so that vantage-point differences can deepen understanding. In other words, we invest concerted energy into challenging the rigid academic space and territory that have been carved up and mapped over the last century. Transgressors have redefined and used many mainstream disciplinary conceptions in refreshing ways, some of which we illustrate later. In so doing, they have been able to create new vantage points beyond disciplinary boundaries that contest the mundane vocabulary that individual disciplines have canonized. Disciplines may or may not get an intellectual shot in the arm from outside vantage points. Usually they do, but creative bursts emerge from within disciplines as well. With borderlands, things are different, and we contend borders cannot be understood within disciplinary boxes. Territorial, institutional, and symbolic borders are constantly emerging, getting reconstructed, and contested. No one vantage point can handle the complexities of time and space therein.

This introductory chapter is divided into five parts. First, we discuss the variety of ways in which borders are an integral feature of the human condition. We argue that although borders appear to be a necessary feature of social organization, they also exist as both a source and product of human conflict. Second, we discuss two types of border discourses, one material and the other metaphorical. Third, we tap into imaginative thinking on borders that transgresses canonized disciplinary vocabularies. Fourth, we explore how maps might be redrawn to reflect an increasingly integrated global system. Finally, we conclude our chapter with an outline of this collection's contributions, whose authors put elements of our approach into practice.

Borders and the Human Condition

Borders are at once essential to the human enterprise and an indicator of its greatest failures. In their most commented-upon guise as the territorial limits of nation-states, borders generally reflect either (1) the inability of culturally distinct groups to get along with each other well enough to form a single government or (2) the ability of one or more national groups to exclude or enclose another group or groups. That said, without borders, the world as we know it would cease to exist. In this section, we discuss borders and boundary-establishing processes with regard to several ubiquitous features of human society: language, the division of labor, and association. We then return to a brief consideration of national boundaries as but the most prominent, visible manifestation of border-making processes that are implicated in the other aspects of social organization we discuss.

Borders and Language[3]

We need borders. In the first instance, this is because human inquiry and knowledge depend upon the development and use of language to make sense of the world, and language depends upon borders to construct the concepts required for cognition and communication. Through language, humans express and transmit concepts derived from their experiences of nature and society. These concepts may be expressed in a variety of ways in language, but for the sake of simplicity we will limit our discussion here to words, their most typical symbolic form. Words are discrete entities, separated from one another by semantic boundaries that permit one word to correspond to meaning X, whereas another word corresponds to meaning Y, such that X and Y can be distinguished from one another.[4] This process of semantic "bordering" is crucial to human cognitive development, for it is through the acquisition of word-based language that individuals come to perceive order in an inchoate world of sensual experience. It is also crucial to the development of society, for all human relationships and social projects depend upon the ability of individuals to communicate conceptually with one another.

Although in some ultimate sense an individual's cognitive development is unique and solitary, language-learning is an intrinsically social process. Each individual is taught the words of the language of her elders and her peers and is thus apprenticed into a shared system of meanings that she did not herself intend or create (though she subsequently uses this linguistic and cultural inheritance to express her creativity). Just as language acquisition is an inherently social process, depending as it does upon interaction between two or more interlocutors, so is the process of semantic bordering that it presupposes. Again, although in some plausible first instance a unique individual proposed a conceptual distinction between two or more objects she encountered in nature and subsequently attempted to represent that distinction to other persons through some kind of aural or visual symbol, both the concepts and the symbols used to represent them had to be understood and accepted by her interlocutors in order for ongoing communication to ensue.

The task of establishing consensus regarding the proper conceptual distinctions to be made and the semantic boundaries that need to be imposed in order to preserve them is not a straightforward one, but intrinsically involves a great deal of negotiation. This is because the recognition of distinction, whether among observable objects and actions or intangible principles and internal states, is a subjective act whose communication requires interaction among a variety of individual subjectivities. The perceptions, intentions, and interests of these many individuals do not necessarily coincide but may in fact collide and compete. Meaning does not leap out from nature or fall from on high to become implanted in human consciousness in the form of an unadulterated word, which is then used by all human beings who have received it in like manner. Rather, the meaning of any word in a language is the ongoing historical product of a series of contestations and negotiations among the many individuals and groups who have used it to communicate with one another. Like other social processes, the process of semantic bordering takes on a political character to the extent that its participants exercise individual or collective power to defend their interests and achieve their ends.

Thus, although the imposition of semantic borders is necessary in order to establish the conceptual distinctions that permit cognitive development and social communication, the determination of these borders is also political. As such it is fraught with the possibility of conflict, discontinuity, domination, and injustice. The semantic borders between concepts shift over time as a consequence of the interplay of the subjective positions taken by the participants in a discourse in which given concepts are present. The meanings of words, therefore, are not fixed but instead reflect the continuous relocation of the socially determined boundaries that separate them from other words. Where semantic boundaries are located and how they are determined have consequences that are not "merely" semantic. This is especially the case with certain concept categories involving race, gender, sexuality, and nationality, upon which social hierarchies are often built.[5] In addition, these boundaries do not neatly separate concepts, but rather allow for considerable conceptual "bleed-through" or "overlap" between words that border one another in semantic space. This may be especially so when the position of semantic boundaries is hotly contested among parties to a discourse, such that there is insufficient consensus to permit unqualified distinctions between concepts.

When Bonnie Urciuoli (1995: 539) notes that "borders are places where commonality ends abruptly," we may simultaneously evaluate her statement in two different but related ways. First, it may be interpreted as a reflection of the human attempt to discipline a continuous, undifferentiated universe into a set of discrete, bounded entities that may be described by language. Second, we may take it as a reflection of the social conflict inherent in determining where boundaries should be established. Nonetheless, we must constantly remind ourselves that semantic borders—because of the complexities of both the world and the human mind, as well as the impossibility of achieving stable consensus on the meanings of words—are imperfect, riddled with holes, ambiguities, and inconsistencies. The distinction implied by the existence of a semantic-conceptual border is thus not absolute but relative, contingent, dialectic. Words are defined as much by what they mean as by what they don't. On the one hand, the boundary between two closely related but apparently distinct concepts fades when each is considered relative to a third concept that differs from the other two in a similar way. On the other hand, hybrid concepts arise or are "discovered" that straddle or transcend semantic boundaries and call into question the reality of the distinctions those boundaries demarcate. Thus, although from one vantage point commonality ends at the border, from others the border is itself imperceptible.

Borders and the Division of Labor

Not only are borders and boundary-making processes essential to human cognition and communication, but they are also intrinsic to another fundamental social process that has permitted the development of modern societies: the division of labor. This process was the subject of much of the writing of Karl Marx, Emile Durkheim, and Max Weber, the three great "classical" theorists of modernity. The division of labor refers, of course, to the process by which productive tasks become separated and more specialized, and may be conceived of in narrow, economic terms or broader social terms, where it becomes synonymous with the term *social differentiation.* In both senses, the division of labor presupposes the establishment of material and mental borders (1) among functions and roles; (2) among the institutions that carry out society's functions; and (3) among the individuals who occupy specific roles within institutions. All three theorists concurred that the division of labor was crucial to the growth in productivity that accompanied and furthered industrialization, which at the same time profoundly transformed social organization. In addition, each theorist recognized social ills that resulted from the division of labor in modern society.

For Marx, the division of labor in industrial capitalist society depended upon divisive arrangements that resulted in multiple alienations, exploitations, and conflicts. These social divisions included (1) the imposition of private property; (2) the separation of mental from manual labor; (3) the rise of antagonistic social classes whose contributions to and rewards from production systematically diverged; and (4) the market-driven competition among capitalist firms, on the one hand, and among workers themselves, on the other. At the same time, in Marx's work we see that the capitalist division of labor releases productive forces of such intensity that they annihilate nation-state boundaries on the way to establishing a world market, thus "destroying the former natural exclusiveness of separate nations" (Marx and Engels 1972: 196). Some of Marx's intellectual heirs have, of course, reworked the question of the division of labor and national boundaries as they have discussed boundaries between different "zones" of the world economy—core, peripheral, and semiperipheral—or have argued that a "new" international division of labor has replaced the old international division between the cosmopolitan countries and their former colonies (Frobel, Heinrichs, and Kreye 1980; Wallerstein 1974).

For Durkheim, the progress of the division of labor is accompanied by increased mutual interdependence of the functional parts of the social organism—a generally healthy development that he referred to as "organic solidarity." At the same time, however, he finds that organic solidarity was not always sufficient to overcome the dissolution of a common morality that he believed integrated premodern societies. Under modern conditions, human communities were increasingly fragmented by the many functional boundaries that crisscrossed them. This fragmentation, in turn, could give rise to anomie and its attendant social pathologies (Durkheim 1984). Thus, Durkheim views the division of labor positively in the sense that it was a necessary part of the progress and overall health of a cooperative society but remains troubled by the possibility that resultant social isolation could produce tragic outcomes—such as suicide—for a growing number of individuals.

Weber recognizes that the progress of the division of labor coincided with the rationalization of social life. For rationalization to be achieved, social differentiation needed to occur in such a way that elements of society were increasingly constituted as discrete, bounded entities that could be subjected to measurement and control. Bureaucracy typified this sort of rationalization in Weber's work (1946). In bureaucracy, we find borders everywhere enforced—between its specialized offices, different levels of hierarchical authority, between agencies with distinct administrative responsibilities, and between administrators and those who are administered.[6] Weber marvels at the efficiencies gained through the compartmentalization of tasks achieved through the division of labor but is also alarmed at the dehumanization of social relations that arise in an administered society. The borders delineating the compartments to which individuals were consigned could become an "iron cage" inhabited by "specialists without spirit, sensualists without heart" (Weber 1930: 182).

Borders and Association

Another essential feature of human societies, in addition to language and the division of labor, involves borders and the border-making process: the tendency of humans to form social groups for a wide range of purposes. From the association of individuals, groups emerge and, whether formally or informally, distinguish their members from those of other groups by establishing social boundaries within which certain types of solidary relations may be assumed, at least in principle, and outside of which they may not. These group identities and the solidarities they foster mobilize resources for collective action in ways that would be difficult to imagine in a world in which such particularistic identities and solidarities did not exist, that is, in a world of universal humanity in which all manner of social distinctions had been erased. As Weber notes in *Economy and Society*, the social relationships that motivate group formation may be either communal or associative, where the former refers to relations based on sentiment or tradition and the latter refers to relations based upon a common rational interest. Groups vary in terms of their desire and ability to exclude outsiders and promote internal cohesion. According to Weber, the exclusion of outsiders from the in-group relationship "[provides] the parties to it with the opportunities for the satisfaction of spiritual or material interests [through] cooperative action or by a compromise of interests" (1978: 43). To the extent that limiting group membership allows members to develop strong affectual bonds and trust, members of bounded groups are able to mobilize resources for their individual or collective projects that might not otherwise be available to them.[7] The motives for closure of in-group relationships vary widely, from the intimately affectual in the case of erotic relationships, to the spiritual in the case of shared religious belief, to the cultural and historical in the case of ethnic groups and nationalities, to pecuniary interest in the case of the business enterprise. It is no accident, however, that the major component institutions of contemporary society— marriage, the firm, the nation-state—are bordered organizations based upon closed relationships in which "participation of certain persons is excluded, limited, or subjected to conditions" (Weber 1978: 43). In a sense, the historical strength and vitality of these institutions derives in large measure from the borders that surround them.

Although the establishment of bounded groups is an essential feature of human sociability and identity-formation, we also find this process at the root of considerable social conflict. Borders and bordering are especially troubling to the moral impulses of universalist humanism, for they promote segregation as a principle of social organization. In his famous "Letter from Birmingham Jail," Martin Luther King, Jr., borrowed from the writings of Martin Buber and Paul Tillich to denounce state-sponsored segregation as sinful because it "substitutes an 'I-it' relationship for an 'I-thou' relationship and . . . relegates persons to the status of things" and because it constitutes "the existential expression of man's tragic separation, his awful estrangement, his terrible sinfulness" (King 1964: 85). In postmodern discourse, we find this sentiment echoed in concern for the social construction of "the Other," whose difference justifies her exploitation and domination.[8]

Linking the notion of bordering with that of segregation calls attention to the fact that the benefits accruing to members of exclusionary groups can come at the expense of those who are excluded, particularly if the exclusion is forcible. With regard to African Americans, Manning Marable (1992) discusses how ethnicity and race represent flip sides of the segregation coin, one morally positive, and the other morally repugnant. According to Marable, African American ethnicity "was derived from the cultural synthesis of the population's African heritage and its experiences in American society, first as slaves and subsequently as sharecroppers, as industrial laborers, and by the 1980s, as the core of the postindustrial workforce in the declining central cities of North America" (1992: 188). In other words, African American ethnicity was the creation of a cultural group identity by the group itself. Race, however, was something that was done to African Americans for the benefit of whites: "Race is a totally different dynamic, rooted in the structures of exploitation, power, and privilege. 'Race' is an artificial social construction, which was deliberately imposed on various subordinated groups of people" (1992: 188).[9]

We see this distinction appearing in a different form and with regard to other groups in the work of a number of sociologists who have been investigating the social and economic ramifications of the growth of immigrant ethnic "enclaves" or "niches" in the major U.S. cities. Alejandro Portes and his collaborators, especially, discuss the advantages that accrue to groups that are able to use ethnic boundaries to create distinct economic enclaves within which their members enjoy advantages unavailable to them outside the enclave (Portes 1995; Portes and Bach 1985; Portes and Zhou 1992).[10] Roger Waldinger's (1996) notion of economic niche is similar to Portes's enclave insofar as it describes the way in which "occupational closure" quickly sets in around types of work in which immigrants become concentrated. This closure involves "networks of information and support [which] are bounded by ethnic ties" (Waldinger 1996: 21). Unlike Portes and his coauthors, however, Waldinger describes the flip side of such niches: the ethnic boundaries that surround them work against the entry of other groups, including African Americans, such that internal solidarity is transformed into external discrimination.

As employed by Marble, both the concepts of ethnicity and race involve bordering processes, but each operates in an opposite direction from the other. For African Americans, the ethnic borders around their cultural identity separated them from white Americans but did not imply the subordination and exploitation of whites by blacks. The racial borders that were created around black Americans, conversely, were imposed by whites not for the purpose of establishing and consolidating a white cultural identity but rather to dominate blacks and exploit their labor. In this formulation, when the black power movement arose in the wake of the civil rights movement, its separatism needed to be viewed not as the imposition of borders around whites (so as to confine them) but rather as the erection of boundaries of cultural defense and identity around black Americans. Because of the power differential between the black minority and the dominant white majority, blacks could be segregated by whites, could segregate themselves, but could not be the segregators of whites.

National Boundaries

In the previous discussion, we saw that bordering processes may involve diverse and contradictory elements, including association, identity, trust, separation, exclusion, domination, and exploitation. In the modern period, the notion of borders is most intimately bound up with the concept of nation, which is typically taken as the fundamental cultural, linguistic, political, economic, and moral unit of analysis for the mainstream social sciences. National borders are presumed to enclose internally homogeneous cultural, political, and economic spaces and segregate such spaces from other distinct national spaces (see also Chapter 2, this volume). Before we deconstruct this dubious presumption, we should first acknowledge that even if we accept it, we may attach sharply divergent meanings to it. On the one hand, bordered nation-states represent the consolidation of groups that share similar traits upon which they base their political and cultural identities. On the other hand, because nation-state boundaries have often been the fruit of military conflicts, with the victors imposing their borders on the vanquished, national territories intrinsically reflect the domination and subordination of peoples excluded and bound by the powerful. Of course, we must also recognize that the vanquished nation whose borders have been imposed upon it by a victorious neighbor, colonizer, or invader may also be the victorious party in conflicts with peoples or nations further down the ladder of international power. Thus, although Mexico's northern border was imposed upon it by the United States and Mexicans are confined by the armed might of their northern neighbors, the Mexican state itself plays a subordinating role with respect to Guatemala, such that its own southern border policies restrict the movement and residence of Central Americans.

Yet, nation-states, like all social groups, are not really internally homogeneous—multiple distinctions exist on the inside with regard to region, ethnicity, gender, and class. Moreover, even when they are established by military force, their borders are never fixed permanently, either in terms of their spatial positioning or in terms of their relative/differential porosity and functional purpose. The fratricidal conflicts involved in the redrawing of the map of the former Yugoslavia are the most dramatic recent example of each of these statements about national borders.

Aside from questions of internal diversity and military conflict, other developments described in the various social science literatures call into question the meaning of national borders in ways that inform our understanding of the current processes at work between the United States and Mexico. These developments are associated with terms such as *globalization, deterritorialization,* and *transnationalization.* We will refer to these concepts and others later in this introduction as we discuss how thinkers of various disciplinary persuasions are drawing new maps of the world. Now, however, we turn our attention briefly to the parallel discourses on borders that have arisen in the social sciences, on the one hand, and in literature and literary criticism, on the other.

A Split Discourse on Borders

Academic talk about borders comes in two special strands. Version 1 is old-style border studies, grounded in history and the empiricism of the social sciences. Version 2 is new-style literary studies.[11] Each version seems to know little about the other. Our collection hopes to remedy that gap with a new sort of merged version. Version 1, old-style border studies, has a deeper history but a relatively narrow spatial agenda. It studies literal territorial borders, usually binational ones. Version 2 has a shorter history, but its intellectual agenda is extremely broad, considering space, time, and philosophies that challenge modernist notions. Much of Version 2 is about literary and critical ideas, rather than observable places or researchable people and things. In its imaginative and engaging prose, we find eloquent writing and occasional gems of brilliance.

Version 1 studies are frequently historical or public-policy oriented, focusing on things that know no borders like the environment, water, sewage, and health. Others focus on borders as institutional laboratories, studying binational institutions, regional political economy, comparative elites, and policy implementation challenges on immigration and trade.[12] More recently, a burgeoning but speculative literature about the North American Free Trade Agreement (NAFTA) and the European Union has emerged. Scholars tend to be interdisciplinary, though some collections address the "status of borderlands studies" inside social science disciplinary terms (see Stoddard 1975–1976). The history of the border is sometimes told in terms of trade relations and economic policies affecting its development (Tamayo and Fernández 1983). Labor and human rights issues are taken up, more and more in gender guise, especially with regard to the maquiladora program (Carrillo and Hernández 1985; Fernández-Kelly 1983; Iglesias Prieto 1985; Peña 1997; Tiano 1994; Ruiz and Tiano 1987), because next to nationality, gender often is the next most convenient basis for which to construct wage differences (Staudt 1998). Some effort has been made by Version 1 scholars to construct border typologies as heuristic devices for facilitating cross-national comparisons. Oscar Martínez, for example, conceptualized four kinds of borders. The U.S.-Mexico border is interdependent, he says, as opposed to other borders that he classified as alienated, coexistent, or integrated (1994: 6–10). Geographers have also contributed to conceptualizing the diversity of border regions, drawing on the famous work of historian Frederick Jackson Turner, who wrote *The Significance of the Frontier in American History* (selections in Gradus and Lithwick 1996). John Friedmann (1996) distinguishes between frontiers that are static (like the U.S.-Mexico border), dynamic (in a Turner-like sense), settlement, and extractive (both of the last two contain discussions of Amazonia). Border typologies continue to be constructed (see, for example, Chapters 2 and 3 in this volume).

With regard to Version 2 border talk, we must first direct our attention to the commanding presence of Gloria Anzaldúa, especially given her work's intimate connection to the territorial borderlands that inspire this collection. The 1987 publication of her book of poetry *Borderlands/La Frontera: The New Mestiza* by a small feminist press broke new ground in its linking of the concept of borderlands with multiple spaces of human existence. She makes this project quite explicit in the preface:

> The actual physical borderland that I'm dealing with in this book is the Texas-U.S. Southwest/Mexican border. The psychological borderlands, the sexual borderlands and the spiritual borderlands are not particular to the Southwest. In fact, the Borderlands are physically present wherever two or more cultures edge each other, where people of different races occupy the same territory, where under, lower, middle, and upper classes touch, where the space between two individuals shrinks with intimacy.

We hear the echo of Anzaldúa's declaration that "to survive the borderlands
. . . you must be a crossroads" fairly frequently in critical literary discussions of borders. A recent essay by cultural critic Nelly Richard, for
instance, contains a section titled, "The Border as a Frontier of Identity and
a Transcultural Crossroads" (Richard 1996). In that essay, she raises the
question of the delinking of identity and geography as culture becomes
deterritorialized in the postmodern world of flows of people, commodities,
and images, a possibility Anzaldúa seems to be aware of in her verse: "to
live in the Borderlands means to put *chile* in the borscht, eat whole wheat
tortillas, speak Tex-Mex with a Brooklyn accent" (1987: 194). At the same
time, in Version 2 border talk, borders remain a distinctly territorial concept, and some authors make quite specific references to the parallels
between nation-state boundaries and boundaries in other realms of human
experience. John Welchman, for example, believes that "the poetic is the
agency of the border," but wonders about the extent to which the border
concept may be "translated across various theories and practices, of thinking the limits, the edges, of the psychological rather than the nation-state"
(1996: 173). In spite of the "unscientific" character of this metaphorical
discourse on borders, we find the same fascination with and concern for the
anomalous situations borders present as we do in the social science discourse on borders. Thus, Welchman speaks of the "ineffability of functions
that can only take place in transgressive space" and "the fuzzy limits of the
interstice" (1996: 173), while U.S. and Mexican demographers hold binational conferences that seek to overcome their inability to collect meaningful data on many concrete social phenomena that are important to the border but whose "transnationality" defy operationalization and measurement.

   Border academic talk speaks not only about boundaries between those
spaces called nations but also about lines, walls, crossers, and mirrors within them (see Gutiérrez 1995 for an empirical work using the "walls and
mirrors" metaphor). Writers evoke borders as "sites of creative cultural
production" (Rosaldo 1989: 208). At a distance from the heartland, these
spaces at the margins provide mixing and crossing opportunities—even
"visions" that mix autobiography with surveys and thick description of
"cultural bumping" (Vélez-Ibáñez 1996). Within border spaces, one can
clearly observe the everyday reinvention of life, practices that often remain
obscure in the heartlands or mainstream. Attempts to exercise hegemony
through comprehensive ideological and institutional projects strain to be
effective. Anthropology's classical norms are changing, among those norms
the definitions of culture that treat cultures as containment zones. Attention
now turns to "zones of difference within and between cultures [making]
borderlands . . . central areas for inquiry" (Rosaldo 1989: 28). But where do
those boundaries get drawn, and do they subsume or submerge other
bounded identities? Does the new hybrid, or the transformation, break
down the old "I-it," as earlier discussed, or "us-them" long prominent in

studies of colonialism, or even the internalized colonialism once prominent in studies of ethnicity in the United States? Does it produce a sense of belonging that surpasses older constructions? Does it situationalize identity so much that identity no longer has a center or a stable grounding? Our contributors take up some of the obvious complications that Rosaldo's conceptual challenge poses as we revisit cultural production at borders.

At borders, people, money, and goods cross in commonplace ways, often with utter disregard for official rules and regulations. Also at borders, the "public transcripts"[13] of "what's happening" are multiple—different governments and different people working at different levels and even in different languages. Cracks in border enforcement are everywhere visible. These cracks—brought about by the absence of a single authority capable of seamlessly regulating behavior on the border—create pockets of uncontrolled space in the official hierarchies (Crozier 1964) or underneath the grid as "hidden transcripts" (Scott 1990). And these differences reflect one another in mirrorlike ways. Borders operate "something like counter-sites . . . in which the real sites are simultaneously represented, contested, and inverted" (Foucault 1986: 24; Soja 1989). We use these conceptual insights in this collection within thematically focused contributions on territory, social identity, and policy institutions. And we want, in this collection, to know about real places, peoples, and things.

Although we accept that there are no definitive statements, as was assumed in modernist thought, we do not accept that discourse is everything, central, and privileged. We, along with our contributors, believe that it is possible to integrate the literary sparkle and expansive agenda of Version 2 border talk into an empirically grounded social science discourse. We want to build bridges in our gaze at borders, focusing especially on nationalism, citizenship, and culture. We generally look for political, economic, and social explanations for what we study, and we relish the adventure of analyzing evidence, however multiple or unusual the sources. We do not dismiss the terminology of culture, contested as it is, but rather we embrace it in all its complexity. In so doing, we find insights within that large grab-bag of writing labeled postmodern, but we operate at the margins of that bag as well. So, we are now on to imaginative but grounded talk on nationalism, citizenship, and cultures. In this regard, we cannot help but critique the edifice on which comparative analysis in the social sciences is based: the nation-state.

New Ways of Talking About Borders

The notion that borders are limited to lines that divide one political economy from another has been hotly contested across and in between a variety of disciplinary fields. Part of the contestation involves questions about, or new names for, terminology long taken for granted, like *nation/nationalism, citizenship,* and *culture.* Disciplinary crossers have contested the canonical way mainstream disciplinary thinkers have used and interpreted these concepts.

Nationalism

Nationalism was once considered a powerful force for pride, self-determination, and independence. It provided sentimental foundations for the modern state, an entity usually traced to European origins and defined in Weberian ways as legitimate authority in territorial space. Modernization theorists studied the rise of nationalism and documented shared communication patterns. Theorists of the left, though, viewed nationalism as the hook that a territorially based dominant class uses to mobilize labor (see selections in Hutchinson and Smith 1994: sect. 2).[14] When area studies scholar Benedict Anderson historicized nations as "imagined communities," he spoke a language that appealed to but extended beyond the left. By imagined communities, Anderson means for us to understand that nations that now seem so fixed in their political identities and boundaries were once just imaginations that took languages, schools, and force to make coherent. His language embraces but simultaneously criticizes enumerated communication patterns within a bordered space as historical constructions (1983). Postcolonial scholars in turn would criticize Anderson for identifying a process that emerged from colonizer countries as universal (Chatterjee 1993; Williams and Chrisman 1994). Still, his imaginative angle was here to stay.

Part of the imagination of it all involved gendered imagery. Only recently, with the flowering of feminist theorizing in international relations, have the contested social constructions of the nation gotten their gender tags. For Cynthia Enloe, nationalisms have "typically sprung from masculinized memory, masculinized humiliation and masculinized hope" (1989: 44). More directly, states were founded using warfare, an extension of politics of, by, and for men. In their metaphoric and symbolic appearances, women are implicated in nationalism (McClintock 1996; Anthias and Yuval-Davis 1989). Christine Sylvester plays with domestic imagery in how she situates women's homelessness and the homelands men make, simultaneously using the stark language of apartheid (1994). However, several ironies pervade the way many analysts think about women. First, they fall back on using the state categories that men made. Collections cover women in men's political machinery that has muted women's voices for the long haul of history: in China, Kenya, and Argentina, among scores of others (Nelson and Chowdhury 1994; Basu 1995; Rai and Lievesley 1996; but see Pettman 1996). Second, even as men used domestic and family imagery to symbolize national difference, state makers constructed historical lines between public and private in ways that excluded female voice and agency (McClintock 1996: 261–262; Eley and Suny 1996: 27). By crossing the public-private border, analysts expose more fully the massive gendered social construction that states have wrought. For Geoff Eley and Ronald Suny, gender terminology is indispensable theoretically, yet in discourse about nationalism, readers find its "astonishing absence." Eley and Suny go on: "Anxieties about the health of the nation, or its demographic future and productive efficiencies, or the stabilities of the social fabric, commonly translate into a politics directed to and against women, whether through systems of mother-and-child welfare, through rhetorics of family values, or by policy offensives around reproductive health, the regulation of sexuality, or the direct control of women's bodies" (1996: 26–27). Books such as *Feminist Nationalisms* begin to give women agency in more nuanced constructions of nationalism (West 1997).

Although the national embrace has clear implications for how men and women experience the nation and live their everyday lives, people make their histories amid the confines of crisscrossed institutional lines. A good place to look is at borders and border crossing, whether across *la línea* or "between two islands." As Sherri Grasmuck and Patricia Pessar (1991) show for the islands of Hispaniola and Manhattan, men's and women's experiences are different not only in national terms but in households, with gender-distinctive interests and motivations to root or to leave the spaces where they sojourn.

Some metaphoric scholars go so far as to reduce nations to "politicized ethnicity" or a "fiction" or "fantasy" (in Peterson 1995). However fantasized initially, imagination takes on a material life of its own complete with political and educational machinery. Nationalism can be historicized and periodized. Antonio Gramsci joins the material and the cultural together in calling the ideological component of that machinery "hegemony." The ideological apparatus produces real results in education, economic, and civic terms, for better or worse. Eley and Suny call this "imaginative ideological labor" the "novelty of national culture" (1996: 8). In the meantime, the once lauded terminology of nationalism has assumed derogatory, suspect, and ominous overtones, with the "perverse extension of nationalism into racialized forms of political and cultural address" (1996: 3). Even more bluntly, J. E. Spence cites novelist John LeCarre's *Our Game:* "While we're pulling down the economic borders, these ethnic crazies are putting up national borders" (1996: 439).

Citizenship and old, new, and tenuous borders, always constructed and invented, problematize the movement of labor, "national" values, and exiles. Citizenship can be viewed in various ways. In legal terms, U.S. citizens hold rights and obligations, with citizenship a matter of birth or of naturalization, where the latter depends not only upon being legally admitted to the country, but also upon passing official tests (in English) on the flag, U.S. history, and the structure and functions of U.S. government institutions. Citizens are idealized as obedient to laws, including tax obligations; they offer their lives to defend the nation. They share values, a waxing and waning set of principles, heroes, and mythic stories of the past. In other terms, we are citizens if we earn (Shklar 1991, drawing on T. H. Marshall), if we have the resources to invoke citizens' rights. But even those economic notions are contained within nation-states.

Among all disciplines, political science has perhaps been most obsessed with the demarcation of national sovereignty and authority at boundaries. It confines border talk to phenomena anchored in national terms. In this century-old discipline, early treatment took the nation as the unit of analysis, or subunits therein. People studied France, India, Mexico, or the United States, among many others. Colonies had little interest for political scientists, even area studies scholars among them, until those colonies moved on their national ways. (The same could not be said for anthropologists, fascinated with colonized peoples.) Research, teaching, and training took on national overtones, for better or worse, with disproportionate influence exerted from the United States (Spender 1981). The American Political Science Association (APSA), adopting an expansive and ambitious hemispheric name despite its U.S. site, was born in 1903. Its organizational structure and journal gave space to the study of "foreign" governments, especially their constitutions (Staudt and Weaver 1997). International relations (IR) emerged as a subfield in U.S. political science during the interwar years, as analysts and practitioners aimed to understand foreign relations in what is thought of as the anarchic context of nation-states. For the most part, IR scholars take borders for granted as they study the behavior of nation-states. The field has been jointly dominated by two groups: those who assume states operate according to some rational model and a cadre of behavioralists searching for numeric patterns in "numeric metaphors" (Stone 1997). Postpositivist critics attacked this thinking, among them feminist theorists (Ashley and Walker 1990; Peterson 1992; Lapid and Kratochwil 1996; also see Agnew and Corbridge 1995).

In the postwar period, non-U.S. study was lodged in "comparative" terms, subsequently grouped within world area studies such as Asia, Africa, and Latin America or analyzed cross-nationally. For decades, study of the state diminished, its machinery relegated to the professional field of public administration. Then, with help from historical sociologists, the state was brought back into analysis (Evans, Skocpol, and Rueschemeyer 1985), only to become a fetish that turned attention away from questions of people's own agency, democratic accountability, and the considerable variation among weak and strong states. Increasingly, states are viewed as embedded in society (Migdal, Kohli, and Shue 1994), but we remain worried that this theoretical advance will reify the territorial boundaries states have made without attention to all those in-between spaces, language crossings, and cultural hybridizations generated by or transcending such boundaries. At territorial borders states are simultaneously porous and Goliath-like, with all the symbolic trappings of their authority. Borderlanders counter national hegemony in ways that need to be understood (Staudt 1998).

As a critic from within, former APSA president Theodore Lowi has called attention to another multidisciplinary problem that affects our understanding of borders: the statistically fed "rational choice" models that have dominated not only U.S. political science but other disciplines as well. The term *statistics*, according to Lowi, "takes its name from state and statist" (1992: 3). The nation-state collects, analyzes, and reports data through censuses and surveys that are representative, usually at the national or subnational levels. Complicating matters further, official data are organized in different ways, displaying peculiar national preferences for indicators and measurements of features differently prioritized. Rational choice models—which typically involve the economic rationality of *men,* not women—can do violence to our understanding of reality in all its complexity, including the complexity of social identity and culture, unless we conceive of multiple rationalities. The "rational man" idea erases vantage points, but vantage points are always plural. Those that "man" state institutions manage a territorial space that draws lines between, rather than nourishes those Bhabha-like in-between spaces of "women and other aliens" (the connectedness of those two terms is discussed in Nathan 1987). Several of the contributors to this volume suggest the need to draw new kinds of borderlines and define new kinds of citizenship. They indicate that the places to start looking are in and between households at the grassroots of practice (see Chapters 3 and 6, particularly).

Culture

Anthropologists have contested the extent to which political community coheres around culture. At the same time, the boundaries defining culture have become less clear, and not just to anthropologists. Scrutiny of the terminology of culture has been taken up by analysts in history, sociology, and international relations as well. For Eley and Suny, "culture is more often not what people share, but what they choose to fight over," although elsewhere they say it is the "informal, practical, and unconscious territory of everydayness" (1996: 9, 21). These conflicting statements are both true, of course: everyday experiences differ markedly by gender, class, race, ethnicity, and nationality, however these categories are socially constructed. Internally homogeneous cultures are hard to find in the modern world.

Cultural analysis was once used to explain nonhegemonic groups especially. Between and within nations, Renato Rosaldo insightfully remarks,
"full citizenship and cultural visibility appear to be inversely related. When
one increases, the other decreases" (1989: 198). Yet anthropology, once relegated to studies of southern countries, now finally "comes home from the
tropics" (Latour 1993: 100) as northern-based scholars visit upon their own
homelands insights they once reserved for the "exotic" peoples of the
south. Ironically, for Veronica Stolcke, cultural identity, once "a peculiar
obsession only of anthropologists, has now come to occupy a central place"
in the policy discourse of northern countries as their national identities are
called into question by the arrival of southerners from the former colonies
(1995: 2). If anthropologists don't deal with culture "up north," disciplinary
crossers will (in fact, they already have).

This growing interest in cultural analysis on the part of nonanthropolo-
gists has been noted with some bemused concern by Ulf Hannerz:

> Suddenly people seem to agree with us anthropologists; culture is every-
> where. Immigrants have it, business corporations have it, young people
> have it, women have it, even ordinary middle-aged men may have it, all in
> their own versions. . . . One might have thought that this success story of
> what has so long been a favorite concept of theirs should make anthropol-
> ogists very happy. Actually, at present it seems rather to make us nervous
> for a variety of reasons. Despite a winning streak, and to a degree because
> of it, the culture concept seems perhaps more contested, or contestable,
> than ever. (1996: 30)

Drawing New Maps

Gazing from the center, the capitol building, or the census bureau, officials
make maps with the sort of ease that distance allows. The maps that portray
borderlands sensitively have yet to be drawn, however, according to
Rosaldo. "Human cultures are neither necessarily coherent nor always
homogeneous; . . . our everyday lives are crisscrossed by border zones,
pockets, and eruptions of all kinds" (Rosaldo 1989: 207). Our border intellectual platter is thus full of gender, class, ethnicity, and nationality lines
and creative sites.

As we approach the millennium, new patterns in the global political
economy call old-style national territorial borders into question. Such patterns have been summed up with the term *globalization*, itself a contentious
term and subject to deep and layered analysis, including that of resistance
(Mittelman 1996; selections in Gills 1997). Capital crosses borders with
impunity—even with the blessings of national policies and mainstream
political parties. After all, borders contain worker pools with nationally

managed minimum wage and benefit packages (not to mention environmental regulations). But migrants counter the hegemonies of border controls.

Global cities operate as autonomous command-and-control centers for transnational capital. In these global cities, populated with domestic and international migrants (documented and otherwise), informalized jobs emerge simultaneously with modern, high-technology communication (Sassen 1994; Staudt 1998). People are on the move in lots of directions, so much so that Rouse put parentheses in a word once whole: (im)migration (1995). Circular migration contributes to the deterritorialization of the nation-state such that in some countries migrant residents act like citizens and in others migrant citizens live outside national territory (Basch, Glick Schiller, and Blanc, 1994; Blanc, Basch, and Glick Schiller, 1995). Former Haitian president Jean-Bertrand Aristide refers to "Haitians in the United States as constituting a 'tenth province' in addition to the nine within the national territory of Haiti" (Richman 1992: 190; also see Kearney 1995: 553; Rouse 1991). The highly educated are drawn to high-salary regions; labor moves back and forth, recreating new identities in the process; unauthorized labor can comprise significant proportions of the economically active within national populations (Vale and Matlosa 1995; UNRISD 1995). Nineteenth-century documents like the birth certificate and passport, "born in the nationalist nineteenth century," no longer have the same meanings; they make claims for labor market participation as much as attest "loyalty to a protective nation-state" (Anderson 1994: 322–332). Aihwa Ong's analysis shows how the rich create their own cultural capital (1992). But what struggles does that leave for the poor majority? Regional trading blocs (called "free trade") proliferate, among them NAFTA and other geographic clones in process.

In material terms, borders have concrete, even ruthless meaning for working people's lives. Divided and contained within borders, workers experience obscenely different wages and living standards. These containment zones offer numerous opportunities to elites: for extracting excessive value from labor; for pricing goods and services at startlingly different rates. To what extent do crossers take comparative advantage of these zones? With all this movement of money, people, and things, one might imagine a new kind of community or at least a new kind of flexibility at territorial borders. Paradoxically, those lines are now policed with a new sort of ferocity, as Timothy Dunn (1996) shows for the U.S.-Mexico border.[15] Cultural and linguistic markers—the dress codes—draw subtle lines within those borders that separate people: the authorized, the unauthorized; the haves, the have-nots (Nathan 1987).

Bureaucratic machinery, itself a series of vertical and horizontal lines with specified jurisdictions, maintains surveillance over multiple borderlines. The mark of modernity, after all, is the establishment of surveillance, defined as "the supervision of the activities of subject populations in the political sphere . . . [through] direct [means] . . . but more characteristically it is indirect and based upon the control of information" (Giddens 1990: 100). This need for surveillance is indicative of a refusal to acknowledge the inadequacy and imperfection of borders in sociocultural terms.

Although the governments of nation-states do not appear to be flagging in their efforts to control the movements of "subject populations" across their borders, the growth of transnational communities and diasporas seems to pose a substantial challenge to state authority. Whether or not they are conscious of the political ramifications of their actions, hundreds of thousands of Mexicans and nationals of other countries lead lives that are firmly rooted in communities both inside and outside the territory of the United States (Guarnizo 1995; Portes 1996; Rouse 1991; M. P. Smith 1994; R. Smith 1992). These transnationals have refused to remain captive in the labor reserves established by the national boundaries separating the core of the capitalist world-system from its periphery. True free traders, migrants force the labor market to clear in spite of its state-sponsored segmentation. Néstor Rodríguez (1996) recognizes and applauds the "autonomy" of the makers of a transborder Mexican diaspora—they live their lives for themselves where they choose regardless of the functional imperatives of the capitalist state. In his view, the U.S. government and Mexican transmigrants are engaged in a veritable "battle for the border" that will determine who is really globalizing the world and for what purposes.

Although researchers who study transnational communities sometimes argue that their existence poses a direct contradiction to sovereign state authority, other interpretations are possible. If Mexico-U.S. transnationals do not possess meaningful social and political rights of citizenship in both countries and if undocumented Mexicans living in the United States are hounded by the state and left vulnerable to exploitation by employers, then perhaps what we are seeing is not migrant "agency" or "autonomy." Instead, we may be witnessing an instance of Herbert Marcuse's "repressive tolerance" brought up-to-date for the *fin del siglo:* the state tolerates a certain, limited flow of undocumented migration across its borders but represses undocumented labor within them, thus preserving a low-wage labor reserve both domestically and internationally. (See, for example, Cooper's [1997] excellent account of the policed exploitation of Mexican immigrant workers in the U.S. meatpacking industry.) Or perhaps, as Avalos and Welchman (1996: 188) suggest, "for the state itself the border is a necessary fiction . . . put forward as a theatre of purity and legitimacy, a kind of semi-permeable membrane whose gauze is woven by the officers and apparatuses of state surveillance."

The U.S.-Mexico borderlands cannot be disciplined with one way of knowing; their map cannot be drawn from any single vantage point. Perhaps here more than in most topics of inquiry, the divisions of social life do "not respect them [disciplines] and ideas flow across them" (Gregory 1994: 11). At the margins of disciplines, much fruitful, creative production occurs; this is where thinkers straddle the lines, build the bridges, make the exchanges. "Marginal sites thus resist knowing in the sense celebrated in modern culture, where to 'know' is to construct a coherent representation that excludes contesting interpretations and controls" (Ashley and Walker 1990: 263).

An Outline of Chapters

The contributors to this collection are among those who challenge their disciplinary core from its margins. They offer a way of knowing based on those margins of creative production. Their writing is accessible and evocative, with respect for and celebration of how the "boundaries between formal intellectual inquiry and imaginative writing are becoming blurred" (Geertz, quoted in Gregory 1994: 4). Analytically, they focus on gender, culture, and ethnicity; on policy consequences traced from core to periphery; and on the seemingly marginal borderlanders who reveal "weapons of the weak." (Scott 1990) To a large extent, they speak with the voice of an interpretive tradition, immersing themselves in language and ways of knowing from vantage points outside the power mainstream.

We have organized the individual chapters into four thematic sections. The first section of the book, of which this chapter is part, addresses varying conceptions of borders and the rise of international borders in the modern era. In a theoretically provocative Chapter 2, Víctor Zúñiga discusses the establishment and maintenance of states' external political borders that complement the eradication of their internal "social" borders, examining the U.S.-Mexico border as an example of the former and the situation facing Mexico's resurgent indigenous population with regard to the latter. Sharp contradictions face the modernity project. One of the paradoxes of the internal borders separating indigenous and nonindigenous peoples is their endurance after 500 years of conquest and the twentieth century's enshrinement of egalitarian principles in the Mexican constitution.

In the second section, contributors write about economic and social organization at different points along the Mexico-U.S. border. In Chapter 3, Michelle A. Saint-Germain discusses public policy interests that transcend the territorial boundary and, consequently, require an institutional *re-presentation*. Next, David Spener and Bryan R. Roberts use a survey of small-scale entrepreneurs in their comparative analysis of five border cities. In Chapter 4, they periodize border economic transactions and conclude that trade liberalization redefines the border in ways that make it a "staging ground" for heartland business initiatives. Olivia Ruiz then explores the concept of *lo transfronterizo* (transborderness) in Chapter 5. She draws on multiple sources that allow analysis of spatially specific knowledge that motivates and sustains different kinds of cross-border visits. In the final chapter of this section, Kathleen Staudt, with Angélica Holguín and Magda Alarcón, compares two *colonias* at the peripheries of urban space on both sides of the border in El Paso–Ciudad Juárez. They ask why Mexico-based residents get public services sooner than those based in the United States. The answers are found in fragmented U.S. federalism, atomized individualism, and political powerlessness among residents, many of whom are noncitizens.

In the third section of this book, contributors examine identity and symbolic borders. In Chapter 7, Julie A. Murphy Erfani analyzes how marginalized peoples are reinventing space and identity in Mexico City, despite persisting modernist ideologies of national identities and nation-states. Next, in Chapter 8, Bradley J. Macdonald analyzes the relationship among graffiti, identities, and resistance in Los Angeles. His focus on urban space and its artistic lines shows not only individual creativity but the revitalization of everyday life. In the final chapter of this section, Pablo Vila takes up linguistic lines, ethnic identification, and discursive struggles in his discussion of the competing meanings of the label "Chicano" in El Paso. As a term, "Chicano" is tangled up in class, Mexican heritage, political resistance, and cultural treason, as respondents' voices reveal in rich and charged English and Spanish.

The final section of this book is titled "Debordering and Rebordering." The two chapters it contains address the nature of the transformations that U.S.-Mexico borderlands are experiencing at present. In Chapter 10, Mathias Albert and Lothar Brock analyze economic, multistate, and social dimensions of global debordering processes where "debordering" refers to the increasing permeability of national borders and the inability of states to do much about it. Finally, David Spener and Kathleen Staudt offer a concluding chapter in which they argue that although debordering processes are undoubtedly at work globally and along this particular border, the weight of contributions in this volume indicates that the systematic differences between Mexico and the United States will continue to express themselves in the next century in new and perhaps even more stark ways at their shared boundary.

Notes

1. Over fifteen years ago, anthropologist Thomas Weaver pointed border scholars in this direction when he argued that we should consider that "the line

which separates societies can be the center rather than the edge" (Weaver 1983: 251).

2. Taking a broader view of borders and borderlands has empirical as well as theoretical implications. For instance, a recent study of the incidence and patterns of accidental or violent deaths among undocumented border crossers that was conducted by the University of Houston was able to account only for those deaths that occurred in the *municipios* and counties that abutted the border itself (Eschbach et al. 1997). Over the past several years in Texas, however, numerous news stories have reported deaths of Mexican migrants at points well into the interior of the state, where deaths have resulted from, among other causes, dehydration in the ranch lands of south Texas and suffocation in tractor-trailer compartments and railcars away from the border. These deaths are presumably caused at least in part by the ways in which the border is policed by U.S. authorities. Thus, the many deaths that the University of Houston's study was able to document must be considered merely a lower-bound estimate since the study excluded "border-related" deaths that did not occur in the immediate vicinity of the border itself.

3. This section on borders and language reflects our own rough synthesis of various general and, to a certain extent, mutually contradictory influences. Readers may recognize traces of the ideas of Peter Berger and Thomas Luckmann (1966), Ferdinand De Saussure (1959), Jacques Derrida (1973), Michel Foucault (1984), Antonio Gramsci (1971), Stuart Hall (1992), and Karl Marx and Frederick Engels (1947).

4. Words, of course, are also separated by aural and visual borders in speech and in writing. The process of creating morphological and phonological distinction, as the founders of semiotics remind us, is arbitrary, since there is no natural or logical link between the external features of words and their meaning.

5. A good example of this appears in Pablo Vila's discussion of the use of the ethnic label "Chicano" in Chapter 9 of this book.

6. And, of course, it is the responsibility of state bureaucracies—the military along with customs and immigration services—to administer and enforce the external borders of the nation-state. See Víctor Zúñiga's discussion in Chapter 2.

7. Here we are referring to the concept of "social capital" discussed by James Coleman (1988), Frances Fukuyama (1995), and Alejandro Portes (1995).

8. Similarly, Marx believed that the division of labor in society that created antagonistic social classes was morally repugnant. His vision of an ideal society presupposed the abolition of classes and the surpassing of the division of labor. Communist society was to be, in many senses, a borderless society.

9. David Montejano (1987) makes essentially the same distinction between ethnicity and race with regard to Mexicans in the United States in his widely acclaimed historical account of Anglo-Mexican relations in Texas.

10. Also of interest is Barth's (1969) more general discussion of how ethnic groups establish and maintain boundaries.

11. Other distinctions among border studies "types" have been made in the literature. See, for example, Alvarez (1995).

12. Academic researchers, most of them based at the U.S.-Mexico border, founded the Association for Borderlands Studies (ABS). For two decades now, ABS has brought together several hundred people annually, connecting them in between conferences by means of an academic journal (Stoddard 1992). Various journals publish border-oriented work, among them the *Journal of Borderlands Studies, Frontera Norte, Río Bravo,* and *Estudios Fronterizos.*

13. James Scott (1990) uses the term *public transcripts* to refer to the official discourse on events and the symbolism surrounding them.

14. As we discuss later, it is merely a short leap forward to gaze at these differently valued labor and conscription pools in global economic terms.

15. Perhaps, as Nevzat Soguk (1996) seems to suggest, the state is acting materially on the bodies of migrants at the border in order to legitimate its discourse about itself in the face of the multiple threats to its sovereignty that globalization represents.

References

Agnew, John, and Stuart Corbridge. 1995. *Mastering Space: Hegemony, Territory and International Political Economy.* New York: Routledge.

Alvarez, Robert R. 1995. "The Mexican-U.S. Border: The Making of an Anthropology of Borderlands." *Annual Review of Anthropology* 24: 447–470.

Anderson, Benedict. 1983, 1991. *Imagined Communities.* London: Verso.

———. 1994. "Exodus." *Critical Inquiry* 20, no. 11: 4–27.

Anthias, Floya, and Nira Yuval-Davis. 1989. "Introduction." In *Woman—Nation—State,* Floya Anthias and Nira Yuval-Davis, eds. London: Macmillan, 6–11. Reprinted in *Nationalism,* John Hutchinson and Anthony D. Smith, eds. New York: Oxford University Press, 312–316.

Anzaldúa, Gloria. 1987. *Borderlands/La Frontera: The New Mestiza.* San Francisco: Spinsters/Aunt Lute Press.

Ashley, Richard K., and R. B. J. Walker. 1990. "Speaking the Language of Exile: Dissident Thought in International Studies." *International Studies Quarterly* 34, no. 3: 259–268.

Avalos, David, and John C. Welchman. 1996. "Response to the Philosophical Brothel." In *Rethinking Borders,* John C. Welchman, ed. Minneapolis: University of Minnesota Press, 187–199.

Barth, Fredrik. 1969. "Introduction." In *Ethnic Groups and Boundaries,* Fredrik Barth, ed. Boston: Little, Brown, and Company, 9–38.

Basch, Linda, Nina Glick Schiller, and Cristina Szanton Blanc. 1994. *Nations Unbound: Transnational Projects, Postcolonial Predicaments and Deterritorialized Nation-States.* North Ryde, Australia: Gordon and Breach Publishers.

Basu, Amrita, ed. 1995. *The Challenge of Local Feminisms.* Boulder: Westview Press.

Berger, Peter L., and Thomas Luckmann. 1966. *The Social Construction of Reality.* New York: Doubleday and Company.

Bhabha, Homi. 1994. "Narrating the Nation." In *Nationalism,* John Hutchison and Anthony D. Smith, eds. New York: Oxford University Press.

Blanc, Cristina Szanton, Linda Basch, and Nina Glick Schiller, 1995. "Transnationalism, Nation-States, and Culture." *Current Anthropology* 36, no. 4: 683–686.

Carrillo, Jorge, and Alberto Hernández. 1985. *Mujeres fronterizas en la industria maquiladora.* Mexico City: Secretaría de Educación Pública and Centro de Estudios Fronterizos del Norte de México.

Chatterjee, Partha. 1993. *The Nation and Its Fragments: Colonial and Postcolonial Histories.* Princeton: Princeton University Press

Clifford, James. 1994. "Diaspora." *Cultural Anthropology* 9, no. 3: 302–338.

Coleman, James. 1988. "Social Capital in the Creation of Human Capital." *American Journal of Sociology* 94 (supplement): s95–s120.

Cooper, Marc. 1997. "The Heartland's Raw Deal: How Meatpacking Is Creating a New Immigrant Underclass." *The Nation* (February 3): 11–17.

Crozier, Michel. 1964. *The Bureaucratic Phenomenon.* Chicago: University of Chicago Press.

De Saussure, Ferdinand. 1959. *Course in General Linguistics.* New York: Philosophical Library.

Derrida, Jacques. 1973. *Speech and Phenomena: And Other Essays on Husserl's Theory of Signs.* Evanston: Northwestern University Press.

Dunn, Timothy J. 1996. *The Militarization of the U.S.-Mexico Border 1978–1992: Low Intensity Conflict Doctrine Comes Home.* Austin: University of Texas, Center for Mexican American Studies.

Durkheim, Emile. 1984. *The Division of Labor in Society.* New York: Free Press.

Eley, Geoff, and Ronald Suny, eds. 1996. "Introduction: From the Moment of Social History to the Work of Cultural Representation." In *Becoming National: A Reader,* Geoff Eley and Ronald Suny, eds. New York: Oxford University Press.

Enloe, Cynthia. 1989. *Bananas, Beaches and Bases.* Berkeley: University of California Press.

Eschbach, Karl, Jacqueline Hagan, Néstor Rodríguez, Rubén Hernández-León, and Stanley Bailey. 1997. "Death at the Border." Working paper WPS 97-2. Houston: Center for Immigration Research.

Evans, Peter B., Theda Skocpol, and Dietrich Rueschemeyer. 1985. *Bringing the State Back In.* New York: Cambridge University Press.

Fernández-Kelly, Mária Patricia. 1983. *For We Are Sold, I and My People: Women and Industry in Mexico's Frontier.* Albany: State University of New York Press.

Foucault, Michel. 1984. "Truth and Power." In *The Foucault Reader,* Paul Rabinow, ed. New York: Pantheon Books, 51–75.

———. 1986. "Of Other Spaces." *Diacritics* 16: 22–27.

Friedmann, John. 1996. "Introduction: Borders, Margins and Frontiers: Myth and Metaphor." In *Frontiers in Regional Development,* Yehuda Gradus and Harvey Lithwick, eds. Lanham, Md.: Rowman and Littlefield.

Frobel, Folker, Jurgen Heinrichs, and Otto Kreye. 1980. *The New International Division of Labor.* Cambridge, UK: Cambridge University Press.

Fukuyama, Frances. 1995. *Trust: Social Virtue and the Creation of Prosperity.* New York: Free Press.

Giddens, Anthony. 1990. *The Consequences of Modernity.* Cambridge: Polity Press.

Gills, Barry K., ed. 1997. "Globalisation and the Politics of Resistance." *New Political Economy* 2, no. 1.

Gradus, Yehuda, and Harvey Lithwick, eds. 1996. *Frontiers in Regional Development.* Lanham, Md.: Rowman and Littlefield.

Gramsci, Antonio. 1971. *Selections from the Prison Notebooks.* New York: International Publishers.

Grasmuck, Sherri, and Patricia R. Pessar. 1991. *Between Two Islands: Dominican International Migration.* Berkeley: University of California Press.

Gregory, Derek. 1994. *Geographical Imaginations.* Cambridge: Blackwell.

Guarnizo, Luís Eduardo. 1995. "The Mexican Ethnic Economy in Los Angeles: Capitalist Accumulation, Class Restructuring, and the Transnationalization of Migration." Unpublished manuscript.

Gupta, Akhil, and James Ferguson. 1992. "Beyond 'Culture': Space, Identity, and the Politics of Difference." *Cultural Anthropology* 7, no. 1: 6–23.

Gutiérrez, David. 1995. *Walls and Mirrors: Mexican Americans, Mexican*

Immigrants, and the Politics of Ethnicity. Berkeley: University of California Press.

Hall, Stuart. 1992. "The Question of Cultural Identity." In *Modernity and Its Futures,* Stuart Hall, David Held, and Tony McGrew, eds. Cambridge, UK: Polity Press, 273–326.

Hannerz, Ulf. 1996. *Transnational Connections: Culture, People, Places.* London: Routledge.

Holston, James. 1996. "Cities and Citizenship." *Public Culture* 19 (special issue).

Hutchinson, John, and Anthony D. Smith. 1994. *Nationalism.* New York: Oxford University Press.

Iglesias Prieto, Norma V. 1985. *La flor más bella de la maquiladora: Historias de vida de la mujer obrera en Tijuana, B.C.N.* Mexico City: Secretaría de Educación Pública and Centro de Estudios Fronterizos del Norte de México.

Kearney, M. 1995. "The Local and the Global: The Anthropology of Globalization and Transnationalism." *Annual Review of Anthropology* 24: 547–565.

King, Martin Luther, Jr. 1964. *Why We Can't Wait.* New York: Harper and Row.

Lapid, Yosef, and Friedrich Kratochwil, eds. 1996. *The Return of Culture and Identity in IR Theory.* Boulder: Lynne Rienner.

Latour, Bruno. 1993. *We Have Never Been Modern.* Cambridge: Harvard University Press.

Lowi, Thomas. 1992. "The State in Political Science: How We Become What We Study." *American Political Science Review* 86: 1–7.

Marable, Manning. 1992. *Race, Reform and Rebellion: The Second Reconstruction of Black America, 1945–1990.* Jackson: University Press of Mississippi.

Martínez, Oscar J. 1994. *Border People: Life and Society in the U.S.-Mexico Borderlands.* Tucson: University of Arizona Press.

———. 1996. "Introduction." In *U.S.-Mexico Borderlands: Historical and Contemporary Perspectives,* Oscar J. Martínez, ed. Wilmington, Del.: Scholarly Resources, xiii–xix.

Marx, Karl, and Frederick Engels. 1947. *The German Ideology.* New York: International Publishers.

———. 1972. "The Materialist Conception of History." In *Karl Marx: The Essential Writings,* Frederic L. Bender, ed. New York: Harper and Row, 159–229.

McClintock, Cynthia. 1996. "'No Longer in a Future Heaven': Nationalism, Gender, and Race." In *Becoming National: A Reader,* Geoff Eley and Ronald Suny, eds. New York: Oxford University Press.

Migdal, Joel, Atul Kohli, and Vivienne Shue. 1994. *State Power and Social Forces: Domination and Transformation in the Third World.* New York: Cambridge University Press.

Mittelman, James, ed. 1996. *Globalization: Critical Reflections.* Boulder: Lynne Rienner.

Montejano, David. 1987. *Anglos and Mexicans in the Making of Texas, 1836–1986.* Austin: University of Texas Press.

Nathan, Debbie. 1987. *Women and Other Aliens: Essays from the U.S.-Mexico Border.* El Paso: Cinco Puntos Press.

Nelson, Barbara, and Najma Chowdhury, eds. 1994. *Women and Politics Worldwide.* New Haven: Yale University Press.

Ong, Aihwa. 1992. "Limits to Cultural Accumulation: Chinese Capitalists on the American Pacific Rim." In *Towards a Transnational Perspective on Migration: Race, Class, Ethnicity, and Nationalism Reconsidered,* Nina Glick Schiller, Linda Basch, and Cristina Blanc-Szanton, eds. New York: New York Academy of Sciences (vol. 645 of the *Annals of the New York Academy of Sciences*), 119–144.

Paredes, Americo. 1978. "The Problem of Identity in a Changing Culture: Popular Expressions of Culture Conflict Along the Lower Rio Grande Border." In *Views Across the Border: The United States and Mexico,* Stanley R. Ross, ed. Albuquerque: University of New Mexico Press, 68–94.

Peña, Devon. 1997. *The Terror of the Machine: Technology, Work, Gender, and Ecology on the U.S.-Mexico Border.* Austin: University of Texas Center for Mexican American Studies.

Peterson, V. Spike. 1992. "Transgressing Boundaries: Theories of Knowledge, Gender and International Relations." *Millennium: Journal of International Studies* 21: 183–206.

———. 1995. "Reframing the Politics of Identity: Democracy, Globalisation and Gender." *Political Expressions: The Politics of Identity* 1, no. 1.

Pettman, Janet. 1996. *Worlding Women: A Feminist International Politics.* New York: Routledge.

Portes, Alejandro. 1995. "Economic Sociology and the Sociology of Immigration: A Conceptual Overview." In *The Economic Sociology of Immigration: Essays on Networks, Ethnicity, and Entrepreneurs,* Alejandro Portes, ed. New York: Russell Sage Foundation, 1–41.

———. 1996. "Transnational Communities: Their Emergence and Significance in the Contemporary World System." In *Latin America in the World Economy,* Roberto Patricio Korzeniewicz and William C. Smith, eds. Westport, Conn.: Greenwood Press, 151–168.

Portes, Alejandro, and Robert L. Bach. 1985. *Latin Journey: Cuban and Mexican Immigrants in the United States.* Berkeley: University of California Press.

Portes, Alejandro, and Min Zhou. 1992. "Gaining the Upper Hand: Economic Mobility Among Immigrant and Domestic Minorities." *Ethnic and Racial Studies* 15: 491–522.

Rai, Shirin, and Geraldine Lievesley, eds. 1996. *Women and the State: International Perspectives.* London: Taylor and Francis.

Richard, Nelly. 1996. "The Cultural Periphery and Postmodern Decentering: Latin America's Reconversion of Borders." In *Rethinking Borders,* John Welchman, ed. Minneapolis: University of Minnesota Press, 71–84.

Richman, Karen. 1992. "A Lavalas at Home/a Lavalas for Home: Inflections of Transnationalism in the Discourse of Haitian President Aristide." In *Towards a Transnational Perspective on Migration: Race, Class, Ethnicity, and Nationalism Reconsidered,* Nina Glick Schiller, Linda Basch, and Cristina Blanc-Szanton, eds. New York: New York Academy of Sciences (vol. 645 of the *Annals of the New York Academy of Sciences*), 189–200.

Rodríguez, Néstor. 1996. "The Battle for the Border: Notes on Autonomous Migration, Transnational Communities, and the State." *Social Justice* 23, no. 3: 21–37.

Rosaldo, Renato. 1989. *Culture and Truth.* Boston: Beacon.

Rouse, Roger. 1991. "Mexican Migration and the Social Space of Postmodernism." *Diaspora* 1, no. 1: 8–23.

———. 1995. "Questions of Identity: Personhood and Collectivity in Transnational Migration to the United States." *Critique of Anthropology* 15, no. 4: 351–380.

Ruiz, Vicki, and Susan Tiano, eds. 1987. *Women on the U.S.-Mexico Border: Responses to Change.* Boston: Allen and Unwin.

Sahlins, Peter. 1989. *Boundaries: The Making of France and Spain in the Pyrenees.* Berkeley: University of California Press.

Sassen, Saskia. 1994. *Cities in a World Economy.* Thousand Oaks, Calif.: Pine Force Press/Sage.

Schiller, Nina Glick, Linda Basch, and Cristina Szanton Blanc. 1992. "Transnationalism: A New Analytic Framework for Understanding Migration." In *Towards a Transnational Perspective on Migration: Race, Class, Ethnicity, and Nationalism Reconsidered,* Nina Glick Schiller, Linda Basch, and Cristina Blanc-Szanton, eds. New York: New York Academy of Sciences (vol. 645 of the *Annals of the New York Academy of Sciences*), 1–24.

Schneider, Jane, and Rayna Rapp, eds. 1995. *Articulating Hidden Histories: Exploring the Influence of Eric R. Wolf.* Berkeley: University of California Press.

Scott, James. 1990. *Domination and the Arts of Resistance.* New Haven: Yale University Press.

Shklar, Judith. 1991. *American Citizenship: The Quest for Inclusion.* Cambridge: Harvard University Press.

Smith, Michael Peter. 1994. "Can You Imagine? Transnational Migration and the Globalization of Grassroots Politics." *Social Text* 39: 15–34.

Smith, Michael Peter, and Joe R. Feagin. 1995. "Putting 'Race' in Its Place." In *The Bubbling Cauldron: Race, Ethnicity, and the Urban Crisis,* Michael Peter Smith and Joe R. Feagin, eds. Minneapolis: University of Minnesota Press, 3–27.

Smith, Michael Peter, and Bernadette Tarallo. 1995. "Proposition 187: Global Trend or Local Narrative? Explaining Anti-Immigrant Politics in California, Arizona and Texas." *International Journal of Urban and Regional Research* 19: 664–676.

Smith, Robert C. 1992. *Los ausentes siempre presentes: The Imagining, Making, and Politics of a Transnational Community Between New York City and Ticuaní, Puebla.* Ph.D. diss., Columbia University, New York.

Soguk, Nevzat. 1996. "Transnational/Transborder Bodies: Resistance, Accommodation, and Exile in Refugee and Migration Movements on the U.S.-Mexican Border." In *Challenging Boundaries: Global Flows, Territorial Identities,* Michael J. Shapiro and Hayward R. Alker, eds. Minneapolis: University of Minnesota Press, 285–325.

Soja, Edward. 1989. *Postmodern Geographies: The Reassertion of Space in Critical Social Theory.* London and New York: Verso.

Spence, J. E. 1996. "Ethnicity and International Relations." *International Affairs* 72, no. 3: 439–443.

Spender, Dale, ed. 1981. *Men's Studies Modified.* New York: Pergamon Press.

Spivak, Gayatri Chakravorty. 1994. "Can the Subaltern Speak?" In *Colonial Discourse and Post-Colonial Theory: A Reader,* Patrick Williams and Laura Chrisman, eds. New York: Columbia University Press, 66–111.

Staudt, Kathleen. 1998. *Free Trade? Informal Economies at the U.S.-Mexico Border.* Philadelphia: Temple University Press.

Staudt, Kathleen, and William Weaver. 1997. *Political Science and Feminisms: Integration or Transformation?* New York: Twayne/Macmillan.

Stoddard, Ellwyn. 1992. "Legitimacy and Survival of a Professional Organization: The Association of Borderlands Scholars." *Journal of Borderlands Studies* 7, no. 1: 92–121.

———, ed. 1975–1976. "The Status of Borderlands Studies." *Social Science Journal* 12, no. 3 (special issue).

———, ed. 1975–1976. "The Status of Borderlands Studies." *Social Science Journal* 12, no. 3 (special issue).

Stolcke, Veronica. 1995. "Talking Culture: New Boundaries, New Rhetorics of Exclusion in Europe." *Current Anthropology* 36, no. 1: 1–24.

Stone, Deborah. 1997. *Policy Paradox: The Art of Political Decision Making.* New York: W. W. Norton.

Sylvester, Christine. 1994. *Feminist Theory and International Relations in a Postmodern Era.* New York: Cambridge University Press.

Tamayo, Jesus, and Jorge Luís Fernández. 1983. *Zonas fronterizas.* Mexico City: Centro de Investigación y Docencia Económicas.

Tiano, Susan. 1994. *Patriarchy on the Line: Labor, Gender, and Ideology in the Mexican Maquila Industry.* Philadelphia: Temple University Press.

United Nations Research Institute for Social Development (UNRISD). 1995. *States in Disarray.* Geneva: UNRISD.

Urciuoli, Bonnie. 1995. "Language and Borders." *Annual Review of Anthropology* 24: 525–546.

Vale, Peter, and Khabale Matlosa. 1995. "Beyond the Nation-State: Rebuilding Southern Africa from Below." *Harvard International Review* 17, no. 4: 34–37, 83–84.

Vélez-Ibáñez, Carlos. 1996. *Border Visions.* Tucson: University of Arizona Press.

Waldinger, Roger. 1996. *Still the Promised City? African Americans and New Immigrants in Postindustrial New York.* Cambridge: Harvard University Press.

Wallerstein, Immanuel. 1974. *The Modern World System.* New York: Academic Press.

Weaver, Thomas. 1983. "The Social Effects of the Ecology and Development of the Border Region." In *Ecology and Development of the Border Region: Second Symposium of Mexican and United States Universities on Border Studies,* Stanley Ross, ed. Mexico City: Asociación Nacional de Universidades e Institutos de Enseñanza Superior, 233–270.

Weber, Max. 1930, 1992. *The Protestant Ethic and the Spirit of Capitalism.* London: Routledge.

———. 1946. *From Max Weber: Essays in Sociology.* New York: Oxford University Press.

———. 1978. *Economy and Society: An Outline of Interpretive Sociology.* Berkeley: University of California Press.

Welchman, John C. 1996. "The Philosophical Brothel." In *Rethinking Borders,* John C. Welchman, ed. Minneapolis: University of Minnesota Press, 160–186.

West, Lois. 1997. *Feminist Nationalisms.* London: Routledge.

Williams, Patrick, and Laura Chrisman, eds. 1994. *Colonial Discourse and Post-Colonial Theory: A Reader.* New York: Columbia University Press.

2

Nations and Borders: Romantic Nationalism and the Project of Modernity

Víctor Zúñiga

In this chapter I undertake a theoretical examination of the meaning of national borders in both of their manifestations: the establishment and maintenance of external borders and the eradication of internal borders. Since the end of the eighteenth century, attempts have consistently been made to establish external borders as secure symbols of nation-states. At the same time, nation-states have sought to erase their internal borders as a precondition for constituting themselves as liberal, representative democracies. Each of these processes signals the state's desire to territorialize history and transform mythical nations into earthly ones. Although both processes are territorial in nature and presuppose one another, it is useful to analyze them separately. The eradication of internal frontiers implies the homogenization of space in social, political, and cultural terms. The imposition of external borders, however, implies quite the opposite, that is, the promotion and maintenance of spaces that are socially, politically, and culturally distinct. By analyzing these dialectically related processes here, I wish to draw attention to some of the sharpest contradictions facing the project of modernity. With regard to the question of external borders, I consider the case that is the explicit object of attention in this volume: the U.S.-Mexico border, which is strikingly fraught with many of the

Portions of this chapter were published previously under the title "Elementos teóricos sobre la noción de la frontera: Reflexiones en torno a la tésis de Michel Foucher," which appeared in 1993 in *Frontera Norte* 5, no. 9: 139–146. Thanks are given to the publisher, El Colegio de la Frontera Norte, for granting permission to include several translated passages of that article in this chapter. Translated by David Spener.

contradictions inherent in the attempts of nation-states to establish their external boundaries. To illustrate the unresolved problems of eliminating internal borders within nation-states, I discuss the attempts being made by the indigenous peoples of Mexico (fifty-four different ethnic groups with a population estimated at around 12 million individuals) to exercise territorial autonomy within Mexico. Both cases permit us to make international comparisons and include, within the same text, quite diverse theoretical and critical perspectives.

The External Borders of Nation-States

The rise of the nation-state in history was predicated upon the invention of territorial boundaries. This process has been described in an erudite fashion by Michel Foucher (1986) in his pioneering thesis, *L'invention de frontières*. In this section, I present several of the theoretical elements of Foucher's thesis as well as a few of my own reflections inspired by them and apply them to the case of the U.S.-Mexico border. In turn, I consider (1) the border as an ideal type, (2) the historically heterogeneous reality of borders, and (3) the various ways in which border spaces may be constituted.

The Ideal Type

Currently, the dominant meaning assigned to the term *border* is that of a spatial sheath enveloping the nation-state. This meaning is the fruit of a long and complex history involving both territorial and social space. Its history is particularly visible on the European continent; actually, it is visible only on the European continent. The border as a spatial wrapper surrounding the nation-state (the nation as a space governed by a single power and inhabited by a homogeneous mode of social life) presupposes three historical events: the existence of the state, the creation of the nation, and the technical capacity to open and close the nation's frontiers. To draw a border is to confront an adversary (this is only possible when internal adversaries have been suppressed), and in order to do this it was necessary to create a line-drawing mechanism that was sufficiently effective in times of war and sufficiently useful in times of peace. To close a border is an eminently military function, whereas the opening of a border by a state presupposes the effective operation of fiscal and customs operations, the formation of a bureaucracy loyal to a central authority. In this ideal type, the sovereign— the king or his bourgeois successors—has the capacity to impose his will over all the territory of the kingdom (Aron 1962). Thus, borders ideally are political representations of space according to ruling-class beliefs, ideologies, and desires revolving around the idea of limits (Mairet 1978).

The Historically Heterogeneous Reality of Borders

From the empirical point of view, however, *L'invention de frontières* demonstrates that "political border" is an extraordinarily variable notion because it is home to so many different geohistorical realities. Foucher walks the reader through a variety of historical border situations, ranging from the Etruscan rites that demarcated the difference between sacred spaces—those that were inhabited by the gods—and earthly spaces, through the French invention of the "borderline" within which the sovereignty of a people—conceived as a single will—was exercised. Smuggling, illegal migration, international border disputes, and military movement in "ambiguous" zones are contemporary social facts that demonstrate the distance that exists between the ideal-typical border and the world's multiform border reality.

Throughout history, the particular ways in which national spaces have been represented politically have depended upon how dynastic families or triumphant nationalist revolutionaries see themselves. For example, Carlos V of Spain and his court imagined themselves to be governors of a discontinuous territory upon which "the sun never set." The most powerful Chinese dynasties had no place for the idea of a dividing borderline: how could they when they considered themselves to be the center of humanity? For these dynasties, borders were the unpopulated regions that surrounded (and therefore protected) the territory under their control. The founders of the United States did not think of their nation as being bounded. Instead, they viewed their young nation as advancing outward in waves toward the West and South.

In reality, there are only a few societies in the history of the world that have specialized in producing borders. These have included the Chinese, Ottoman, British, French, Portuguese, Spanish, German, and Russian empires. The Catholic church, the first transborder entity in history, also appears on the list, with its long track record in establishing the borders of parishes and dioceses. The United States, for its part, constitutes a special case in the history of the production of borders. To the extent that Americans for more than a century regarded their frontier as the point of contact between "civilization and barbarism" (Turner 1987), they invented a new way of creating borders: filling empty spaces (defined as such so as to justify expansion). But the great majority of contemporary nation-states have not established their borders; they have suffered them. Their borders are the inheritance of a colonial past, the fruit of the carving up of the world's territory by the great powers or of a unilateral, single-state arrangement (the Treaty of Guadalupe Hidalgo, for example).[1]

If borders have arisen historically as the result of a variety of hegemonic projects undertaken by monarchs and nationalists, in the contemporary period we are struck by the multiplicity of border types around the world:

- Minuscule borders (600 meters between Macao and China) and grandly extensive borders (20,000 kilometers that formed the perimeter of the recently extinct Soviet Union)
- Hermetic borders, whose mission is to separate and divide absolutely (the Berlin Wall, the electronic barriers between Russia and Turkey, and the border between the two Koreas)
- Legitimate, or "cold," borders (Canada–United States) and conflictive, or "hot," borders (Colombia-Venezuela, Iraq-Kuwait)
- Vacant border regions (Mexico-Belize) versus highly populated ones (Brazil-Uruguay)
- Relic borders (the ancient German border in Lorraine)
- Absurdly imposed borders (Niger/Nigeria)
- Borders that favor a more or less symmetrical relationship between two nation-states (Brazil-Argentina, Algeria-Morocco), between two empires (United States–Russia), between two regional powers (China-India), or between two societies on the road toward constituting states (Ethiopia-Sudan, Afghanistan-Pakistan)
- The borders that stimulate decidedly asymmetric relations between a nation and an unfinished state (Algeria-Niger, Egypt-Sudan), between an empire and an unfinished state (former Soviet Union–Afghanistan), or between a nation and an empire (Mexico-United States)

Moreover, a quick glance around the world indicates that human societies continue to actively reinvent and redraw their borders. Without getting into the details of the current situation facing the former Soviet Union and some of the countries that remained under its geopolitical sway for several decades, we note the following:

- In Africa today, disputed territorial boundaries affect nearly one-fifth of the continent's surface.
- In South America, new borders have been created throughout the twentieth century, in spite of the fact that borders began to be fixed during the eighteenth century, and the nation-states of the continent have been in existence for more than a century and a half.

- In Asia, from the Middle East to Indonesia, it can be demonstrated that practically no state is exempt from disputes regarding its territorial limits.

These examples remind us that there is nothing "natural" about borders. Nonexistent in nature, national borders are human fabrications that shift, rise, and fall as a consequence of ongoing contestation between different societies.

Conceptualizing Border Spaces and Cross-Border Interaction

According to Foucher, understanding borders requires constructing a social geography of bounded space. As a bounded space—a place where nation-state "envelopes" intersect—border space is both diatopic and diachronic; yet as a space of adjacencies, it is a syntopic and synchronic space as well. A border is a diachronic and diatopic space in the sense that in it diverse times and diverse spaces converge. In other words, it is at once a place and its multiple coordinates. Foucher (1986: 46–47) utilizes two diatopically and diachronically dense cases in order to illustrate the importance of these notions:

> The Berlin Wall, a separating border, which has the function of dividing two parts of the city and preventing migration, is also a place in which Germany is split in two, where Europe is divided, and moreover is one of the borders where two military pacts and two planetary ideological systems separate themselves. . . . The Mexico-U.S. border separates two States, but at the same time divides Anglo-Saxon America from Latin America, a military superpower from a Third World state.

In both cases, there are multiple times and spaces, distinct coordinates that situate themselves on different geopolitical and historical planes. The production of a border cannot be understood without taking into consideration its diatopic and diachronic dimensions.

Nonetheless, a border is a syntopic and a synchronic space in the sense that it is a specific place with one specific time. Both the Berlin Wall and the U.S.-Mexico border constitute unique places with histories that are distinct from the histories of their respective nation-states. The history of the two Berlins could not have happened in the rest of Europe. What occurs in Tijuana–San Diego cannot repeat itself in any other part of the United States or Mexico. Border spaces are unique syntopic combinations produced by particular moments in the history of two nation-states or two nation-state projects. Not surprisingly, there is a great deal of variation in the types of combinations that are produced along different borders around the world as well as at different points along the same border. On each border, and at diverse points along a single border, singular syntheses are produced that must be the object of particular observations. For this reason, a border and the diverse neuralgic points that compose it must be seen as a complex confluence of adjacencies.

The Mexico-U.S. border, as an example of a legitimate, diatopically asymmetrical border, produces very interactive syntopias (i.e., meeting places of a unique set of confluences). As the Mexican state increased its presence along the space of the border—a long process of "federalization" of the northern frontier (Ceballos 1991) that was initiated during the dictatorship of Porfirio Díaz and reinforced after the Mexican Revolution—the United States found itself obliged to modify its conception of its southern border. No longer was it the crest of an outwardly rolling wave. Instead, it was transformed into a line of diatopic and diachronic confluences (Maciel and González de la Vara 1990). This was a historical novelty that the expansive American state has yet to digest.

Tito Alegría (1989: 61) argues that the flows of interaction and the barriers inhibiting them on the Mexico-U.S. border are driven by "the adjacency of differences." If we add Jorge Bustamante's concepts of "internationality" and "asymmetry" to the equation, we expand the heuristic capacity of Alegría's proposal. In the case of decidedly asymmetric borders, perceived as legitimate and with densely populated crossing points, interaction is intensified without erasing differences or weakening the separating functions of the marked frontier. In other words, the intensity of the interaction does not erase the borders. What happens is the opposite: the asymmetry is often the condition for interchange. Interaction and internationality, nonetheless, tend to be nonexistent with respect to "vacant" borders between two symmetrical state entities or to be prohibited in those border regions that have eminently separating functions and are perceived as illegitimate (Iraq-Kuwait and the old border between the two Germanys).

Nineteenth-Century Liberalism
and the Eradication of Internal Borders

Although Mexico's national political and historical discourse has constantly dealt with the meaning of its northern border with the United States, it has seldom dealt openly with the question of ethnic borders within its territory (Barth 1976). Until very recently, the idea of ethnic diversity in Mexico had no place in the official version of the national imagination. In fact, a legal constitutional discourse on the question of ethnic borders does not appear until 1987. This is odd given that Mexico is a society in which ethnic, religious, moral, and historical diversity is quite obvious to both natives and foreigners alike. Until recently, the national discourse reflected a belief that the homogeneity of Mexicans was the product of nature, of an implacable *mestizaje* (blending of races) that links all citizens.

This lack of discussion of ethnic boundaries between Mexicans is not accidental. One of the driving ideological forces motivating the elites who conceived the Mexican nation was the idea of *inclusion* (Wolfe 1992). But the idea that had such an impact in Mexico is not that version of inclusion that is usually translated into systems of "assimilation" (so characteristic of U.S. society). As is known, north of the Río Bravo del Norte/Río Grande, the politics of inclusion took the form of systems of incorporation of "others" into a dominant national project. The idea that was so successful in Mexico, however, is that other form of inclusion that engenders a plethora of legal and rhetorical discourses: an idea based on the passion for *formal equality*. Behind the convictions that have been expressed from the speeches of Miguel Hidalgo y Costilla to the reforms of Article 4 of the Mexican Constitution can be observed declarative forms whose central message is always the same: all Mexicans are identical before the law.[2] Through their use of these forms, Mexican jurists, intellectuals, elected representatives, and governors have tried to erase from the collective imaginary all the borders that impeded the construction of the national community. Nobody can deny the great political legitimacy behind the ideas of equality and inclusion. So powerful are their political legitimacy that they have played a crucial role in attempting to implant democracy in a society that had inherited authoritarian traditions from three centuries of colonialism and counterreform. At the level of ideology, Mexico was born from the rubble of New Spain as a nation of free, equal, and property-owning men (Vázquez 1979).[3]

Liberal thought establishes a clear relation between formal equality, social inclusion, and democracy. From 1821 onward, the historical justification for the Mexican nation has been equality. In contrast, it was thought, differentiated societies are those that accept exclusions that prevent all individuals from exercising their rights. In short, democratic equality supposed social equality. Starting from this powerful ideological impulse, replete with liberal ideals and convictions, it was believed that there were no social barriers that deserved to survive. As such, for the nineteenth-century men who conceived of Mexico, the project of constructing a secular, democratic, and republican society had no rival. Mexicans shared this impulse with their U.S. and European contemporaries. In fact, this passion for inclusion is and has been the quintessential politics of modernity in its original conception. In their official histories, the processes of inclusion are told not as an imposition of a new faith in the individual and his or her forces, as a war in favor of equality and its blessings, but rather as natural processes, inevitable historical flows.

> The public stories that modern liberal democracies tell and retell empha-
> size the gradual triumph of inclusion. Once upon a time, it is said, such
> societies were ruled by privileged elites. Governing circles were restricted
> to those of the correct gender, breeding, education, and social exclusive-
> ness. All this changed as a result of those multiple forces usually identi-
> fied by the term democracy. (Wolfe 1992: 309)

At the end of time, we will all look like one another because the ideal is
that of similarity, the eradication of all internal borders. This nineteenth-
century faith appears to persist with great vigor in the present day, as some
of the most important philosophers and writers in Mexico have noted:

> Processes of inclusion have always been the ones which have prevailed.
> No autonomy has managed to survive this historical process, given, as
> Fray Bartolomé de Las Casas used to say, "there is only one humanity."
> (Trabulse 1996: 101)

> There are no indigenous rights, there are only the rights of Mexicans.
> There is a General Constitution of the Republic: only one Republic, only
> one Fatherland. . . . [The Indians] may maintain their customs, their cook-
> ing, their religion, their superstitions. But with regard to the question of
> laws, there is only one. (Henestrosa 1996: 4)

> What is Mexico? A group of strange peoples and cultures clashing with
> one another? No, Mexico is a nation that has historically been united
> using the instruments that, without having intended to, its conquerers and
> colonizers gave it: language, religion, and the blending of races
> [*mestizaje*]. This is its culture, no longer indigenous nor *criolla* nor *mesti-
> za,* but Mexican. (Zea 1996: 352)

> It is not about us all being the same and that we all consume Coca-Cola or
> Pepsi-Cola. Equality is not standardization, it is equality before the law
> and economic equity. I believe that we should still aspire to that end, and
> that it is all about modern values, which are valid for all men, Indians and
> non-Indians. (Villegas 1996: 337)

Liberal discourse affirms that borders are undesirable. Nonetheless,
differences survive in spite of the historical impulse—real or imagined—
toward equality. If borders persist, then they have to be explained. The first
means of explaining the persistence of internal borders supposes that they
are historical remnants. The idea of "remnant" makes it possible to define
borders as mere unfinished business, as pending tasks or vestiges from the
past, delays in the ineluctable historical process of inclusion, as affirmed by
Martha Robles (1996).[4]

The second narrative route, the most liberal of all, explains internal
borders as the result of individual decisions. Modern societies, so it is said,
offer all the formal conditions for individuals to be free and exercise their

right to equality; if in spite of this differences persist (poverty, subjugation, illiteracy, etc.), it is because individuals do not want to make use of the resources that democracy has put within their reach. In sum, we are all equal. A nation is composed of equal men and women. This is the most legitimate political ideal and, according to modernity's evangelists, part of the inevitable march of history. As a result, those who are different because of their isolation and ignorance must be conceived as holdovers, stragglers in the forward march of history; those who because of stubbornness and close-mindedness want to remain different must be conceived as pariahs, as groups that exclude themselves from the nation.

The political position of Mexican indigenous peoples—their condition of invisibility and silence—has enormously facilitated the fiction that Mexico is a mestizo country, a country where internal borders have been eliminated, or if they have not been completely eliminated, these borders exist within a well-integrated mosaic. Existing borders have been perceived, in the official discourse, as folkloric or idiosyncratic features that complement one another, creating a portrait that corresponds to the national ideal: a set of common social customs, aspirations, and languages that promote cohesion.

The Fragmentation of Space and the Collapse of the Romantic Notion of Nations and Borders

By placing the ethnic question on the national agenda, the indigenous peoples of Mexico have revitalized the political notions of territory, barrier, border, and difference. In so doing, they have introduced into Mexico's political imagination the most advanced and promising possibilities for reconstituting the modernist project: the rebirth of the local, the valorization of identities, the reconstitution of space, the limits to consumption, the perfecting of democracy, the symbolic force of differences, and the transformation of the idea of the rule of law. In sum, the political visibility of the Mexican indigenous peoples introduces, first and inevitably, a renewal of the idea and the promise of nationhood (Bonfil Batalla 1979). Their voices entirely recreate the cultural geography of the nation and the way in which this geography is conceived.

Collective identities are essentially unique combinations of temporal (historical) dimensions and of spatial (territorial) dimensions. Common history and common territory—this pair permits affective, symbolic, and intersubjective recognition among human beings. Nonetheless, throughout history, the forms of belonging and the sense of belonging, in both their spatial and temporal dimensions, have been possible only when these have human stature, that is, when they refer to identifiable social spaces (native lands, hometowns) and when they touch traditions and narratives that are name-able and memorable (habits, proverbs, stories, legends). This is the source of the recognition of identities, as Raymond Williams (1982) shows upon inquiring as to the nature of nationalities.

The Spatialization of Human Experience

Although the romantic idea of the nation, in all of its versions, derives entirely from traditional forms of belonging, it introduces, at the end of the eighteenth century in almost all the American nations and in the nineteenth century in the European nations (Anderson 1991), an artificial form of belonging that attempts to replace a multitude of local identities with a supralocal form of identification called "nation." This process of replace-ment, which Ernst Gellner (1988) relates with moving coldness, goes hand in hand with faith in progress and modernity. The tribe, the clan, the extended family, the city, or the neighborhood are seen as defeated, not by a spiritual or religious "nationality" (e.g., the people of Naples in the fif-teenth century were Neapolitans first and Catholics second) (Poutignat 1992) but by a supralocal, worldly identity.

Romantic nationalism's symbolic violence was accompanied by a seemingly liberatory mission. Local powers were seen as despotic (as, in fact, they were); in response, as a promise, the nation-state viewed itself as a liberating agent and the harbinger of social equality. However, in reality, local powers were replaced by central power, which embodied not the hope that the liberatory power produced but rather the violence that was promul-gated by numerous state apparatuses: centralized professional armies com-mitted to all forms of repression, juridical norms that failed to recognize regional customs and histories, mandatory schooling in the language of the central authority, and medical teams capable of domesticating bodies and minds. All this made it possible to create a "great majority" that would bear, from that moment forward, the name of citizens of the same nation. Because of these contradictions, the romantic idea of the nation is expressed in an ambivalent, dual language, that is, the language of facts and the language of words.

> What I want to emphasize in that large and liminal image of the nation with which I began is a particular ambivalence that haunts the idea of the nation, the language of those who write of it and the lives of those who live it. It is an ambivalence that emerges from a growing awareness that, despite the certainty with which historians speak of the "origins" of nation as a sign of the "modernity" of society, the cultural temporality of the nation inscribes a much more transitional social reality. (Bhabha 1990: 1)

From words, from the official rhetoric, emerges one of the Janus faces that

Homi Bhabha speaks of: the totalization of the national culture. Facts and human sentiments supply the other face: that of earthly pleasure, that of the desire to belong to a group, that of the harm done by domination, that of the sensitivity to gender, that of the language that is spoken versus the language that should be spoken. It is for all this that Bhabha observes unreservedly that the idea of nation is a problem.

The construction of the modern nations has led to a geographical politics of human experience in which not only do individuals define themselves in terms of belonging to a real and symbolic territory that is far from being the "native land" or the *paese* (country) referred to by Williams (1982) and Ruggiero Romano (1994); but also this politics has imposed a cultural geography that spatializes all forms of human experience and tears down all internal borders. Collapsing the temporal dimensions of human life and transforming them into spatial coordinates, the nation is a fundamentally modern construct. As a result of this, David Gross says, "Spatialization has now become our basic modality for organizing and structuring the world" (1992: 65).

The collapse of time accompanies the construction of nations because it is precisely history—collective time—that would impede the cultural homogenization of territory. Local identities are local histories that resisted, as long as it was possible, the collapse of their histories. As such, the nation-project is essentially a geography. The space of the nation is the territory of sameness: no longer are there historic borders, only places, positions in space. Nationality winds up being nothing more than points in space. If a nation is a contiguous and undifferentiated space, anybody who is born in Spain is Spanish, just as anyone who was born in the Soviet Union was Soviet in discursive terms. In this way it was hoped that Mexican indigenous peoples, whether *mixtecos* or *purépechas,* would wind up being Mexicans by virtue of the common territory they inhabited, which, in turn, defined them as a group and assimilated them to the national culture.

When the modes of spatial perception replace the temporal modes of perception, Gross (1992) explains, this produces a disjuncture that has repercussions for all the forms and structures of the cosmology of local cultures. Once this happens, it is easier to conceptualize things according to their contiguity in space than it is to distinguish things based on their differences in terms of time. Social things cease to have a history, only a place. This process, however, is nothing more than a model of modernity, a romantic purpose for the founding of nations according to an appetizing ideological project. Real processes, those that are produced in the framework of real human relations, show the other face of Janus: numerous, anomalous, contemporary phenomena call the national project into serious question.

Contemporary Anomalies

Among the many cultural and political events that have captured the attention of researchers over the past decade, there are a handful that have shattered the conventional geography that has officialized the invention of nations. By conventional geography, I refer to the type of geography that uses the world map to teach schoolchildren "such deceptively simple-sounding beliefs as that France is where the French live, America is where the Americans live, and so on" (Gupta and Ferguson 1992: 12). Here I will refer to the most notable of these phenomena that, owing to their novelty and singularity, have been calling attention to the bankruptcy of nationalism and its fictions.

Perhaps the most noteworthy of all is the phenomenon of the fragmentation of regions, of nations, of cities, of daily life, and even of identities (Gupta and Ferguson 1992). Everything occurred as if the "common histories" and the "common origins" had not had the expected effect on the length and breadth of national, regional, metropolitan, and identity regions. Not everyone wound up being "priests" of their own macrotribes, as Gellner (1988) explains, but rather astounding fissures were produced in the nationalism of the Soviet Union, of Yugoslavia, and of Czechoslovakia. Regionalisms also resurged in Spain, India, Tibet, New Zealand, and Canada. In the same way, the native peoples of Mexico today reclaim autonomy as a political concept, that is, an autonomy based on territory and history (Simposio Indolatinoamericano 1995).

Similarly, on another scale, U.S., French, and English cities appear to the eyes of the observer as sets of disconnected segments. The typical U.S. citizen is stunned to discover neighborhoods in Los Angeles where English is as much a foreign language as Chinese, Korean, or Spanish. And if that were not enough, daily life in the big cities is organized as an immense puzzle that appears to have no form or logic; cities are places where individuals play the role of contradictory, delinked characters, according to the terrain in which they are located (Davis 1990; Entrikin 1991).

This social fragmentation has placed in doubt numerous notions employed in nationalist narratives. Some of them were noteworthy for their vacuity, such as the narrative of "cultural evolution" or of "common patrimony," even the notion of "nationality." In Mexico, these notions are still used, whereas in Canada, Spain, and India they are used with greater trepidation and all because there is no longer a way of imagining a culture as a spatial continuum that extends over a two-dimensional territory. In Mexico, *mexicanidad* is still spoken of very loosely, as a space-filling essence, an idea whose problematic character becomes apparent as soon as it is applied to any other countries: How can one speak of "Guatemalan-ness" in the face of the evidence of the numerous ethnic boundaries that exist in that country? Who would dare to speak of the "U.S.-ness" of that multiethnic, multilingual, and multicultural country known as the United States of America?

International migration has been, without a doubt, one of the most important challenges to the romantic nationalist vision, especially migration that produced an important transfer of population from the poor countries of the south to the rich countries of the north. This sudden presence of Turkey in Germany, of Morocco in France, of Mexico in the United States, and so on, has surprised societies and has given rise to a questioning of the reality and the fiction of borders. The border, taken as an immutable spatial fact, has begun to be used as an essential tool in political and cultural debate (Zúñiga 1998). Cultural borders have shifted as they have followed the footsteps of migrants, giving rise to unimaginably contradictory events.

International migration has made evident two particularly anomalous processes. On the one hand, it has laid bare the logic of spaces. In order to illustrate this, I will make a brief argument, similar to that of a mathematician's logical proof:

Condition: Mexico is the country where they eat *pozole* and they listen to *mariachi* music.

Question: Where is Mexico?

Answer: Where they eat *pozole* and listen to *mariachis*.

Question: Where do you find abundant concentrations of *pozole* and *mariachis?*

Answer: In Chicago and Los Angeles.

This argument is a caricature, but it allows us to show how spaces are being fragmented, how borders are transcended, and how the definitions of culture no longer correspond to spatial surfaces that are more or less homogeneous and contiguous. For this reason, there is no longer a sure way to answer these questions: Where are Morocco, Turkey, and Lebanon? Where is Italian culture? Where are the Berber traditions?

Another anomalous process that comes to light due to international migration has not to do just with space, but with the relationship between time and space (Gutiérrez Estévez 1996). International migrants distort, or "transport," time. Think of the Maya communities in Houston and their funeral rituals, just a few miles from the National Aeronautics and Space Administration (NASA) (Hagan 1994). What is new in Houston: NASA or Mayan funeral rituals? If modernity is synonymous with "the latest" or the most recent and the traditional is equivalent to the antique, the old, the past, then what is the latest in Houston? Not only do migrants distort time, but they collapse spaces as well. There is less real distance between the residents of the San Francisco Bay Area who hail from the Mexican state of Michoacán and their relatives in the sending community of Aguililla (Rouse 1989) than there is between the women factory workers of Ciudad Guadalupe, Nuevo León, and the rich residents of San Pedro Garza García, Nuevo León. This is the result of the new electronic communication technologies, certainly, but also of the international recomposition of enterprises and labor markets. Many inhabitants of Monterrey (*regiomontanos*) are much closer to Houston than to Saltillo (which is only 40 miles away). Real space, the international political boundary, the definition of the nation, immigration controls: none of these things impedes *regiomontanos* from establishing themselves equally in Monterrey and Houston (Hernández 1996). Thus, the anomalous process of the fragmentation of one type of space is accompanied simultaneously by the integration of other types of spaces.

Fears and Doubts

The events observed in numerous societies point toward a recomposition of nationalities and identities imposed by central powers. Nevertheless, fears and doubts remain. Nation-states are born with a promise of human equality democracy that continues to powerfully captivate our attention. The renaissance of local sentiments, the fragmentation of spaces, the return to local traditions and microhistories seem to bring with them an undesirable specter: the return to premodern despotisms and the reign of fanaticism (religious, ethnic, local). In other words, local identities that are based on real human associations will not be erased by the efforts of modern nation-states to assimilate them.

How can modern societies be open to diversity and difference without losing the achievements of liberal democracy, of the establishment of the rule of law, of equality before the law? These are the questions that occupy Jean-Pierre Saez in his introduction to the set of essays that recently appeared (1995) under the title *Identités, cultures et territoires*. If nations are in retreat and democracy is a historical outcome of the construction of nations, how can we save democracy without defending extralocal, national identities? Saez's answers are particularly interesting given the presence of indigenous peoples at the negotiations over the future of the Mexican nation. The author puts forward a political question: how to reconcile "the proliferation of particularisms, the coming apart of nations, the obsolescence of the structures that held nations together, the disarticulation of social groups, the intensification of the demands put forward by minority identity groups" with "the reactions of re-deployment, of aggression, of self-protection or of destructuring, of the growing possibility of interchanges, encounters, communication, cultural mixings, of opening towards the Other that offer our most democratic contemporary societies?" (Saez 1995: 16). With this, Saez takes up the questions expressed by Alain Touraine (1992: 231) in his critical analysis of modernity: "We see how international market logic plays against the speakers representing the new cultural identities. On the one hand, the world seems global; on the other hand, multiculturalism seems to have no limits. Is it possible to close our eyes to these ravages which pose a double menace to the planet?"

The recent breaking up of nations presents us with a dilemma that requires a talented and complex political response. It is a response that must allow us to face and recognize the profound changes that sociologists have called "the crisis of modernity" at the same time that we attempt to save the most appreciated political values of modernity. In other words, we need a politics that avoids throwing the baby out with the bathwater.

The design of this politics requires, in the first place, the recognition of the crisis that is being experienced by the so-called project of modernity. Without recognition of the crisis of the old ways of knowing, of the crisis of the old forms of the social division of labor, and of the weakening of the nation-state, it will be difficult to engender a new politics of nations. Individuals will increasingly search for more disparate identities, and they will try to make sense of their lives by "shopping in supermarkets of reconditioned mystiques and bottled messianisms" (Saez 1995: 19). Individuals will become more conscious of the emptiness of the idea of progress, which now more than ever is associated with dispersion, exclusion, and the rupture of social ties. The universalistic hope that accompanied the idea of progress so strongly promoted by the defenders of modernity seems to make less and less sense to the *michoacanos* who find themselves channeled to California, just as Moroccans, Turks, or Slavs abandon their homelands in order to move into neighborhoods in German, French, and Swiss cities.

There is no doubt in the eyes of the new citizens of a shattered modernity that the great national institutions (the school, political parties, the army, unions, and the police) are incapable of responding to the diversification of identities and the multiplication of logics. These institutions, in their current form, will come to be seen in the same way as national anthems: romantic songs from the nineteenth century.

"Multi-belonging is the contemporary individual's destiny," Saez declares (1995: 25). Will contemporary nation-states be able to respond to this new reality? In Saez's opinion, it is possible to reinvent the cultural and symbolic functions of the nation on the condition that the "politics of identity" are qualitatively renewed; that nations incorporate in an integrated way, with legal force, the "politics of difference"; and that they be capable of mediating the increasing variety of problematic identities that will arise in the future of national societies (Stavenhagen 1988).

Saez finishes his argument by citing numerous field studies conducted in the European Community, Asia, Africa, and Latin America that show that the needed political responses will be found at the level of social microcosms. Many differentiated collectivities now expect the central powers to place the following items on the political agenda:

- The construction and reinforcement of identities upon precise territorial bases that people establish (urban, rural, regional)
- The instrumentalization of images that make local sense, such that a variety of local, ethnic, and political views are represented by the most powerful communication and symbolic apparatuses in society (the mass media, schools, monuments, the national currency, etc.)
- The development of collective interactivities based on tolerance for a diversity of worldviews and identities

The renewal of the idea of nation and of nationality in Mexico has no model or paradigm except for the one that real, active Mexicans construct for themselves. This is and will continue to be the central message that Mexican society will receive from the *huichol, coras, mixes, mazahua, tarahumara, maya, mixtec,* and *chamula* indigenous groups. The political visibility of the Mexican indigenous peoples has asserted that historical reality is functioning according to formulas different from those of classical liberalism. This is the same reality that has not been represented in Mexican law, that instead codifies attitudes very dear to the Mexican elites, including their religious faith in modernity and their passion for progress (Annino 1982). These elites have rejected indigenous reality throughout postindependence Mexican history. Now the hour of opportunity is arriving, as the voices of ethnic difference are speaking up for the first time and their faces are appearing on the scene. All that is missing are ears and eyes prepared to listen and see and minds open to learning. What is missing is the will to hear the new political voices (Johnston 1990).

Toward a Synthesis

Drawing from a variety of theoretical currents, I have attempted to show that the formation of nation-states has been closely linked with the promises of modernity: freedom, equality, and the recognition and bestowing of rights upon the individual. This explains why the creation and enforcement of external borders has presented itself as a synonym for national sovereignty. Borders are guarded in order to preserve laws and traditions, to protect individuals and their rights. At the same time, the eradication of internal borders is rooted in the ideal of democracy. The functioning of democracy supposes the appearance of citizens, educated individuals who are proud of their own nation and respectful of their collective symbols and the law. Democracy promises equality on the condition that individuals and peoples have been made equal and uniform.

The creation of modern states included a dual geographic exercise: level and divide. It is for this reason that the promises of modernity suppose, on the one hand, secure external frontiers that are unmovable, functional, and linear. On the other hand, they suppose that the spaces within national frontiers will be homogeneous, ordered, level, contiguous, and isolated from other national spaces, just as they appear on grade school maps. The literary image in the work of Goethe, analyzed by Marshall Berman, synthesizes this geographical exercise of power: "As Faust surveys his work, the whole region around him has been renewed, and a whole new society created in his image" (Berman 1982: 66–67).

What is currently happening along the U.S.-Mexico border, as well as in the interior of Mexico, serves as an exemplary announcement of the fallacies and contradictions inherent in the promises of nation-states. The cold formality of the external border (the Río Bravo del Norte/Río Grande and the international line), with its customhouses, its contrasts, its police, its bridges, and all its multiple manifestations of the ability to impose separation and control the movement of undesirable people and goods, contrasts with the millions of Mexicans and Central Americans who skip across the border with no one's permission. In the same way, the borders within Mexico between indigenous peoples and the nonindigenous find no legal expression because, according to the law, all Mexicans are equal. Paradoxically, these ethnic, linguistic, cultural, and historical borders are much more stable and insurmountable than state-imposed borders. On the one hand, the Mexico-U.S. border has become one of the most transgressed boundaries in the world. On the other hand, internal ethnic borders within Mexico have not yet been abolished 500 years after the Spanish conquest.

Contemporary states move, dispute, and establish new external borders. Workers and their families trespass, perforate, and profane borders. Capital laughs in the face of state borders. At the same time we are witness to a rebirth of internal borders, which are multiplying with unforeseen vigor. Individuals, social groups, and communities are more and more experiencing the disconcerting fragmentation of their own identities and seek refuge in the only place where history offers it: in a sense of belonging they construct for themselves.

The linear border, understood as the sheath of the nation-state under conditions of equality and fruit of a generally conflictive bilateral arrangement, is not a universal reality: it is an exceptional historical and geographical situation, characteristic of a few European borders in certain specific moments of their history. Consequently, we must see the linear border on its own terms: a state project, a structural type, a sovereign desire. A nation, in turn, is nothing more than the project of specific hegemonic social classes; it represents their faith in modernity. It has been the ideology of certain elites as well as the dream of *independentistas* (pro-independence nationalists) worldwide. Whether revolutionary or reactionary, nation builders have shared a common goal: to build a large and homogeneous community free from internal borders, an interconnected space where differences have been disappeared.

It is a sorry scene. The hegemony over space, the fusion between power and geography, did not last long. The maps of power have turned out to be strangely artificial. Geography could not be separated from real human histories; these histories could not be united and divided at the exclusive whim of those in power. Now in Mexico the *huichol* council of wise men and leaders stridently demands complete autonomy and total control over the sacred territory of its ancestors. It demands that history be converted into geography, whether the central government likes it or not. At the same time in the Deep South of the United States, we find that more than 30,000 Mexicans imagine—in spite of it being against the law—their personal and collective futures in Withfield, Georgia. Not even William Faulkner could have imagined this.

Notes

1. The border set in February-March 1848 between Mexico and the United States was "a compromise border . . . [arrived at] between Americans" (Foucher 1986: 209).

2. Article 4 of the Mexican Constitution was reformed in 1992. It now declares: "The Mexican nation has a poly-cultural composition which draws strength originally from its indigenous peoples." It was not until 1992 that the Mexican government officially recognized that Mexican society is multicultural!

3. In Mexico, Agustín de Iturbide (1822–1823) outlawed the ethnic categories that were used during the Spanish colonial period and forged them all into a single name: Mexicans. With this curious exercise of executive power, he attempted to erase all internal social differences within the nation (Lira 1966). According to Manuel Marzal, something similar occurred in Peru: "The liberal political project, which attempted to suppress all the barriers between *criollos* and *indios* established by the *Cortes de Cádiz,* attempted to assimilate the indigenous population under the generic name 'Peruvians'" (1992: 127–128).

4. The discourse regarding "backwardness" appears to be the preferred political explanation for "difference" not only in Mexico, but throughout Latin America.

References

Alegría, Tito. 1989. "La ciudad y los procesos transfronterizos entre México y Estados Unidos." *Frontera Norte* 1, no. 2.

Anderson, Benedict. 1991. *Imagined Communities: Reflections on the Origin and Spread of Nationalism.* New York: Verso.

Annino, Antonio. 1982. "Il patto e la norma alle origini della legalita oligarchica in Messico." *Nova Americana* 5. Quoted in Ruggiero Romano. 1994. "Algunas consideraciones alrededor de nación, estado y libertad en Europa y América Centro-Meridional." In *Cultura e identidad nacional,* R. Blancarte, ed. Mexico City: Fondo de Cultra Económica, 21–43.

Aron, Raymond. 1962. *Paix et guerre entre les nations.* Paris: Gallimard.

Barth, Fredrik. 1976. "Introducción." In *Los grupos étnicos y sus fronteras,* Fredrik Barth, ed. Mexico City: Fondo de Cultura Económica, 9–49.

Berman, Marshall. 1982. *All That Is Solid Melts into Air: The Experience of Modernity.* New York: Simon and Schuster.

Bhabha, Homi K. 1990. "Introduction: Narrating the Nation." In *Nation and Narration,* Homi K. Bhabha, ed. New York: Routledge, 1–7.

Bonfil Batalla, Guillermo. 1979. "Los pueblos indígenas: Viejos problemas, nuevas demandas." In *México, hoy,* P. González Casanova and E. Florescano, eds. Mexico City: Siglo 21, 97–107.

Bustamante, Jorge. 1989. "Frontera México–Estados Unidos: Reflexiones para un marco teórico." *Frontera Norte* 1, no. 1: 7–24.

Ceballos, Manuel. 1991. *Nuevo Laredo: Visión histórica de temas y períodos en Nuevo Laredo, Tamaulipas.* Nuevo Laredo: Cien años de ser ciudad 1891–1991.

Davis, Mike. 1990. *City of Quartz: Excavating the Future in Los Angeles.* New York: Vintage Books.

Entrikin, Nicholas. 1991. *The Betweenness of Place.* Baltimore: Johns Hopkins University Press.

Foucher, Michel. 1986. *L'invention des frontières.* Paris: Fondation pour les Etudes de Défense Nationale, Collection les 7 Epées, Documentation Française.

———. 1991. *Fronts et frontières.* Paris: Fayard.

Gellner, Ernst. 1988. *Naciones y nacionalismo.* Mexico City: CONACULTA–Alianza Editorial.

Gross, David. 1992. "Space, Time, and Modern Culture." *Telos* 115: 59–78.

Gupta, Akhil, and James Ferguson. 1992. "Beyond 'Culture': Space, Identity, and the Politics of Difference." *Cultural Anthropology* 7, no. 1 : 6–23.

Gutiérrez Estévez, Manuel. 1996. "Alternidad étnica y conciencia moral, el juicio final de los mayas yucatecos." In *De palabra y obra en el Nuevo Mundo,* Manuel Gutiérrez Estévez, Miguel Leon-Portilla, Gary H. Gossen, and J. Jorge Klor de Alva, eds. Mexico City: Siglo 21, 295–322.

Hagan, Jacqueline M. 1994. *Deciding to Be Legal: A Maya Community in Houston.* Philadelphia: Temple University Press.

Henestrosa, Andrés. 1996. "Entrevista a Andrés Henestrosa." *El Nacional,* February 12.

Hernández, Rubén. 1996. *Youth, Street Gangs and International Migration in the Monterrey-Houston Inter-urban Region.* Unpublished report for the North-South Center, University of Miami.

Johnston, Michael. 1990. *On Their Own Terms, in Their Own Voices.* Amherst:

Center for Organizational and Community Development, University of Massachusetts.

Lira, Andrés. 1996. "La extraña anomalía: Realidades indígenas en el México del siglo XIX." In *Archivo General de la Nación: Cultura y derechos de los pueblos indígenas de México.* Mexico City: Fondo de Cultura Económica, 103–118.

Maciel, David R., and Martín González de la Vara. 1990. "La frontera historiográfica: México y Estados Unidos 1968–1988." Paper included in *Memorias del Simposio de Historiografía Mexicanista,* compiled by the Instituto de Investigaciones Históricas, UNAM/Gobierno del Estado de Morelos.

Mairet, Gerard. 1978. "L'idéologie de l'Occident: Signification d'un mythe organique." In *Les idéologies, Tomo 2,* François Châtelet, ed. Verviers: Marabout.

Marzal, Manuel M. 1992. "Del paternalismo colonial al moderno indigenismo en el Perú." In *De palabra y obra en el Nuevo Mundo,* Manuel Gutiérrez Estévez et al., eds. Mexico City: Siglo 21, 127–152.

Poutignat, Philippe y Jocelyne Streiff-Fenart. 1992. *Théories de l'ethnicité.* Paris: PUF.

Robles, Martha. 1996. "Indigenismo y globalización: El peso del atraso." *Excelsior,* February 6: 1, 10–11.

Romano, Ruggiero. 1994. "Algunas consideraciones alrededor de nación, estado y libertad en Europa y América Centro-Meridional." In *Cultura e identidad nacional,* R. Blancarte, ed. Mexico City: Fondo de Cultura Económica, 21–43.

Rouse, Roger. 1989. *Mexican Migration to the United States: Family Relations in the Development of a Transnational Migrant Circuit.* Ph.D. diss., Stanford University.

Saez, Jean-Pierre. 1995. "Introduction." In *Identités, cultures et territoires,* Jean-Pierre Saez, ed. Paris: Desclée de Brouwer, 15–32.

Simposio Indolatinoamericano. 1995. *Derecho indígena y autonomía.* Jaltepec de Candayoc Mixe, Oaxaca, Mexico: Servicios del Pueblo Mixe A. C. SER.

Stavenhagen, Rodolfo, ed. 1988. *Política cultural para un país multiétnico.* Mexico City: Secretaría de Educación Pública–El Colegio de México.

Touraine, Alain. 1992. *Critique de la modernité.* Paris: Fayard.

Trabulse, Elías. 1996. "Los orígenes científicos del indigenismo actual." In *Archivo General de la Nación: Cultura y derechos de los pueblos indígenas en México.* Mexico City: Fondo de Cultura Económica, 77–101.

Turner, Frederick Jackson. 1987. "El significado de la frontera en la historia americana." In *Secuencia, No. 7,* José María Luís Mora, ed. Mexico City: Instituto de Investigaciones Históricas, 187–207.

Vázquez, Josefina Zoraida. 1979. *Nacionalismo y educación en México.* Mexico City: El Colegio de México.

Villegas, Abelardo. 1996. "El criollismo actual." In *Archivo General de la Nación: Cultura y derechos de los pueblos indígenas de México.* Mexico City: Fondo de Cultura Económica, 319–338.

Williams, Raymond. 1982. *Toward 2000.* London: Fontana.

Wolfe, Alan. 1992. "Democracy Versus Sociology: Boundaries and Their Political Consequences." In *Cultivating Differences,* Michele Lamont and Marcel Founier, eds. Chicago: University of Chicago Press, 309–325.

Zea, Leopoldo. 1996. "El problema indígena." In *Archivo General de la Nación: Cultura y derechos de los pueblos indígenas de México.* Mexico City: Fondo de Cultura Económica, 339–352.

Zúñiga, Víctor. 1998. "Representaciones infantiles de la frontera y del espacio nacional." In *Voces de la frontera: Estudios sobre la dispersión cultural en la frontera México–Estados Unidos,* V. Zúñiga, ed. Monterrey, Mexico: Editorial de la Universidad Autónoma de Nuevo León.

Part 2

Economic, Political, and Social Organization on the Border

3

Re-Presenting the Public
Interest on the U.S.-Mexico Border

Michelle A. Saint-Germain

After decades of neglect (benign or otherwise), the southern border region of the United States is attracting renewed attention from policymakers, public administrators, and students. The same is true for the northern border region of Mexico. Yet most accounts describe a top-down (vertical) process on each side of the border, with the national level of government establishing policies for subnational (state, local) units. Little attention has been given to the possibility that these border regions have their own interests, that those interests may diverge from those of their respective nation, and that those interests may be shared (horizontally) across borders. In this chapter I consider how to address shared interests that arise in adjacent border regions that fall under the jurisdiction of different national administrative units. Specifically, I examine how different policy mechanisms treat the representation of the shared interests of the constituencies that populate the U.S.-Mexico border region.[1]

In the first section of this chapter, I briefly define the border for the purposes of this discussion, examine the concept of public interest as important for designing and administering public policy, and apply this concept to the border region. In the second section, I propose a continuum of arrangements for representing border region interests. Alternative public policies can be measured on the continuum to discover the extent to which they acknowledge the existence of and actually reflect a border region public interest. The final section will offer some conclusions about policymaking and public administration in the border region.

This discussion is based on a review of pertinent literature as well as data from research conducted by the author on the U.S.-Mexico border. Specifically, two waves of interviews were conducted with mid-level government officials in the adjacent border cities of El Paso, Texas, and Ciudad Juárez, Chihuahua, during the years 1992–1995. The metropolitan area formed by these two contiguous cities is one of the largest binational settlements in the world. The region shares a long history as well as many common environmental, cultural, and other resources.

The Border

My first task is to describe the U.S.-Mexico border. A boundary is a one-dimensional line surrounding and defining the territory of a nation-state, but a border region includes both the boundary and the region around it as well (Thomas 1994: 94–95). Although there are many possible definitions of the U.S.-Mexico border region, it is useful to indicate some dimensions of the phenomenon being considered here. If the international boundary is about 1,950 miles (3,140 kilometers) long and the border region extends roughly 62 miles (100 kilometers) north and south of the boundary, then it encompasses about 242,182 square miles (628,000 square kilometers). It includes major portions of four U.S. and six Mexican states, twenty-four U.S. counties, and thirty-four Mexican municipalities (Baeza 1985) and as many as 20 million people.

The border region has a geography and a population and has been the target of many public policies and programs. Few studies, however, have considered the question of whether it can be said to form a public and, therefore, have unique public interests, or considered how those public interests might best be manifested in order to affect public policies.

Public Interest(s) at the Border

One of the oldest concerns of policymakers and administrators has been the concept of the public interest. Judith Lichtenberg (1981: 79) remarks that "it is difficult to define the public interest, but it is the goal of public policy." The public interest seems sometimes like the Holy Grail of public officials: it is their sole concern as well as the justification for their existence. A public is a group of people that shares something in common, be it property, concerns, or the negative consequences of the actions of others. Thus, a public interest is a manifestation of what is shared by a public.

Shared experiences may bring a public into existence, but it does not progress beyond a formless condition until it establishes officials and gives them special powers (Dewey 1927). The boundaries of a public thus mark the limits of the effects of conjoint action by its members as well as the limits of the regulatory powers of its officials. A group becomes a public when it lives in a common area, has the same perceptions about the consequences of action, and decides on a solution or goal, for which it appoints officials to act for it in certain circumscribed situations to control the lasting and serious indirect effects of the actions of others (Dewey 1927). In principle, these officials design and implement policies that reflect the interests of the public, and they exercise their functions to benefit the public, not themselves. Although residents of the U.S.-Mexico border region share a common area and common perceptions, they have not as yet been able to appoint officials to act for them, so they have been denied recognition as a legitimate, if unique, binational public.

Using the definitions of the border region and the public interest derived previously, we can now ask whether there are one or multiple publics and, therefore, one or multiple public interests manifested at the U.S.-Mexico border. As an exercise, let us examine these questions with regard to national security and economic policy issues.

National security provides a good example of a policy area where different publics compete for representation of their interests. To most people, national security is a concern of high-level officials in the nation's capital and something best left to the nation's armed forces, which are largely segregated from civilian life. There are few daily reminders of this policy area in everyday life.

At the border, however, one experiences heightened "awareness of the security needs of the state" (Prescott 1987: 171). The goal of the modern nation is the control of territory and the maintenance of territorial integrity. Thus the state attempts to "impose relatively firm boundaries on otherwise porous and unstable geographic edges" (Harvey 1985: 152). For the nation, the border represents "a strategic space, a limit that is always in danger . . . under constant tension" (Montero 1994: 165). Concerns over the ability of the U.S. federal government to control the U.S.-Mexico border date back to a 1930 proposal from President Herbert Hoover to unify border management (Kaiser 1988: 4).

It may be trendy to say that we live in a "world without borders," but the U.S.-Mexico border region has recently been characterized, paradoxically, by the "confirmation of old borders" and the "reimposition of barriers to interaction" (Williams 1993: 213). As economic globalization has seemed to reduce the power of the state, the United States has responded by intensification of the policing function of the state, especially along the U.S.-Mexico border (Andreas 1995). The national government function of law enforcement has been "elevated from 'low' politics to 'high' politics as it takes place at an international boundary" (Andreas 1995: 21).

Indeed, national security policy has recently undergone fundamental shifts with respect to the U.S.-Mexico border. Perhaps the most important is the change in the long-standing Posse Comitatus statute of 1879, which prohibited U.S. armed forces from being used to put down civil disorders or deputized by local officials to carry out law enforcement. Beginning with the Reagan administration, this principle has been steadily eroded by acts of Congress allowing the armed forces to assist civilian law enforcement agencies, especially with respect to drug, customs, and immigration laws (Dunn 1996: 107). An increasing number of joint military-civilian activities are being undertaken along the U.S.-Mexico border, which create a different environment for the people who live there, even if they are not the primary targets of these operations. For example, a U.S. high school student who was herding his family's goats in a west Texas town was shot and killed by four U.S. Marines who were camped out to watch a suspected drug trafficking route. Citizens in the area said "they had never been told that armed forces were in their area on patrol" (Verhovek 1997: 1).

These national security concerns have instigated a "Berlinization" of the U.S.-Mexico border. One witness, testifying at congressional hearings about the impact of federal government policy on local law enforcement officers, charged that U.S. border facilities were "not designed for law enforcement" (Magee 1994: 137). Since then, federal officials have attempted to compensate by adding new technology, such as walls, fences, generator-powered stadium lights, night vision goggles, helicopters, x-ray machines, automatic gate arms, steel columns that rise up out of the ground in front and in back of vehicles to keep them from speeding off, three-sided nail-studded sticks that can be put under rear tires, drug-sniffing dogs, and concrete barriers arranged in a slalom pattern to slow traffic to a crawl. One public manager I interviewed in El Paso remarked, "just crossing the border there and back eats up the whole day."

As can be imagined, interests are perceived differently at the border from a local, as opposed to a national, perspective. The operation of national security policies in the borderland influences the development of the landscape of local community life (Prescott 1987: 77). In the case of the U.S.-Mexico border, this landscape now includes "dangerous fugitives shot and killed at border crossings; violence against street vendors and border agents; patterns of selective enforcement; violent encounters; systematic tolerance of violence; militias/vigilantes; shakedowns of illegal border crossers; murders, rapes, beatings, torture, and robbery" (U.S. House of Representatives 1990: 5–8).

Changes in national security policy tend to have a whiplash effect on the local community where the change is implemented. A national decision to step up security initiatives in some border areas can result in a shift of the targeted activities to other border communities, overwhelming the local residents and law enforcement officials. For example, launching Operation Gatekeeper in western San Diego County resulted in a sharp increase in environmentally related migrant deaths in eastern San Diego County, with thirteen deaths resulting from hypothermia in January 1997 alone

(Eschbach, Hagan, and Rodríguez 1997: 10). One observer quips that "federal officials' job is to maintain the border as a legal boundary (i.e., barrier) while local officials' job is to cope with federal overregulation" (Jamail 1981: 85).

Similar developments have occurred on the northern Mexican border. National security concerns have resulted in an increased presence of existing federal police and military units at the border. In addition, new paramilitary law enforcement units have been created, such as Grupo Beta, often over the protests of local residents.

Paradoxically, the presence at the border of two separate systems of law works to encourage lawless behavior. Currently, persons who commit crimes on one side of the border—whether as minor as motor vehicle violations or as major as murder—can hide out on the other side. There is no courtesy extended to officers of the law in "hot pursuit" of suspects, and extradition agreements are limited, vague, and rarely enforced. Thus, national sovereignty concerns act as a barrier to solving serious border region problems of crime and violence.

Economic policy provides another example of divergent national and local interests colliding at the border. The U.S. government sees the border region as both integral and subordinate to the primary goal of national economic growth (Herzog 1986b: 113) as embodied in the North American Free Trade Agreement (NAFTA). NAFTA was designed to increase the volume of U.S.-Mexico trade and create a positive balance of trade for the United States. To pay for the increased workload for U.S. officials made necessary by the increased volume of economic activity brought about by NAFTA, the federal government planned to impose a federal border crossing fee (in addition to the existing local fee) of $3 per car and $1.50 per pedestrian on those entering the United States. The Immigration and Naturalization Service (INS) felt that the communities that benefit economically from cross-border traffic should pay for border "enhancements," whereas the local inhabitants, already greatly inconvenienced by heightened security measures, saw increased fees as adding insult to injury.

With economic globalization, economic interests at the local or regional level may begin to diverge from those at the national level, and substate units may begin to question the state as a source of political or national identity as well (Agnew 1993: 229–230). The economic impacts of NAFTA on El Paso were not the same as those on the state of Texas or the nation as a whole. For example, for the first two years of NAFTA, Mexican trucks were allowed into the United States but were restricted to commercial zones within 20 miles of the border. In interviews, several U.S. public managers underscored the increased costs to El Paso of providing or maintaining infrastructure such as roads and bridges under the increased weight of trade spurred by NAFTA. Truck traffic on El Paso bridges is up. Heavier trucks are now coming over from Mexico, and drivers unfamiliar with El Paso are traveling on city streets that were not meant to support that kind of weight. There is more illegal truck parking on city streets, which also causes damage. Longer waiting times on the bridges are increasing both air pollution and damage done by heavy trucks. However, these problems found no sympathy from national officials. Rather, concerns about the possible impact of Mexican truck traffic on the national highway system prompted the United States to impose a delay in the implementation of NAFTA provisions that would allow Mexican trucks to travel beyond the restricted border zones (Gross 1995).

Similarly, Mexican border economic interests diverge from Mexican national interests. Mexican national policy includes "economic stimulation, a boost in the average standard of living, reduction of high unemployment, bringing in new technology, creating a highly trained workforce, and generating income to pay off foreign debt" (Vaznaugh 1993: 211–212). One engine of this economic policy is the twin-plant or in-bond plant system, known as maquiladoras. Under this plan, Mexico created special zones at its northern border where foreign (mostly U.S.) companies could build subsidiary plants that import separate components and perform labor-intensive assembly work. The products are then shipped back to the United States as finished goods but are taxed only on the value added. Since 1964, this national plan has transformed small northern Mexican border towns into bustling metropolises. The growth caused by this national policy has had tremendous effects on the natural, built, and cultural environment both in northern Mexican border towns and their U.S. counterparts, including problems of growth management, land management, transportation, environmental impact, and planning (Herzog 1986a: 6).

Negative externalities are the results of action in one jurisdiction that spill over into another jurisdiction. In this case, the national economic policies of both Mexico and the United States have caused negative externalities for their own as well as the other country's border regions, in areas such as population explosion, crime, poverty, unemployment, air pollution, water shortages, lack of housing, poor health, communication, transportation, waste management, and violence (Raat 1992: 192).

These examples show how local interests at the border region diverge from national interests in terms of security (national versus neighborhood) and economics (national versus community). Many other examples could be provided in social, cultural, and other areas of public endeavor. At the same time, however, public managers in El Paso and Ciudad Juárez also recognize many joint interests common to their border communities, as simple as exchanging maps and as complex as developing a joint geographic information system. For example, one public manager from El Paso pointed out that "it makes no sense not to engage in recycling on a regional basis." Managers from both sides of the border point out a number of common goals, such as "providing a safe, secure environment for our citizens to raise families in," and other "basic concerns that all cities have," such as streets to maintain. They also identify common problems such as pollution, pesticides, hazardous wastes, working conditions, water, housing, unemployment, gangs, garbage, transportation, industrial and economic development, plant diseases and predatory insects, poverty, and threats to human and animal health. As one Ciudad Juárez manager explained:

> When El Paso sneezes, Ciudad Juárez gets a fever, or a cold, and I think very soon we're going to see that when Ciudad Juárez gets a cold, El Paso will also get a fever. They don't want to see, many times, the people don't understand how dependent the two cities are, one upon the other. When one gets sick, it goes badly for the other. This will be ever more evident with free trade, if it passes. No, whether it passes or not. (author's translation of original Spanish)

An El Paso manager put it even more firmly:

> As a matter of fact, I think El Paso and Juárez [are] just one city. Too bad we have the river, but other than that, we share the same problems and we cherish the same goals. I think it would be foolish not to [recognize this]. I don't think we will have any alternative other than to work with them if we are to resolve our mutual problems. What happens in Juárez, we also feel it in El Paso, and vice versa.

If the border is an identifiable region, with its own distinct interests, how best can those interests be represented? How can people in the border region have a share in the decisionmaking processes that produce policy and administrative programs? One way is to join forces. One El Paso manager suggested a strategy of "strength in numbers": "El Paso is too small-thinking. We're a big city, but we still think we're small, and can't really get people to pay attention and look at [our interests] as a priority. And I think we need to work with Juárez to do it, because they're at least three times bigger than we are."

Re-Presenting the Public Interest

Boris Graizbord (1983: 10) notes that the border region "pays a price for mixing local, regional, national and international concerns and multiple tensions." The tension at the border is a result of multiple and overlapping publics with diverse interests, only some of which are recognized as legitimate and accorded representation by public policy making and administering officials. As Sergio Montero (1994: 62) asks, "What are the possibilities of harmonizing the people whom the border now divides? Is some kind of union possible? Is it desirable? How would this union function? What are the barriers?"

A variety of strategies for resolving or abating this tension at the border region have been elaborated (e.g., Fry 1988; Herzog 1986a, 1986b, 1991a, 1991b; Ryan 1993; Stoddard 1986; Vaznaugh 1993). With few exceptions, however, most proposals have assumed that the purpose is to negotiate only national interests (compatible or incompatible) or to negotiate local interests as subordinate to a hierarchy of interests within each country. Almost no one begins from the perspective of the border region as one public with common interests that deserve to be manifested and dealt with by the members of that public in relative autonomy. Two exceptions are Herzog (already noted) and Oscar Martínez (1994).

I propose a continuum of possible forms (public policies) that could be used to express public interest for the border region (Figure 3.1). My formulation differs from that of Martínez (1994), who discusses a four-stage borderlands continuum, from alienated through coexistent and interdependent to integrated. Although his sympathies lie with the borderlanders, his models are described almost entirely from the perspective of national rather than local interests. For Martínez, the level of integration "is fundamentally dependent on the relationship between adjoining nations" (1994: 11). Also, he is not focusing on the variety in possible policy instruments and how different instruments can reflect different conceptions of the underlying public interest.

The continuum I propose stretches across nine stages, from the most

Figure 3.1   A Continuum of Public Policies Re-Presenting Border Region Interests

Separate National Interests				Common Binational Interests				Separate Border Region Interests
I								I
I	I	I	I	I	I	I	I	I
1	2	3	4	5	6	7	8	9

Legend: 1. Independent policymaking by each nation
        2. Extraterritorial jurisdiction by one or both nations
        3. General international treaties
        4. Specific binational treaties
        5. Binational institutions for joint implementation
        6. Integrated two-country intergovernmental agreements
        7. Informal two-country local agreements
        8. Formal two-country local agreements
        9. Autonomous border region institutions

extreme situation of the border region divided between two completely independent nations, with no expression of common interests (stage 1), to the other pole of autonomous border region institutions that express the common interests of the inhabitants of the border regions independently of any other political entities or jurisdictions (stage 9). These stages are described in detail in what follows.

1. *Independent policymaking by each nation.* In this situation, two nations independently exercise sovereignty over their territory up to the boundary line. This would probably be the condition existing in a state of war (hot or cold). There is no perception of a transboundary border region. National border regions are not perceived to have any interests different from those of the nation. Although the United States and Mexico cannot be characterized as being at this point right now, it represents a preferred state for some people. Public administrators generally abide by the convention that these artificial but well-marked boundaries promote "peace and better administration" (Prescott 1987: 80) or by the old adage that "good fences make good neighbors." As one Ciudad Juárez manager remarked: "When you say border, do you include El Paso? Well, our agencies could work well across the border, but only as [an informal] type of relationship, because it is at the border precisely that the application of Mexican law ceases, and it is there also that the application of North American law ceases" (author's translation of original Spanish).

This end of the continuum is no longer accepted as unproblematic. Although we still cling to the belief that national policies should promote that nation's interests, a nation's boundaries "are increasingly less relevant . . . to determining whose interest must be considered in formulating [public] policies" (Lichtenberg 1981: 92). It is increasingly difficult to identify any "national" interests based on shared values or culture. Writers now find that "national culture is not an essence but a group of essences, amalgamated, of course, into something amorphous and indivisible, without it mattering that these essences are contrary and opposed to one another in different ways" (Montero 1994: 86–88).

In fact, according to Dale Furnish, "laws that [attempt to] define and enforce a common border suffer constant pressure in a way other laws never do" (1985: 73). The problem with border laws is that they affect a "bifurcated constituency"—they respond to national interests, not the interests of those on (either side of) the border. This unrepresented constituency lives in tension with those laws and eventually contorts the laws to its own "special imperative" (Furnish 1985: 74). Interlocking border region societies and economies give rise to a third society defined by geography, economics, and personal attachments that do not respect the political frontier (Furnish 1985: 82). Thus a vicious cycle ensues: the border region is important and thus affects national life; affected national actors react by imposing national will on the border; national laws conflict with border interests; border residents act to frustrate the law. The border activity both makes the law necessary and guarantees that the law will not solve the problem (Furnish 1985: 75). These sentiments were expressed by a long-time El Paso public manager:

> The border is an intriguing environment, and people who come here from other parts of the country, who plan on changing the environment, get consumed by the environment, and become very frustrated people because they don't study what they have to work with, and they can't adjust and the border's not going to adjust to them. The border will thwart you; I think people on the border will thwart you. You won't be able to, you have to understand the players and the system, and you have to learn how to utilize the players and the system to get things done. You cannot enslave it, holding your hand up to keep the water from coming down the river; you're not going to do that. And it's frustrating. People get very frustrated. I've seen a lot of people, I've hired a lot of people, I've met a lot of people; there are a lot of people here who still don't understand it . . . all they do is complain about the border, the system, the people, and all that. They're not happy and the problem is that they have not taken the time to try and understand the rules of the game and what it takes to accomplish things. It's not that bad. It's not that much different of an environment to work in, because every environment has its own personality. This one, though, has a personality that's foreign to a lot of people, and they can't understand it and they don't want to adjust to it and face the problem.

2. *Extraterritorial jurisdiction.* This is a type of legal arrangement that allows adjudication in the courts of one country of the claims arising against citizens or corporations of that country who are operating in another country. The practice of extraterritorial jurisdiction is said to be justified under internationally accepted principles of nationality, citizen allegiance, state responsibility for nationals, and state interest in citizen welfare (Vaznaugh 1993: 230). One example would be the application of U.S. environmental legislation to actions of U.S. companies in Mexico. Another example is provided by Mexican labor leaders who, under the terms of NAFTA, have recently filed suit against the U.S. telecommunications company Sprint, accusing it of unfair labor practices according to Mexican standards.

This type of approach assumes that the two nations may have some common interests at the border region but lack the will or the mechanisms to express them. Thus extraterritorial jurisdiction advances the interests of two countries separately (Vaznaugh 1993: 224–225) but makes no provision for independent border region interests to be expressed.

3. *General international treaties.* A number of international treaties have been signed by many nations, whether or not they are neighbors such

as the United States and Mexico. These include the Montreal Protocol on Substances That Deplete the Ozone Layer and the Basel Convention on the Control of Transboundary Wastes and Their Disposal. Unlike the first two stages on the continuum, stage 3 treaties assume that nations do have some common interests and have found a way to express them through multinational treaties. Although border (transboundary) regions may be affected by these treaties, it is assumed that each side of the border region has (or can express) no interests other than those of its nation. Implementation mechanisms for these treaties are often left to be self-policed by each signatory. Even when those treaties or agreements have supranational oversight bodies (for example, the General Agreement on Tariffs and Trade [GATT], NAFTA, or the Central Commission for the Navigation of the Rhine), "international regulatory efforts are often designed at a level which is distant from the people whose behavior is targeted, which often results in implementation problems" (Bernauer 1995: 3–4). Additionally, the question of a border region with unique interests apart from those of the nation is not considered by this approach. For example, it is as difficult to move an exhibit of Mexican art from Ciudad Juárez to El Paso as to Peru due to stringent regulations over taking objects of national patrimony out of the country.

4. *Specific binational treaties.* Many examples of binational treaties exist all over the world. These treaties are often more specific than global multinational treaties, since they deal with more limited situations. One example is the Agreement Between the United States and Mexico on Cooperation for the Protection and Improvement of the Environment in the Border Area (the La Paz Agreement). This agreement directs the government officials of each nation "to prevent, reduce, and eliminate sources of air, water, and soil pollution within 50 kilometers of the [boundary]" (Vaznaugh 1993: 221). Like the general international treaties above, this approach assumes that nations do share common interests, but that these joint interests may be especially evident in the regions abutting the international boundary. Nevertheless, it retains the perspective that the articulation of these interests is the sole prerogative of the national level of government, which alone has authority to negotiate international agreements. Concomitantly, it preserves the idea of national sovereignty by instituting parallel but separate implementation systems with each nation. One El Paso county manager's comment reflects this view: "In the border regions, there is no such thing as a county issue. It's almost always *international*" (emphasis added).

5. *Binational institutions for joint implementation.* This approach represents the second milestone on the continuum. The first milestone (at stage 3) marked the progression from an assumption of separate interests to an assumption of shared interests. This second milestone (at stage 5) marks

the progression from proprietary self-implementation to coordinated joint implementation. This is best exemplified by the U.S.-Mexico treaties that established the International Boundary and Water Commission (IBWC). The IBWC is an "institution designed to facilitate joint action while protecting national sovereignty" (Ingram and White 1993: 153). Separate U.S. and Mexican administrators negotiate shared concerns based on national interests and then implement the agreements reached. The national representatives to the IBWC are situated within the foreign affairs ministries of each country. The IBWC has been hailed as "a model of international cooperation," demonstrating the "capacity of both nations to accommodate their political differences in settling potentially divisive problems arising from their common border" (Mumme 1988: 45).

However, in a thorough analysis of the IBWC, Helen Ingram and David White (1993: 153) report that it has been criticized for "its failure to include state and local governments and non-governmental organizations (NGOs) in its decision-making processes." Although the IBWC's name implies that there are common concerns of two nations whose territories meet at a shared international boundary and those concerns are endemic only (or mostly) to the border region, the IBWC does not have any mechanism for directly determining the interests of the border region. Local concerns must be sent up through the hierarchy of subnational governmental units and are accorded little status in the pecking order of government interests. In fact, NAFTA may be eroding what little power and autonomy local governments had in the intergovernmental system in both the United States and Mexico (see Saint-Germain 1995c). As one El Paso manager pointed out:

> We are a metropolitan area of approximately 2 million people, and we share the same resources and environment, and, yeah, there needs to be significant interaction. If the federal governments would just let us interact with a little less interference maybe we could get some things done. Most of our major success is done on the local basis, without having to deal with Mexico City, who does not understand the border, and [without] having to deal with Washington, D.C., who does not understand the border. People [there] do not understand the border. They have no concept of the U.S.-Mexican border if they're not on it and have not been here. It's a different world and they don't understand [that just] because they establish programs or do things that will work somewhere [else], they may not work here; but they don't even bother to come down here and find out what will work. And it's, we say, even the state of Texas, and even Chihuahua City, even Arizona, California, New Mexico, the state offices—although they have a better feel for it than the federal [government]—they still have other problems and priorities; and the border is the border: it's a different place. They have a tendency of not wanting to put their assets in this area because they have a tendency to feel that they're stuffing money down a rat hole, I think. The adage around here is that the

only time they come visit us is when there's an election. And the rest of the time we fool ourselves because they really don't get it. And the other side of the border is very much alike, even though they are in different states in Mexico. But they don't relate to their federal government, they don't relate to their state governments.

6. *Integrated two-country intergovernmental agreements.* In this situation, all three levels of both U.S. and Mexican governments are involved in negotiating transboundary agreements to reflect the interests of the binational border region. Both the United States and Mexico, as federated republics, have federal, state, and local governments. Although the actual intergovernmental functioning of these distinct governmental units is quite different in the two nations, the principle of integrated intergovernmental agreements can obtain nevertheless. That is, entities of the federal, state, and local governments that have overlapping (or coinciding) jurisdiction in the border region, on both sides, join together to negotiate binding agreements that reflect the interests of the transboundary region. For years, El Paso managers attempted to convince the federal Environmental Protection Agency (EPA) that they must take Ciudad Juárez into account when designating air quality standards for the area.

In this formulation, all three levels of government are actively involved and represented, and agreements have formal recognition by all levels of government. Agreements by lower levels of government only, however, would not be recognized as valid. This option would address the problems of the lack of state and local participation identified in the last alternative. It recognizes joint interests not only of two neighboring nations but also of subnational neighboring entities such as states and municipalities. It establishes a process for integrating the interests of both vertical (intranational) and horizontal (international) entities in order to address common interests and negative externalities.

There are still problems with this approach, however, from a local point of view. Historically, national governments usually have considered jurisdictional spillover problems to be local problems, even though the localities are often ill-equipped to address transboundary externalities. Yet localities are reluctant to consider solutions that call for help from upper levels of government, since these move the problem from the arena of traditional local, urban, domestic concerns to the "domain of international relations and foreign policy" (Herzog 1986b: 100). Thus this option can shift the terms of the policy debate away from local concerns and toward national concerns, allow outside interests to capture the debate, and highlight the limited (economic, political, and other) resources of local actors compared to state or national actors. In short, it has all the defects identified for other intergovernmental relations situations in the United States. One El Paso arts administrator identified the situation in these words:

As local communities, we are part of a larger national whole. And so where those national or state regulations are in place, we have to abide by those, and they are not always the most efficient way to go about dealing with local concerns, even when those local concerns are international. Right now, with respective federal regulations in the United States and Mexico, it makes it difficult. I think that very often people that live locally on both sides of the border are more accustomed to dealing with each other in a more informal way and on a more daily basis than national governments give us credit for. And we would be able to deal with things in a more efficient manner, but other rules and regulations step in.

7. *Informal two-country local agreements.* Another milestone marks this stage. Here the progression is to the recognition of two parallel local publics within the border region that have shared interests. Subnational units of government on both sides of the border that share interests join together to elaborate programs and implement them jointly. This approach assumes that local transboundary border regions have interests that they share and that do not necessarily coincide with the national interests of either federal government. Further, it assumes that the people closest to the problems have the best ideas about how to solve them. For example, listening to U.S. federal officials, one could derive the false impression that the Mexican border region is homogeneous, whereas there are really at least three distinct zones: west (Baja California and Sonora), middle (Chihuahua), and east (Tamaulipas). Each zone is much more closely tied to—and reflects interaction with—its U.S. counterpart than to other Mexican border zones or to other zones within Mexico (Raat 1992: 180).

In practice these informal arrangements are a staple of public policy and administration on the U.S.-Mexico border, according to the public managers interviewed. For example, El Paso and Ciudad Juárez water workers do "twinning," spending time with a counterpart to get to know each other and their respective operating systems. Local health department personnel may have the most intensive involvement, in areas such as tuberculosis treatment, child immunization education, binational air quality monitoring, and pest control (e.g., mosquitoes). Some disaster preparedness officials have begun to coordinate drills, although they are frustrated by security and logistics concerns. Juvenile justice authorities often informally return underage nationals to their respective countries. City planners have also been in quite frequent contact and have good working relationships with their counterparts, as do economic development and chamber of commerce officials. From nutrition programs for the elderly to public libraries, services are often provided informally to all residents of the border region. As one El Paso manager pointed out:

I think that especially on the border, the future is in working together. . . .
We know that this is going to happen, that we have to deal with the envi-

ronment. I think El Paso and Ciudad Juárez represent the largest metropolitan statistical area or whatever you want to call it on the border, along the U.S.-Mexico border. I think we are in a unique position to really do some neat things working together. I think it will definitely end up happening, that we will end up working together in the environmental area. It's not stopping at the border; pollution doesn't stop, you know. The air pollution, the water pollution, the recycling problems, they don't stop at the border. We might as well work together, so I think it will happen.

Unfortunately, the very existence as well as the effectiveness of local informal agreements waxes and wanes with changes in personnel; municipal, state, and national elections; and other political and economic developments. In addition, these agreements do not afford any legal standing on which citizens can solve their problems, nor do they provide any legal grounds for government officials to take official actions outside their jurisdictional boundaries.

8. *Formal two-country local agreements.* This approach is substantially like the one just discussed above, with one important difference. Local (subnational) units of government would have the authority to reach formal, rather than merely informal, agreements, which would be binding on the parties and respected by other levels of government. These agreements would be reached by local units of government across the border to realize the transboundary interests of the border region. The agreements so reached would be implemented by both sides conjointly. Although the Mexican constitution has recently been amended to allow for the possibility of such agreements initiated by Mexican municipalities, law in the United States would have to be substantially amended to provide the same prerogatives for U.S. municipalities.

Contiguous subnational authorities often have been involved in formal and informal agreements and projects, both along and across national boundaries. Historically, however, formal agreements have tended to be merely microversions of national diplomatic agreements, whereas informal agreements arose to solve problems created at the periphery by the formal agreements negotiated at the countries' centers. Local public managers are under pressure to conform to the dictates of their national governments while remaining sensitive to the concerns of their cross-border counterparts, on whom they may be more dependent socially and economically. Milton Jamail (1981: 85) adds that it often falls to third-sector organizations (commissions, service organizations, universities, chambers of commerce, professional groups, and local chapters of national groups) to maintain "informal, extra-legal, and unofficial communication and ties" across the border under the present system. Many public and nonprofit service providers, such as alcohol and drug abuse treatment and support groups, work informally across the border to find the best services for their clients.

However, a Ciudad Juárez manager pointed out that cooperation exists now mostly along narrow lines of specialization, which prevents people from getting a holistic view of the border region:

> Planning officials in El Paso have envisioned the need for a specific city department: dealing with international issues, with knowledge of international law. There's a lot of development in this region that used to be done at a binational level, an international level, including transportation, the development of water resources, sewage disposal, sanitation, the management of hazardous materials, environmental protection. What we do in that area is more at an informal level than at a formal level. I think that we need a department . . . related to international issues, to develop policy, international policy, for the solution of the various binational problems that there have been.

A Ciudad Juárez planner highlighted the same concerns:

> This is the first time, I think, in the history of the border, that a serious effort is being made to develop joint programs. Before, there were meetings, but nothing happened, everything remained at the level of plans, ideas, and handshakes. Now we need to create a formal organization to institutionalize this. There isn't one now; everything is done by meetings, perhaps formal meetings, but there is no institution to agglomerate all these efforts. Yes, it would be very important, and even more important would be for it to follow up on everything, so that if anything happened to us, personally, the people who came afterward could continue the relationship. (author's translation of original Spanish)

This ability to conclude meaningful, border-centered formal agreements would allow localities to find holistic solutions to their common challenges, rather than to continue the fragmented approach offered by a patchwork of international treaties, binational agreements, executive agency rules and regulations, and transient, informal arrangements.

9. *Autonomous border region institutions.* This is the final stage that realization of the transboundary interests of the border region can reach. In this form, quasi-autonomous jurisdictions would be set up that encompass entire transboundary border regions (without respect to nationality). A Ciudad Juárez manager explained, "We are all binationals, who just happen to be divided only by a river." One El Paso manager added, "I'd like to see that concept of the border being moved back about 50 miles, open it up here to both cities. It's going to have to happen, especially if this NAFTA agreement goes into effect." All the citizens of the region would have the same voice in deliberating and deciding on public policies and programs for their jurisdiction. Citizens today belong to many overlapping jurisdictions, such as municipalities, states, and nations, not to mention the nearly

80,000 units of government in the United States that regulate such areas as mosquito abatement, transportation, or school districts. One El Paso manager involved in economic development had this to say on the eve of the NAFTA vote in the U.S. Senate in 1993:

> We've got to get away from "mine" and "theirs." You've got to work with your neighbors. There's no other place on the planet that has, that is this close to each other, that is a border city this large, two border cities this large. And say NAFTA doesn't go through, [people say], "what are we going to do now?" But if we start working together now, who cares about NAFTA? We had NAFTA here already. If you look at everything that we've got, we've already got NAFTA, more or less; we've got free trade going across our borders. We shouldn't stop all the efforts that we are doing now and go back into our cocoons.

A Ciudad Juárez manager used almost exactly the same words:

> We can't think in terms of "mine" without having present also the reality of the "other." Very frequently here in this border area, El Paso concepts are applied to speak of the problems of Juárez, and vice versa. The North American functionary—the same as the Mexican functionary—has many problems in doing justice to the other community when making decisions, because it is different, it is the unknown. If someone doesn't know the reality of the other community, they can be very unjust. It works the same way here, [looking] from here to there. So it is very important, ever more important, that the functionaries in this region be experts in the culture of Ciudad Juárez, and that we *juarenses* be experts in the culture of El Paso, of Las Cruces [New Mexico], of the entire [border] region. That reality must be present in our decisions. (author's translation of original Spanish)

This border region jurisdiction would not supplant the other jurisdictions that exist simultaneously to perform other functions but would address important concerns that no other unit could. For example, the University of Texas–El Paso allows Ciudad Juárez residents to pay the same tuition as Texas residents, and many school districts in Texas (and New Mexico) border communities already unofficially provide education to Ciudad Juárez children. One public manager, a lifelong El Paso resident, recommended this solution:

> You've got to start with the little ones, so when they grow up, there's some communication, some appreciation, it's not all just a foreign country. You can't start with adults, I mean, you can try, but it's easier with kids. . . . I look at [this situation] and I think, it's going to happen in twenty or twenty-five years from now in any other city. We are on the edge. [But] we are not as progressive as we should be; we are just chipping away at it.

Thomas Bernauer (1995: 3–4) signals that "the most common solution to problems of externalities and market failures is not available in the case of transboundary [spillovers]: there is no central authority that could solve these problems by simply imposing remedial policies (e.g., taxes, subsidies, emission licenses, prohibitions, product and production process requirements, etc.). There is no legal framework through which producers and victims of externalities could effectively settle their conflicts, for example, by engaging in legal action over liability for pollution." Such a jurisdiction could explicitly address local transboundary concerns that are not now the province of any binational agency or are handled in an uncoordinated and haphazard fashion by many national agencies. It would also overcome the approach of merely technical fixes to problems that need holistic, political solutions. For example, many border managers mentioned the creation of a regional transportation district that would reactivate the old international bus or streetcar system, install a new international light rail system, or perhaps even implement a new binational transportation hub that would serve both civilian and military airline, train, and truck traffic. As one Ciudad Juárez manager envisioned the future:

> We're now creating a zone, not a border zone but a metropolitan zone, that will encompass all the urban areas of Juárez, El Paso, and New Mexico and all the counties that are close by. I think that the criterion will be to develop, hand in hand, the entire region. Because, as I said, realistically, whatever happens to us will have repercussions on them, and vice versa. So I feel that in the future, as much due to free trade as to market globalization, we will have to put forth a thousand efforts, reach a thousand objectives, to make us stand out as a region. It will be very, very important to work on common, bilateral projects. (author's translation of original Spanish)

Some models exist of these types of institutions, mostly in Western Europe. There is some difference of opinion over whether the U.S.-Mexico border region could adopt or adapt such models because of the disparities between the two situations (for an excellent discussion of these issues, see Herzog 1986b, 1991b). One question is whether greater economic integration will bring greater political integration (Graizbord 1983). However, I believe a wait-and-see approach is not correct; rather, one should not be allowed without the other. Arguments are made that the weaker partner (presumably Mexico) would suffer in such an arrangement. Assessments of the economically dependent status of Mexico vis-à-vis the United States, however, do not always hold in the border region, where the population of Mexican municipalities often vastly outnumbers the corresponding U.S. population and where the economies of the U.S. municipalities are dependent on their Mexican counterparts. Neither are Mexican municipalities politically dependent on the United States. And culturally, the border region has evolved a new set of values, so that neither side is experiencing cultural oblivion. The major difficulty facing an autonomous border-region institution is the national sovereignty principle. Any such agency would have to transcend the narrow interests reflected in local power struggles and national political agendas (Herzog 1986a: 5). One El Paso arts manager proposed creating a regional arts service:

> It will have to be well established what the mission is, what the goals are, and whether it will be able to achieve its goals. At first, it's going to take a lot of time without any results. You'd have to know who the players are. It would have to fully represent the needs on a local basis, as well as on a civic basis. This is a valley that really belongs closer together. We have to realize that when we look only to New York, or Los Angeles, or Chicago, or Houston, we are only looking at half the pie, a 180-degree view. Why should we lose 180 degrees? We need to look also to Ciudad Juárez, Monterrey, Guadalajara, Mexico City, Zacatecas. . . . We have to recognize what is going on, on the other side, not only to acknowledge it but to encourage a stronger dialogue to reinforce the entire region. I feel bound to provide a regional service.

One model in the United States is the council of governments (COG) organization used in many metropolitan areas, a voluntary association in which local (municipal, county, and special district) governments devolve authority upward to an umbrella organization for specific purposes, such as coordination of regionwide planning and infrastructure projects. Although COGs do not have much official authority to act independently, a structure with more autonomy and more authority could be evolved from existing practices. This kind of organization could also be the realization of the model of the public sphere as an energy field proposed by Charles Fox and Hugh Miller (1995). In this model, public administrators and other members of a public with a robust subculture engage in discourse to find solutions to problems of public policy and administration. One El Paso manager captured these sentiments by calling for the formation of a binational chapter of the American Society for Public Administration: "And now with this NAFTA, I think, we're going to have to build it. It's not just a matter of whether we want to or not, or whether we need to do it, [but] to protect the public interest, to have somebody speaking out."

If "the primary good that we distribute to one another is membership in some human community" (Walzer 1981: 1), then the creation of autonomous border region institutions would recognize the human community that forms a public in the U.S.-Mexico border region. Members of that human community would have a greater say in both paying for and receiving the goods and services to be allocated. This represents a more

Aristotelian definition of public interest, in which individuals participate in democratic activities to decide not for themselves separately but for the community generally (Walzer 1981: 16) and thereby improve both themselves and the community at the same time. Local alliances for the public interest could form alternative responses to the often disastrous consequences of national and international policies for border regions.

Conclusion

There is a need for studies of the evolution of the role of boundaries and their changing functions (Prescott 1987: 173) so that strategies can be devised to address their problems. With the advent of NAFTA, all three nations (the United States, Mexico, and Canada) will not only study each other more closely but also study their own composition, institutions, and mechanisms more closely; all three will become more self-conscious of their own making and remaking (Smorkaloff 1994: 99).

This examination of possible policies points to the need for public officials at all levels of government in nations that share borders to better understand each other's policymaking and administrative systems. In particular, local public managers in border regions must be able to work with one another across artificial boundaries not only to find solutions to common problems but also to strengthen local autonomy (Saint-Germain 1995a). International bodies such as the World Bank are promoting the "devolution" of responsibilities from higher to lower levels of government; in Mexico this movement has been called "decentralization" (Rodriguez 1993). In order to fashion successful border region policies, local public managers must learn not only about new administrative and policy skills but also about the structure and culture of administration in the entire border region at the same time. This in turn implies a need for revitalization of the study and teaching of comparative administration in order to train those future public policy makers and administrators (Saint-Germain 1995a).

Finally, those who study the border must no longer presume to be addressing only a national audience, with national interests. The process of defining or ascertaining interests—especially public interests—must change. It is time to widen the border discourse to admit all from the wider transboundary border region who have an interest in the outcome.

Notes

1. Support for this research was provided in part by the University of Texas at El Paso and by the Fulbright Border Lecturer Program.

References

Agnew, John. 1993. "The United States and American Hegemony." In *Political Geography of the Twentieth Century: A Global Analysis,* Peter J. Taylor, ed. New York: Halsted Press, 207–238.

Andreas, Peter. 1995. "The Retreat and Resurgence of the State: Liberalizing and Criminalizing Cross-Border Flows in an Integrated World." Paper presented at the American Political Science Association, Chicago.

Baeza, Arturo Licón. 1985. "Las normas jurídicas como reglas del juego en la frontera." In *Rules of the Game and Games Without Rules in Border Life,* Mario Miranda Pacheco and James W. Wilkie, eds. Mexico City: ANUIES, 41–49.

Bernauer, Thomas. 1995. "Managing International Rivers." Paper presented at the American Political Science Association, Chicago.

Dewey, John. 1927. *The Public and Its Problems.* Chicago: Swallow Press.

Dunn, Timothy J. 1996. *The Militarization of the U.S.-Mexico Border 1978–1992: Low Intensity Conflict Doctrine Comes Home.* Austin: University of Texas, Center for Mexican American Studies.

Eschbach, Karl, Jacqueline Hagan, and Néstor Rodríguez. 1997. "Death at the Border." Working paper. Houston: University of Houston, Center for Immigration Research.

Fox, Charles J., and Hugh T. Miller. 1995. *Postmodern Public Administration: Toward Discourse.* Thousand Oaks, Calif.: Sage.

Fry, Earl H. 1988. "Subnational Units in an Age of Complex Independence: Implications for the International System." In *Centralizing and Decentralizing Trends in Federal States,* C. Lloyd Brown-John, ed. Lanhan, Md.: University Press of America, 75–88.

Furnish, Dale Beck. 1985. "Border Laws and Other Artificial Constraints." In *Rules of the Game and Games Without Rules in Border Life,* Mario Miranda Pacheco and James W. Wilkie, eds. Mexico City: ANUIES, 73–94.

Graizbord, Boris. 1983. "Integracíon, diferencias regionales e interdependencia en la frontera de México con Estados Unidos." *Demografía y Economía* 17, no. 53: 1–20.

Gross, Gregory. 1995. "Safety Worries Hold Up Cross-Border Trucking." *San Diego Union Tribune,* December 19, p. 1.

Harvey, David. 1985. "The Geopolitics of Capitalism." In *Social Relations and Spatial Structure,* D. Gregory and J. Urry, eds. London: Macmillan, 128–163.

Herzog, Lawrence A. 1986a. "San Diego–Tijuana: The Emergence of a Trans-Boundary Metropolitan Ecosystem." In *Planning the International Border Metropolis: Trans-Boundary Policy Options in the San Diego–Tijuana Region,* Lawrence A. Herzog, ed. San Diego: Center for U.S.-Mexican Studies, University of California–San Diego, 1–12.

———. 1986b. "Trans-Boundary Metropolitan Ecosystem Management in the San Diego–Tijuana Region." In *Across Boundaries: Transborder Interaction in Comparative Perspective,* Oscar J. Martínez, ed. El Paso: Texas Western Press, 96–116.

———. 1991a. "Cross-National Urban Structure in an Era of Global Cities: The U.S.-Mexico Transfrontier Metropolis." *Urban Studies* 28, no. 4: 519–533.

———. 1991b. "International Boundary Cities: The Debate on Transfrontier Planning in Two Border Regions." *Natural Resources Journal* 31, no. 3: 587–608.

Ingram, Helen, and David R. White. 1993. "International Boundary and Water

Commission: An Institutional Mismatch for Resolving Transboundary Problems." *Natural Resources Journal* 33, no. 1: 153–175.

Jamail, Milton H. 1981. "Voluntary Organizations Along the Border." *Mexico– United States Relations* (special issues), S. K. Purcell, guest ed. *Proceedings of the Academy of Political Science* 31, no. 1: 78–87.

Kaiser, Frederick M. 1988. "Border Management Reorganization." In *Border Management Reorganization and Drug Interdiction,* Congressional Research Service, ed. Washington, D.C.: U.S. Government Printing Office, 1–36.

Lichtenberg, Judith. 1981. "National Boundaries and Moral Boundaries: A Cosmopolitan View." In *Boundaries: National Autonomy and Its Limits,* Peter G. Brown and Henry Shue, eds. Totowa, N.J.: Rowman and Littlefield, 79–100.

Magee, R. Michael. 1994. "Statement." In *The Mexican Border: Impact on Local Law Enforcement in the United States,* U.S. House of Representatives, Committee on Government Operations, Subcommittee on Information, Justice, Transportation, and Agriculture, ed. Washington, D.C.: U.S. Government Printing Office, 133–145.

Martínez, Oscar J. 1994. *Border People: Life and Society in the U.S.-Mexico Borderlands.* Tucson: University of Arizona Press.

Montero, Sergio Gomez. 1994. *The Border: The Future of Post-Modernity.* San Diego: San Diego State University Press.

Mumme, Stephen P. 1988. *Apportioning Groundwater Beneath the U.S.-Mexico Border.* San Diego: Center for U.S.-Mexican Studies, University of California–San Diego.

Prescott, J. V. R. 1987. *Political Frontiers and Boundaries.* London: Allen and Unwin.

Raat, W. Dirk. 1992. *Mexico and the United States: Ambivalent Vistas.* Athens: University of Georgia Press.

Rodriguez, Victoria E. 1993. "The Politics of Decentralization in Mexico: From *Municipio Libre* to *Solidaridad.*" *Bulletin of Latin American Research* 12, no. 3: 133–145.

Ryan, Richard W. 1993. "The North American Free Trade Agreement and Intergovernmental Management on the U.S.-Mexico Border." Paper presented at the Western Political Science Association, Pasadena, California.

Saint-Germain, Michelle A. 1995a. "Problems and Opportunities for Cooperation Among Public Managers on the U.S.-Mexico Border." *American Review of Public Administration* 25: 93–117.

———. 1995b. "Public Sector Impacts of NAFTA on U.S. and Mexico Border Cities." Paper presented at the American Society for Public Administration, San Antonio, Texas.

———. 1995c. "So Near and Yet So Far? Similarities and Differences Among Public Managers on the U.S.-Mexico Border." *Public Administration Review* 55: 507–516.

Smorkaloff, Pamela Maria. 1994. "Shifting Borders, Free Trade, and Frontier Narratives: U.S., Canada, and Mexico." *American Literary History* 6, no. 1: 89–102.

Stoddard, Ellwyn R. 1986. "Problem-Solving Along the U.S.-Mexico Border: A United States View." In *Across Boundaries: Transborder Interaction in Comparative Perspective,* Oscar J. Martínez, ed. El Paso: Texas Western Press, 57–79.

Thomas, Bradford L. 1994. "International Boundaries: Lines in the Sand (and the

Sea)." In *Reordering the World: Geopolitical Perspectives on the 21st Century,* George J. Demko and William B. Wood, eds. Boulder: Westview, 97–99.

U.S. House of Representatives, Committee on Foreign Affairs, Subcommittee on Human Rights and International Organizations. 1990. *Allegations of Violence Along the U.S.-Mexico Border.* Washington, D.C.: U.S. Government Printing Office.

Vaznaugh, Richard. 1993. "Extraterritorial Jurisdiction—Environmental Muscle for the North American Free Trade Agreement." *Hastings International and Comparative Law Review* 17, no. 1: 207–240.

Verhovek, Sam Howe. 1997. "After Marine on Patrol Kills a Teen-ager, a Texas Border Village Wonders Why." *New York Times,* June 29, p. A16.

Walzer, Michael. 1981. "The Distribution of Membership." In *Boundaries: National Autonomy and Its Limits*, Peter G. Brown and Henry Shue, eds. Totowa, N.J.: Rowman and Littlefield, 1–35.

Williams, Colin H. 1993. "Conclusion: Unresolved Issues." In *The Political Geography of the New World Order,* Colin H. Williams, ed. London: Bellhaven Press, 210–215.

4

Small Business, Social Capital, and Economic Integration on the Texas-Mexico Border

David Spener and Bryan R. Roberts

In this chapter we revisit the conceptualization of the U.S.-Mexico border as an integrated economic region with a unique cultural identity. We do so by examining the activities of small-scale entrepreneurs and their enterprises in five border-region cities—El Paso, Laredo, and San Antonio, Texas; Ciudad Juárez, Chihuahua; and Nuevo Laredo, Tamaulipas—in light of changes in the dynamic of border economic development.[1] We base our discussion on the results of the first phase of a multiyear research project on small- and medium-scale enterprises in the Texas-Mexico border region, which we have been conducting with colleagues at the Colegio de la Frontera Norte (COLEF) in Tijuana, Baja California.[2] It is our contention that the role of the small-scale sector in transborder integration has been insufficiently studied, especially when compared with the great attention in the literature paid to the border industrialization (maquiladora) program. Trade liberalization, culminating in the creation of the North American Free Trade Area on January 1, 1994, has fundamentally altered the way in which the small-scale business sector operates on the border; old border business niches have either been eliminated or threatened, while new opportunities for cross-border activity have presented themselves. The responses of border entrepreneurs to the changed economic situation have repercussions that are not themselves strictly economic. As they engage in new patterns of cross-border commercial exchanges, small-scale entrepreneurs not only build upon preexisting, transborder network ties—they establish new ones. In so doing, this class of social actors helps integrate international economic space in new ways and contributes to the redefinition of the border as a distinct sociocultural region.

In recent years, the border between Mexico and the United States has been the subject of intense scrutiny, both in academia and public policy circles. In the literature, visions of the border emerge along a continuum between two poles. One pole stresses the stark differences in levels of economic development and national power and the cultural differences these imply along the only international boundary where first and third worlds meet (e.g., Weintraub 1992). In this vision, the border demarcates the limits of two separate and competing social systems and constitutes a zone of conflict between them. This vision is prominent in many popular press treatments of the border, particularly with regard to "the tide" of poor Mexicans migrating north of it and the "giant sucking sound"[3] of good U.S. jobs moving south of it. The opposite pole visualizes the border as an artificial imposition that attempts, with varying degrees of success, to divide those inhabitants of both sides who previously were one people and who, in large measure, continue to share a common language, culture, and historical trajectory. In this vision, the border constitutes a region unto itself, distinct from both the rest of Mexico and the United States. Robert Alvarez (1984: 120), for example, maintains that the border region constitutes "a true social system and . . . a society organized around the flow of people conditioned by historical as well as socio-cultural and economic factors."

Tito Alegría (1989), Jorge Bustamante (1989), and Víctor Zúñiga (1993) each recognize the centrality of state power in structuring the social and economic functioning of the border and furthermore recognize the complex ways in which local social actors on either side find ways in which to integrate "binational space" to their own best advantage. Zúñiga (1993) conceptualizes the border as a project of states that simultaneously circumscribes separate national spaces yet permits their partial integration on a selective basis. In doing so, he synthesizes Alegría's (1989) notion of the significance of spatial "adjacency" with Bustamante's (1989) account of the "asymmetry of power" between Mexico and the United States at the level of the state as well as between the economic and social actors of civil society on opposite sides of the border. The term Zúñiga coins to express the border social system in theoretical terms is *asymmetric adjacency*. This term captures an important essence of the border as a social system, namely that "border processes" on the Mexican side typically arise in response to initiatives emanating from the United States, whether from its government or actors in its civil society.

With this theoretical framework in mind, let us now describe, in schematic form, how the combined state projects of Mexico and the United States structured the social and economic functioning of their shared border from the late 1960s through the early 1980s and how that functioning began to change as a result of trade liberalization in the 1980s and 1990s.[4] As part of this description, we will indicate how the functioning of the border has structured the possibilities for small-scale entrepreneurship in both periods. In looking at the activities of entrepreneurs in both periods, we must bear in mind the relationship of their social identities to the structural possibilities for action. In particular, we will explore the extent to which entrepreneurs of Mexican ancestry residing in the Texas border cities have been able to successfully play upon their personal, professional, and cultural connections to Mexico to advance their enterprises.

The Border and Binational Trade Restrictions

Social and economic development along the U.S.-Mexico border in the twenty-five years preceding the creation of the North American Free Trade Agreement (NAFTA) was largely driven by two related factors, which we describe here in a highly stylized fashion. First, substantial barriers were maintained against the free flow of goods, services, and people between the two countries. Second, capitalist development had proceeded at quite a different pace in each country, giving rise to radically unequal income levels, standards of living, and production capabilities on opposite sides of the border. On the Mexican side of the border, the peculiarities of this situation led to the growth of the various maquiladora industries: electronics, apparel, and auto parts, among others. On the U.S. side, it led to substantial growth in the trade and transportation/distribution sectors.

Because wage levels in Mexico were lower than in the United States (with underemployment, if not open unemployment, higher) and because Mexican workers were not legally free to seek higher-wage jobs in the United States, U.S. firms found it profitable to employ Mexican workers on Mexican soil to produce certain labor-intensive goods for sale in the U.S. market. Due to Mexico's prohibition on foreign ownership of factories in the interior of Mexico and because of the special tariff exemptions granted by U.S. Customs to in-bond goods produced in Mexico's northern border region, foreign-owned export factories (maquiladoras) were concentrated primarily along the U.S. border. In the case of the maquiladoras, the legal exceptions granted to the northern Mexican border provided opportunities for U.S. capitalists to make higher profits by crossing into Mexico. Similarly, the border offered new wage-labor opportunities to Mexican *fronterizos* (borderlanders) as well as to migrants from the interior of Mexico.

Because the Mexican government had erected trade barriers against the entry of most foreign goods and because Mexico's level of development did not permit the production of many high-quality consumer and capital goods, Mexican consumers and businesses were motivated to cross the border to purchase goods not available in Mexico. This led to growth in retail and wholesale establishments in U.S. border towns that served customers from Mexico. Demand for goods sold by these establishments was, in turn, enhanced by the growth of maquiladora production and concomitant population growth in Mexican border cities. In this way, the historical peculiarities of the border offered Mexicans access to goods that were unavailable (or overpriced) in Mexico. At the same time, it provided a special market base to U.S.-side retailers and wholesalers.

The growth of the maquiladoras on the Mexican side and of wholesale/retail trade and the transportation/distribution sector on the U.S. side depended upon the border functioning in a particular, selectively permeable way. Capital and inputs for assembly could flow from the United States into northern Mexico, and assembled goods could flow back from Mexico into the United States. U.S. goods could not flow easily into Mexico; neither could many goods produced in the Mexican interior flow easily into the United States. Inputs for maquiladora assembly had to be shipped from the U.S. interior to the border, dropped by trucks on the U.S. side, stored in warehouses, and then taken across the border by short-haul trucking firms. Maquiladora output then had to be shipped back across the border and into the U.S. interior in a similar fashion. Here again, the economic functioning of the border in this period offered specific business opportunities to entrepreneurs on both sides that would not have existed had it functioned differently.

In Mexican border cities such as Nuevo Laredo and Ciudad Juárez, the principal opportunities for small-scale entrepreneurship during this period could be divided into two categories. First, a growing number of small-scale enterprises were needed in both commerce and the services sector to meet the consumption demands of populations that were growing apace with the rapid industrialization brought on by the maquiladora program. Second, entrepreneurs could find opportunities as brokers of goods, smuggled or legal, for buyers in both their own cities and in the Mexican interior. Because much of this second type of activity took place clandestinely, it is difficult to estimate its extent, both in terms of the value of goods and number of people it employed. Nonetheless, qualitative accounts of this brokering activity lead us to conclude that it was a vital part of the regional economy (see, for example, Anderson and de la Rosa 1991; Hellman 1994).

In Texas border cities such as Laredo and El Paso, small-scale business opportunities in the period preceding trade liberalization were concentrated in retail and wholesale trade, with a large portion of the sales from both going to Mexican consumers and firms. In March 1982, on the eve of the Mexican economic crisis that provoked the country's change in trade/development paradigms, about half of El Paso and Laredo business establishments were concentrated in retail/wholesale trade (U.S. Bureau of the Census 1982). Later that year, the devaluation of the Mexican peso caused drastic reductions in sales in this sector, leading analysts to conclude that more than 40 percent of retail sales in El Paso were to Mexican consumers (Institute for Manufacturing and Materials Management 1991). In Laredo, data from the Texas Department of Commerce indicated that gross business sales in all sectors declined by over 50 percent from 1981 to 1982 (Spener 1995). Since Mexican state regulation of foreign business activities on Mexican soil presented a substantial deterrent to pursuing customers in Mexico itself, small businesses on the Texas side of the border were obliged to *receive* Mexican customers, both private and commercial, in their establishments in Texas. Although this meant, for example, that El Paso entrepreneurs were unable to pursue potentially lucrative opportunities to sell, say, in Chihuahua, it also provided Texas border businesses with a ready-made customer base requiring little in the way of market research and development. One longtime El Paso merchant described the "old" border business environment to us as a "field of dreams: build it and they will come." Thus, although cross-border trade was in principle "unfree" during this period, a great deal of trade did occur out of cities like Laredo and El Paso, in a sense precisely because of the restrictions in place.

The Border at the Cutting Edge of Trade Liberalization

By the mid-1980s the role of the border region in the binational economy began to change in important ways. As both national governments liberalized their trade policies, much of the historical "exceptionalism" of the border was rendered obsolete. In conjunction with becoming a party to the General Agreement on Tariffs and Trade (GATT), the Mexican government began to allow the import of goods from the United States without prohibitively high tariffs. The United States also loosened restrictions on some Mexican goods entering its territory. These events, which culminated in the negotiation of NAFTA, changed the "permeability" of the border in ways that were important for the future of border development. First, U.S. goods became increasingly available to Mexican consumers and businesses *in Mexico:* they would no longer be obliged to cross the border in order to gain access to higher-quality products once available only in the United States (indeed, major retail chains such as Wal-Mart, Price Club, and K-Mart have all opened stores in Mexico's larger cities).[5] It also meant that existing maquiladoras could sell more of their output on the domestic Mexican market: previously, maquiladoras were largely prohibited from competing with Mexican manufacturers for domestic sales (Wilson 1992). Second, it meant that much of the border maquiladoras' advantage over the rest of Mexican manufacturing in selling to the United States was eroded. Trade liberalization lowered the tariff on many Mexican goods entering the

United States, thus reducing the price advantage enjoyed by maquiladora products due to their special tax status. Combined with a repeal of the prohibition on foreign ownership of businesses in the Mexican interior, this meant that factories located in the Mexican interior could produce competitively for export to the United States.[6]

Because of trade liberalization, future economic development in the border region has begun to take place on a different basis in accordance with the new ways in which the border functions. The social actors that make development possible have had to seek new opportunities that freer trade presents and abandon niches that a more open border has made obsolete. In this regard, large-scale enterprises have gained an advantage to the extent that their financial resources are greater and their geographical "reach" more extensive than that of smaller enterprises. Thus, larger businesses have been more able to actively access the interior markets of either country than smaller ones and have not always required a border location in order to do so. Our interviews with small business people in Laredo, El Paso, and San Antonio confirmed the threat to their operations posed by larger, international businesses based in the interior of the United States. Because of the moves of major U.S. retail chains into interior Mexican cities, private Mexican consumers now have less incentive to shop in the stores of Texas border retailers, who were already facing intense competition from these same chains in their local market. In addition, the Mexican customs authority's 1992 lowering and intensified enforcement of per-person duty-free import limitations from $300 to $50 for goods taken into the Mexican interior created another disincentive for Mexicans to purchase goods from retailers in Texas border cities.

At the same time that the Mexican government has liberalized trade policies, it has tightened its policies of fiscal control over business and has professionalized its customs service. Mexican companies are now being forced to pay corporate income taxes and must show receipts for both purchase and payment of import tariffs on goods and equipment purchased in the United States if they wish to deduct these as business expenses. This hurts Texas border merchants by making it even less attractive for Mexican firms to purchase many goods in the United States. The Mexican customs agency's policy of enforcing the lower $50 duty-free limit on personal imports may also have hurt merchants' sales to Mexican companies. Many interior Mexican businesspeople mix business with pleasure on their trips to Texas. Often they bring their families across the border to shop and see the sights on the U.S. side and at the same time take advantage of the visit to pick up needed items for their businesses. Thus, making retail shopping on the U.S. side less attractive also decreases the attractiveness to businesspeople of making purchases of supplies of products and equipment in the Texas border cities.

Businesses in El Paso, San Antonio, and Laredo have also been hurt by deals between larger U.S. and Mexican companies to "cut out the middle-man" on the border. Some major U.S. manufacturers have already either cut off or given less favorable terms to their licensed distributors in the border cities that historically have served the Mexican market for them. This is because the manufacturers have either begun to sell directly into Mexico themselves or have licensed new distributors for their products in Mexico, eliminating the need for the Texas border intermediary. As we mentioned earlier, an important entrepreneurial role in Mexican border cities like Nuevo Laredo has been played by the unofficial commodity broker who has enabled U.S.-side companies to access Mexican business customers and Mexican businesses to access U.S. products without actually traveling to the United States or having knowledge of the U.S. market. This niche, too, has been undermined by trade liberalization, as goods become increasingly available to firms in the Mexican interior and as the Mexican government tightens its business taxation policies.

Small-Scale Enterprise in the New Trade Environment

Although changes in the binational trade regime pose a threat to some of the traditional business niches at the border and may put small-scale entre-preneurs at a disadvantage vis-à-vis their larger competitors, the research literature on entrepreneurship also suggests that some small-scale enterprises may enjoy distinct advantages over larger, more bureaucratic firms in seizing upon new opportunities for cross-border trade. The small-scale enterprise is often viewed as one of the most promising vehicles for mobilizing local skills and capital and promoting regional growth (Hansen 1990, 1991). Several interrelated factors are identified as underlying the potential of small-scale enterprise. The first of these is organizational flexibility. Since work relations in these enterprises are close, there is no bureaucratic division of labor, and workers typically possess a range of skills. The small-scale enterprise can, potentially, quickly adapt to market fluctuations and move to exploit new opportunities. Second, the small-scale firm can combine territorially with both small- and large-scale firms in a variety of flexible subcontracting arrangements that allow each unit to specialize and yet adapt efficiently to changes in demand (Piore and Sabel 1984). Third, the small-scale enterprise is often a family firm in which unpaid or under-paid family labor is used as an investment to help expand the enterprise and to diminish the risks entailed by having large wage commitments. These factors played a part in the initial success of the small-scale industrialization of Emilia-Romagna, a region in northern Italy, a case often cited as exemplifying the potential contribution of small-scale enterprise to development (Capecchi 1992).

There is another dimension to the success or failure of small-scale enterprise and that is its capacity to make use of what James Coleman (1988) calls its "social capital." Successful small-scale entrepreneurship among immigrants in the United States, for example, has been shown to hinge on the availability of supportive social relationships in the place of destination, particularly those that can provide access to economic opportunities (Tadao Tsukashima 1990). Relationships between the small-scale enterprise and the local community are often close and positive since the small-scale enterprise provides job opportunities and usually obtains some of its supplies in the community (Escobar 1986).

The social capital needed for successful entrepreneurship raises the issue of the role of ethnic enterprise in the United States. In comparing Cuban and Mexican migrants to the United States, Alejandro Portes and Robert Bach (1985) argue that the relative economic success of the Cubans is based on the ethnic enclave, or the capacity of Cubans to dominate economic activities in the Miami area through kin and community relations. In contrast, Mexican migrants in the United States were found to be more likely to be employees of other ethnic groups and have little control of business in the cities and neighborhoods where they reside. Other studies, however, have documented the existence of Mexican entrepreneurial enclaves in cities in California and Texas, led in some instances by Mexican immigrants themselves and in others by U.S. natives of Mexican ancestry (Alvarez 1990; Chapa and Cárdenas 1991; Hansen and Cárdenas 1988).

An additional point to bear in mind in exploring the link between social capital and successful entrepreneurship is that social and community relationships, although facilitating achievement, can ultimately prove restrictive because of the obligations that the use of one's social capital normally entails. Individuals seeking to be socially and economically mobile must, for instance, negotiate the tricky path between too much and too little involvement in family and community ties. This is a particularly crucial issue for the small-scale enterprise, which is often a family-based enterprise. The long-term interests of certain family members are often sacrificed to both the short-term interests of the family business and its longer-term planning.

In this vein, Elena Hernández and Fernando Pozos (1997) report that in Guadalajara, the response of many local entrepreneurs to the 1980s economic crisis was to reduce nonlabor expenses and sell off other family assets in order to plow the proceeds into their financially strapped businesses. These authors refer to this practice as *patrimonialismo*, that is, entrepreneurs regarding their businesses not only as a vehicle for their economic aspirations but also as the family's patrimony that must be preserved. The results of this strategy were equivocal. On the one hand, family businesses and the jobs of family members were saved. On the other hand, many entrepreneurs did not make or were not able to make the necessary investments in technological reconversion to be able to compete effectively in the free trade market of the 1990s, and many of the businesses that survived the crisis have failed in its aftermath.

A similar story can be told regarding a Laredo wholesaler whose family business had been selling electronics supplies into Mexico since the 1950s. The year before the big peso devaluation hit in 1982, the company's sales had reached $7 million, and most of this amount was to Mexican firms. Since that time, its gross sales have never exceeded $4 million. The firm survived because of its ability to rely on the labor of six family members from three generations whose unremunerated labor contributed both to the firm's lack of debt at the time of the devaluation and its holding of $500,000 in cash reserves, which were plowed back into its operations. Moreover, incomes to family members could be reduced following the devaluation such that the business could be sustained even in the face of an enormous drop in sales. As with the Guadalajara firms studied by Hernández and Pozos, this firm's owners postponed technological upgrading: they did not computerize their accounting and inventory operations until 1993.

It is also important to remember that the social capital that small-scale entrepreneurs draw upon is not necessarily limited to the local communities in which they reside. As Mark Granovetter (1973) points out in his study of the job market, in some situations it can be advantageous for the economic actor to participate in social networks in which relationships are less intense but more geographically far-flung. Social capital in the form of intense, local networks may reduce a small firm's need for financial capital in its day-to-day operations or enable it to weather a crisis but may prove less useful to entrepreneurs obligated to pursue new clients and suppliers in a wider market. Current economic conditions on the border seem to be pushing existing small-scale enterprises in precisely this latter direction as trade barriers fall. In the face of intensifying competition from big retail chains and international manufacturers, certain small-scale enterprises may be able to use their greater flexibility and existing social network ties on both sides of the border to access the wider markets they need to stay in business and prosper in the future. Texas border businesses headed by Mexican immigrant or Mexican American entrepreneurs (of which there are many) may be in a particularly good position to expand their markets in this way, particularly if they have had active, long-standing relationships with firms or trusted individuals in Mexico's interior.

Of course, not all small-scale entrepreneurs on the border are veterans of the "old" border trade model who are seeking to adapt to the new regimen. Many started businesses in the period leading up to NAFTA in order to take advantage of opportunities that liberalized trade engendered.

Owners and managers of these newer businesses may also seek to maximize the return on their social capital as a way of competing with larger enterprises whose capital assets of other types (financial, productive, human) exceed their own. This newer group of entrepreneurs may differ from the older group in that many are themselves new to the border, having relocated there from the interior of either Mexico or the United States. The social capital of newcomer entrepreneurs is more likely to consist of personal and business ties to points "inland" from the border, which they may capitalize upon by using the border as a staging ground giving them easy access to both countries. These newcomer entrepreneurs are also likely to be more highly educated than older border entrepreneurs and generally have a more cosmopolitan outlook, in the classic Mertonian sense.[7]

In looking at the role of social capital in explaining entrepreneurial behavior at the border, we must not forget that it is not only entrepreneurs of Mexican descent who are able to benefit from having it. Although Anglo entrepreneurs in Texas border cities may not have the cultural and familial connections with Mexico that those of Mexican ancestry possess, they may have experience working or living in Mexico at earlier points in their careers, which they have been able to turn to their advantage as trade has been liberalized.[8] Furthermore, we have interviewed Anglo entrepreneurs providing professional services (engineering and architecture, in these cases) in San Antonio, Laredo, and El Paso who have been "recruited" by Mexican firms to do work in Mexico. Once there, the firms of these Anglos were able to build upon their connections with the owners of the firms that recruited them to find other clients on the Mexican side. Owners of these "recruited" firms report that the *personal* relationships that they developed with their initial clients have proven to be as important as the quality of their work in advancing their business in Mexico.

Until this point, we have been discussing the ways in which entrepreneurs' social capital can be utilized to augment or substitute for the other kinds of capital that they may possess in limited quantities. Here we see how the process may work in more complex ways. In these latter cases, the initial contact between entrepreneur and customer is based primarily on meritocratic selection, but the personalized working relationship subsequently developed augments the entrepreneurs' theretofore limited social capital. For certain kinds of small businesses, such as those U.S.-side firms selling high-tech products or providing higher-level professional or business services, this route to establishment of social network ties in Mexico may be particularly important.[9] That this would be the case for companies going into Mexico should not surprise us, given the oft-attested importance of the personal aspect in conducting business there.[10]

Small-Scale Enterprise on the Border:
Flexibility and Social Capital on the Eve of NAFTA

As we have suggested above, small businesses in the cities of the Texas border region and their counterparts in the Mexican border cities such as Ciudad Juárez, Nuevo Laredo, Reynosa, and Matamoros played a special role in integrating binational economic space when there were substantial barriers to trade between the United States and Mexico. This role consisted of the informal brokering of foreign goods into Mexico, whether these goods were made in the United States, East Asia, or Europe. Most typically, these were final consumer goods, although a substantial number of businesses in the Texas border cities also supplied Mexican businesses with a variety of capital goods, parts, and equipment. In this section, we briefly summarize some of the empirical results of the study we have conducted with our colleagues at the Colegio de la Frontera Norte.[11]

Microempresas *on the Mexican Side:*
Ciudad Juárez and Nuevo Laredo

From November 1992 through January 1993, COLEF surveyed 800 microenterprises (small businesses with 15 or fewer employees) in both Ciudad Juárez and Nuevo Laredo. In each of these cities, the vast majority of enterprises surveyed were engaged in either wholesale/retail trade or the provision of a service, with only around 10 percent in either city operating as manufacturers. The businesses surveyed were all officially registered, aboveboard firms—informal enterprises were deliberately excluded from the sample. This is significant to the extent that we presume that informal enterprises (those that operate outside the bounds of official government regulation) are more likely than their formal counterparts to engage in illicit activities, including the movement of contraband imports into Mexican territory.

The results of the COLEF survey are striking in two aspects relevant to our discussion of binational economic integration, interfirm trade networks, and social capital. First, very few of the microenterprises surveyed were enmeshed in interfirm networks that extended beyond the local market. Nearly 90 percent of the enterprises surveyed in each city sold goods or services directly to the public residing in their own city. Second, the vast majority in both cities were principally supplied by large-scale wholesale/retail trade enterprises, which were also located in town. Almost none of the enterprises surveyed in either city worked as subcontractors to other firms, and only a small percent provided goods or services to affiliated companies.

Second, most Juárez and Nuevo Laredo microenterprises did not maintain a direct or intense relationship with suppliers or clients on the U.S. side of the border. Although the enterprises surveyed in both cities reported that around 40 percent of products they purchased for their businesses came from the United States, only between 30 and 40 percent used *any* supplier located in the United States, and only around 15 percent in either city reported that their principal supplier was located across the border. This discrepancy can be accounted for by the small firms' reliance upon larger wholesale/retail suppliers who take care of importing U.S. goods into the Mexican border cities.[12] Indeed, most of the operators of these small enterprises *never* crossed the border for business reasons. This also accords with the fact that almost none of the firms surveyed had U.S.-side businesses as clients. Other results from the survey provided additional indicators of the microenterprises' lack of dynamic linkage with the U.S. side of the border: very few of the operators of these businesses spoke English, and less than a quarter in either city had ever been employed in the United States.

Based on these results, it appears that the potential advantages accruing to small-scale enterprises—their flexibility and ability to extend their markets and find new niches based on social network connections—had not generally enabled *microempresas* in Nuevo Laredo and Ciudad Juárez to take advantage of opportunities that trade liberalization might have afforded them. We therefore speculate that they are constrained by a number of factors that often affect small-scale enterprises in the context of a developing country. The technology needed to provide the goods or services required by the market is usually too expensive for it to be purchased by a small-scale entrepreneur. The most profitable segments of the market were dominated by large-scale enterprises, such as multinational manufacturers and supermarket chains. Under these conditions, the small-scale enterprise is left to supply the low-income demand for "convenience" shopping or for basic goods such as shoes or garments, which can be produced with less expensive technology (Roberts 1978). The mass production of these basic goods in low-wage countries, such as those of Asia, has been reported to undermine even this market for local small-scale enterprise (Blim 1990). In fact, Mexican consumer purchases of cheaply made Asian shoes and garments are a key ingredient in the ability of the downtown shopping districts of El Paso and Laredo to survive competition from bigger retail chains both in Mexico and in newer shopping malls on the U.S. side.

Small Business on the U.S. Side: El Paso, Laredo, and San Antonio

In the summer of 1993, we conducted a telephone survey of nearly 700 chamber of commerce members in El Paso, Laredo, and San Antonio, including members of the Hispanic Chamber of Commerce in both El Paso and San Antonio.[13] Nearly all the businesses surveyed were small by both U.S. and Mexican standards, and around two-thirds of the total sample had fifteen or fewer employees. Like the Mexican microenterprises surveyed by COLEF researchers, all firms in the sample were officially registered businesses operating in the formal economy. Also similar to the situation obtaining in Ciudad Juárez and Nuevo Laredo was the very low representation of manufacturing firms in our sample in each of the Texas cities: as with their Mexican counterparts, the small-scale sector in these three cities was dominated by wholesale/retail and services firms.

Our purpose in conducting the survey was to uncover (1) the extent to which small businesses in these cities had Mexican firms as clients or suppliers; (2) whether the Texas businesses dealt with Mexican clients/suppliers immediately across the border, in the Mexican interior cities, or both; (3) the extent to which businesses that did trade with Mexican firms actively sought out clients or suppliers in Mexican territory (as opposed to waiting for the Mexicans to cross the border to them); and (4) if businesses headed by persons of Mexican ancestry or persons with social network connections in Mexico were any more or less likely to actively pursue trade with Mexican firms than those headed by non-Mexicans.

The answer to our first question was straightforward: the large majority of small businesses we surveyed in Laredo and El Paso did business with Mexican firms. Not surprisingly, further away from the border in San Antonio, only about a third of businesses reported trading with Mexican firms. We must interpret the figures for San Antonio correctly, however. Although the proportion of firms in San Antonio that traded with Mexico was considerably lower than in either Laredo or El Paso, it is important to bear in mind the much larger size of the San Antonio economy. According to the Census Bureau, in 1993 San Antonio (Bexar County) had over twice as many private business establishments as El Paso (El Paso County) and around nine times as many as Laredo (Webb County) (U.S. Bureau of the Census 1993). Thus, the absolute number of Mexico-trading firms in San Antonio was about the same as in El Paso and much greater than in Laredo. Not surprisingly, given the asymmetry of the conditions of development of their respective countries, the Mexican microenterprises surveyed in Nuevo Laredo and Ciudad Juárez were much more likely to be supplied by U.S. firms than to have them as clients, whereas the situation in the Texas cities was exactly the reverse: small businesses in El Paso, Laredo, and San Antonio were about three times as likely to sell to Mexican firms as to be supplied by them.

The answer to our second question was also clear: the Mexican businesses that were customers or clients of the firms we surveyed in El Paso, Laredo, and San Antonio came to the Texas border region from all over Mexico. Texas businesses selling to Mexican firms were about as likely or, in the case of San Antonio, about three times as likely to sell to firms based in cities like Guadalajara, Monterrey, and Mexico City as they were to sell to firms in the Mexican border city nearest to them. A significant minority of these businesses in El Paso and Laredo did not sell to firms in Ciudad Juárez or Nuevo Laredo at all. This finding has important implications for our understanding of the scope of entrepreneurial networks on the border. It shows us, first of all, that business establishments in the Mexican border cities did not play any real gatekeeping role in the process of U.S.-Mexican economic integration, at least as it involved small businesses in Texas. Texas border firms did not necessarily access the Mexican market via transactions with Mexican border businesses, such as the brokers mentioned earlier. When taken in conjunction with the results of the COLEF microenterprise survey, this finding further confirms that there appeared to be little *local* complementarity between the small business sectors of Nuevo Laredo–Laredo and Ciudad Juárez–El Paso. Finally, it indicates that the relevant entrepreneurial networks in which Texas border entrepreneurs were enmeshed extended into the Mexican interior and were not limited to family, friends, and acquaintances immediately across the Río Grande/Río Bravo del Norte.

Answering the third question of how actively the small businesses in the Texas cities pursued Mexican business is not entirely straightforward because there are many mechanisms for exploiting the Mexican market from the U.S. side of the border. In our survey, we measured only one dimension of this pursuit: did the business ever send its personnel across the border into Mexican territory in order to make sales calls on clients or to contact suppliers? Because so few of the Texas small businesses had Mexican suppliers, here we focus on the extent to which they made sales calls in Mexico. The results from the survey indicated that although large numbers of firms had Mexican businesses as clients, most firms never sent personnel across the border in search of or to call on clients: only about a quarter of the firms surveyed in Laredo, just over a third in El Paso, and about 10 percent of those in San Antonio had ever done so. From this we conclude that most small firms in the Texas border region continued to sell to Mexican businesses on a "build it and they will come" basis that was the modus operandi of an earlier period in border trade history. Another indication of the Texas firms' continuation of the old way of doing business was that in each of the three cities, less than 10 percent operated an establishment of any kind on Mexican soil, and only 15 percent or fewer had employees based in Mexico.

Finally, an issue of primary interest for us has been the extent to which persons of Mexican ancestry, whether immigrants or Mexican Americans, have benefited from the increased entrepreneurial opportunities brought about by trade liberalization. Mexicans in the Texas border region, because of the protectionist trade barriers erected by the Mexican government, were for many years deterred from playing an entrepreneurial brokering role between the U.S. and Mexican economies. Groups such as the Texas Association of Mexican American Chambers of Commerce, the League of United Latin American Citizens, and the National Council of La Raza all lobbied for NAFTA in large measure because they believed that it would benefit U.S. Mexicans who, by virtue of their bilingual and bicultural abilities, would be well positioned to take advantage of the new entrepreneurial and professional opportunities offered by freer trade with Mexico (Spener 1996).

Logit regression analysis of our survey data showed that, net of the branch of economic activity in which it was engaged, small businesses (those with fifteen or fewer employees) in these three Texas cities were less likely than larger businesses to extend sales efforts into Mexican territory unless they were operated by entrepreneurs who had significant social or cultural links to Mexico.[14] At the same time, certain kinds of businesses—especially those in business and professional services, transportation, and wholesale trade—were much more likely to be actively selling in Mexican territory than were other business types such as retail stores, eating and lodging establishments, construction companies, and real estate agencies. In fact, branch of economic activity was a much stronger predictor of propensity to make sales trips into Mexico than were the sociocultural characteristics of individual entrepreneurs. And although entrepreneurs with social and cultural connections to Mexico were more likely to be active on the Mexican side than those who did not have such connections, data from the 1990 U.S. Census show that Mexican immigrant and Mexican American entrepreneurs were especially concentrated in the types of businesses—retail trade establishments, restaurants, and personal services enterprises—that were least likely to avail themselves of the opportunities afforded by the Mexican market.

Our regression analysis of the data also seemed to confirm what informants in qualitative interviews had suggested to us, namely, that newcomers to the border region, whether from interior points in the United States or in Mexico, were more likely to engage in cross-border business activities than those who grew up on the border itself. Qualitative interviews had already indicated that these newcomer entrepreneurs tended to be better educated, more cosmopolitan, and better connected to major supplier or customer markets on either side of the border than were entrepreneurs who were native to the border region and inured to its traditional ways of doing business. Thus, although social and cultural factors did seem to play a role in determining a Texas firm's propensity to act entrepreneurially toward the

Mexican market, it was not unequivocally the case that the firms most likely to be active in Mexico were any more likely to be headed by entrepreneurs who were bilingual, bicultural natives of the border region.

Conclusion

Throughout this chapter we have emphasized how the changing projects of two adjacent nation-states—Mexico and the United States—have structured the possibilities for economic action on the part of small-scale entrepreneurs along the border between the two countries. We have argued that the trade liberalization that began in the mid-1980s and culminated in the creation of the North American Free Trade Area in 1994 has changed the relations of exchange between entrepreneurs on opposite sides of the border from one another. Formerly, Mexican entrepreneurs or their representatives crossed into the Texas border cities in search of needed goods and services, and Texas border entrepreneurs "received" them, selling them foreign manufactures or providing services based on more advanced U.S. technologies. Now, to a large extent these same goods and services have become available in Mexican territory itself, particularly in the major population centers of Mexico City, Monterrey, and Guadalajara. This, of course, is because U.S. firms have become freer to market their goods, set up their own business establishments, and purvey their services on Mexican soil.

For small-scale entrepreneurs on the U.S. side of the border, this change represents both a challenge and an opportunity. On the one hand, long-standing businesses that have historically served the Mexican market using old-style "build it and they will come" strategies find themselves in danger of being bypassed by larger-scale retailers and manufacturers who no longer need a border intermediary to sell to Mexico. On the other hand, small-scale businesses themselves are free to compete in the Mexican market now, and may, on the basis of their flexibility, familiarity with Mexican ways of doing business, and sociocultural ties to Mexico, be in a particularly advantaged position to do so relative to larger concerns. Many of the smaller-scale businesses going into Mexico, however, are owned and operated by entrepreneurs who are new to the border and have chosen a border location as a convenient staging ground for conducting business in both the United States and Mexico. In many cases, these newer businesses compete with local firms of longer standing. Although both types of businesses may have limited supplies of financial and productive capital relative to larger competitors, owners or managers of the newer small businesses are likely to possess more human capital (higher education, a greater variety of work experiences) than their competitors who are native to the border region. Although both native and newcomer entrepreneurs build upon their "social capital" to achieve business success, newcomers to the border region frequently build upon a different kind of social capital than natives, relying primarily on a social network that is more geographically extensive than that of border natives, consisting of professional and social ties to firms and individuals in major cities in the interior of either or both countries. Other newcomer entrepreneurs may start with little in the way of social network connections to Mexico but may acquire them after having gained access to the Mexican market by other means. This route may be particularly common for providers of high-level professional services whose clients are likely to be major Mexican companies or wealthy individuals.

Before trade liberalization in the 1980s, the economic forces at work in the border region tended to foster fairly intense, localized integration of international space along the international line itself. The maquiladora program was, after all, intended to function as an enclave, and the movement of persons, goods, and equipment that it entailed took place within a fairly reduced area in the border twin cities. Many Mexican residents of the border zone were able to cross the border legally as often as they wished to shop and conduct business in Texas border cities, and many did so illegally as well. Small-scale businesses on the Texas side benefited from having these border Mexicans as both customers and workers. Legitimate brokers and *fayuqueros* (smugglers) on the Mexican side had close dealings with small businesses on the Texas side, serving as intermediaries between interior Mexican firms and the Texas border entrepreneurs, who, in turn, were intermediaries between interior U.S. firms and Mexican customers. No wonder the border has emerged in the consciousness of both nations as an isolated and exceptional place unto itself, neither Mexican nor "American," exactly, but rather a curious admixture of both.

Trade liberalization changes the political economy of the processes of spatial integration at the border in ways that, as Bustamante (1989) reminds us, are asymmetric. The maquiladora program is no longer an exceptional enclave along Mexico's northern border so much as it is the model for the entire country's export-led reindustrialization. Binational commerce is no longer required to take place at the international boundary itself but allows for interior U.S. companies to penetrate far into the interior space of Mexico. Increasingly, the Texas border cities are becoming staging grounds for newer firms whose business is not at the border itself but in the major Mexican population centers like Guadalajara, Monterrey, and Mexico City. As a result, the border region, especially on the U.S. side, is becoming a more cosmopolitan place, and connectedness to points beyond the immediate border region are required for economic success. To the extent that small-scale entrepreneurs build upon their existing social networks or establish new ones in order to extend their business further into the interior of Mexico or the United States, they participate in the redefinition of the border as a region with a distinct cultural identity. Until recently, this cultural identity had been the combined product of the border's relative lack of integration with the rest of U.S.-Mexico society and the peculiarities of the largely local integration of its own Mexican and U.S. segments.

Collective identities are constructed by local social actors struggling with the structural constraints imposed upon them by the forces of international political economy. The class of small-scale entrepreneurs on the border has a potentially important social role to play in the new processes of economic integration under way between the United States and Mexico. Insofar as they rely upon their existing relationships and identities to integrate economic space, they will participate in the border's sociocultural preservation; insofar as they are obliged to forge new relationships and identities for themselves, these entrepreneurs will participate in its social and cultural transformation.

Notes

1. Although it is located more than 100 miles from the international line, we include San Antonio, Texas, in the border region because it serves as the economic and cultural capital of south Texas (i.e., of *Mexican* Texas) and is home to hundreds of businesses that are headed by persons of Mexican ancestry or that trade with Mexican companies. San Antonio is also a prime U.S. destination for Mexican tourists and businesspeople.

2. This research has been funded by the Ford Foundation's Mexico City and New York offices. Our principal Mexican collaborators during the first phase of this project were Jorge Carrillo, Alfredo Hualde, and Jorge Santibáñez. From November 1992 to January 1993, our colleagues in Mexico conducted a large-scale survey of 1,200 microenterprises (businesses with fifteen or fewer employees) in Ciudad Juárez, Nuevo Laredo, and Tijuana. Face-to-face interviews of business owners or managers were conducted using a standardized questionnaire covering a wide range of topics. On the U.S. side, our research consisted of a telephone survey of owners of 700 small businesses who were chamber of commerce members, covering a more limited range of topics in the three Texas cities, as well as approximately seventy-five in-depth interviews with entrepreneurs in these cities who had dealings in Mexico or with Mexican firms. This work was conducted during 1993. Because we did not cover the cities in southern California in the U.S. portion of the research, we omit a description of the situation prevailing in Tijuana's small-scale sector.

3. The phrase "giant sucking sound" was coined by Texas billionaire Ross Perot in his populist, anti-NAFTA crusade in 1993.

4. Throughout this chapter we describe the situation that prevailed along the Texas-Mexico portion of the U.S.-Mexico border. The situation obtaining in Baja California Norte and Sonora was somewhat different given the Mexican government's granting of exceptional tariff status to these states isolated from the Mexican interior. For a good description of the heterogeneity of the trade regimes in place along Mexico's northern border over the last two centuries, see Jesús Tamayo and José Luís Fernández (1983).

5. See U.S. International Trade Commission (1990) for a chronology of liberalization in the U.S.-Mexico trade regime prior to the creation of NAFTA.

6. See Patricia Wilson (1992) for a chronology of changes in the maquiladora program.

7. Here we refer, of course, to Robert Merton's famous study of "locals" and "cosmopolitans" in a small New England town (Merton 1949).

8. Here we use the term *Anglo* in its colloquial sense, referring to anyone on the border who is not of Latin American descent.

9. In this sense we can invert the title of Coleman's (1988) now famous article, "Social Capital in the Creation of Human Capital," and note that human capital may also, given the right circumstances, beget social capital.

10. See, for example, Robert Barnstone (1993).

11. For a more complete description of the methodology and empirical results of the study, see Harley Browning, Bryan Roberts, and David Spener (1994); Spener (1995); and Jorge Carrillo, Alfredo Hualde, and Jorge Santibáñez (1993).

12. Much of this importation appeared to occur extralegally, since microenterprises in both cities reported that only a third to half of the foreign goods they purchased had passed legally through Mexican customs.

13. Laredo's Hispanic Chamber of Commerce was an active but small, fledgling organization at the time of our survey. Thus, we did not use its membership list as part of our sampling frame. Notwithstanding our failure to purposively sample members of the Hispanic Chamber of Commerce, because the majority of Laredo's population, including its population of businesspeople, is of Mexican ancestry, most of the business owners or operators we interviewed were Spanish-speaking Latinos.

14. Such links consisted of one or more of the following: (1) having been raised by Mexican immigrant parents; (2) having spoken Spanish at home and with family and close friends while growing up; (3) having lived in Mexico as an adult or young adult; and (4) having a living parent, child, or sibling who resided in Mexico.

References

Alegría, Tito. 1989. "La ciudad y los procesos trasfronterizos entre México y Estados Unidos." *Frontera Norte* 1, no. 2: 53–81.

Alvarez, Robert. 1984. "The Border as Social System: The California Case." *New Scholar* 9: 119–133.

———. 1990. "Mexican Entrepreneurs and Markets in the City of Los Angeles: A Case of an Immigrant Enclave." *Urban Anthropology* 19: 99–124.

Anderson, Joan, and Martín de la Rosa. 1991. "Economic Survival Strategies of Poor Families on the Mexican Border." *Frontera Norte* 6, no. 1: 51–68.

Barnstone, Robert. 1993. "¡Viva la diferencia!" *Texas Monthly* (December), pp. 66ff.

Blim, Michael L. 1990. "Economic Development and Decline in the Emerging Global Factory: Some Italian Lessons." *Politics and Society* 18: 143–163.

Browning, Harley, Bryan R. Roberts, and David Spener. 1994. *Cross-Border Socioeconomic Linkages and Small-Scale Enterprise: The U.S. Perspective.* Report to the Ford Foundation, Mexico City office.

Bustamante, Jorge. 1989. "Frontera México–Estados Unidos: Reflexiones para un marco teórico." *Frontera Norte* 1, no. 1: 7–24.

Capecchi, Vittorio. 1992. "Un caso de especialización flexible: Los distritos industriales de Emilia-Romagna." In *Los distritos industriales y las pequeñas empresas,* vol. 1, B. Pyke and J. Sengenberger, eds. Madrid: Ministerio del Trabajo y Seguridad Social, 33–59.

Carrillo, Jorge, Alfredo Hualde, and Jorge Santibáñez. 1993. *Reporte de investigación: Las particularidades de las microempresas en la frontera México–Estados Unidos: Una perspectiva transfronteriza.* Tijuana, Baja California Norte: Colegio de la Frontera Norte.

Chapa, Jorge, and Gilberto Cárdenas. 1991. *The Economy of the Urban Ethnic Enclave.* Austin: Lyndon B. Johnson School of Public Affairs, University of Texas.

Coleman, James. 1988. "Social Capital in the Creation of Human Capital." *American Journal of Sociology* 94 (supplement): s95–s120.

Escobar, Agustín. 1986. *Con el sudor de tu frente: Mercado de trabajo y clase obrera en Guadalajara.* Guadalajara: El Colegio de Jalisco.

Granovetter, Mark. 1973. "The Strength of Weak Ties." *American Journal of Sociology* 78: 1360–1380.

Hansen, Niles. 1990. "Innovative Regional Milieux, Small Firms, and Regional Development: Evidence from Mediterranean France." *The Annals of Regional Science* 24: 107–123.

———. 1991. "Factories in Danish Fields: How High-Wage, Flexible Production Has Succeeded in Peripheral Jutland." *International Regional Science Review* 14, no. 2: 109–132.

Hansen, Niles, and Gilberto Cárdenas. 1988. "Immigrant and Native Ethnic Enterprises in Mexican American Neighborhoods: Differing Perceptions of Mexican Immigrant Workers." *International Migration Review* 17: 226–242.

Hellman, Judith Adler. 1994. *Mexican Lives.* New York: New Press.

Hernández, Elena, and Fernando Pozos. 1997. "Patrimonialismo empresarial y restructuración productiva: El caso de los empresarios de Guadalajara, 1980–1994." *Estudios Sociológicos* 15, no. 44: 489–511.

Institute for Manufacturing and Materials Management. 1991. *Paso del Norte Regional Economy: Socioeconomic Profile.* El Paso: University of Texas–El Paso.

Merton, Robert K. 1949. *Social Theory and Social Structure.* Glencoe, Ill.: Free Press.

Piore, Michael J., and Charles F. Sabel. 1984. *The Second Industrial Divide.* New York: Basic Books.

Portes, Alejandro, and Robert Bach. 1985. *Latin Journey.* Berkeley: University of California Press.

Roberts, Bryan R. 1978. *Cities of Peasants.* London: Edward Arnold.

Spener, David. 1995. *Entrepreneurship and Small-Scale Enterprise in the Texas Border Region: A Sociocultural Approach.* Ph.D. diss., University of Texas at Austin.

———. 1996. "Small Firms, Social Capital, and Global Commodity Chains: Some Lessons from the Tex-Mex Border in the Era of Free Trade." In *Latin America in the World Economy*, Roberto Patricio Korzeniewicz and William C. Smith, eds. Westport, Conn.: Greenwood, 77–100.

Tadao Tsukashima, R. 1990. "Cultural Endowment, Disadvantaged Status, and Economic Niche: The Development of an Ethnic Trade." *International Migration Review* 15: 333–354.

Tamayo, Jesús, and José Luís Fernández. 1983. *Zonas fronterizas*. Mexico City: Centro de Investigacíon y Docencia Económicas.

U.S. Bureau of the Census. 1982, 1993. *County Business Patterns*. Washington, D.C.: Census Bureau.

U.S. International Trade Commission. 1990. *Review of Trade and Investment Liberalization Measures by Mexico and Prospects for Future United States–Mexican Relations: Investigation No. 332–282: Phase I: Recent Trade and Investment Reforms Undertaken by Mexico and Implications for the United States*. Washington, D.C.: U.S. International Trade Commission.

Weintraub, Sidney. 1992. "North American Free Trade and the European Situation Compared." *International Migration Review* 26: 506–524.

Wilson, Patricia A. 1992. *Exports and Local Development: Mexico's New Maquiladoras*. Austin: University of Texas Press.

Zúñiga, Víctor. 1993. "Elementos teóricos sobre la noción de frontera: Reflexiones en torno a la tésis de Michel Foucher." *Frontera Norte* 5, no. 9: 139–146.

5

Visiting the Mother Country:
Border-Crossing as a Cultural Practice

Olivia Ruiz

The U.S.-Mexico border represents a singular case in the study of ethnic formation. On the border, we find not only two nationalities but also a number of diverse social groups that constitute these two nationalities. In particular, multiple Mexican identities coexist on the border, ranging from fourth-generation Chicanos to new immigrants from the states of Mexico's indigenous south. We have yet to fully investigate and understand the constitution of Mexican identities in this region. We must still learn more about the day-to-day aspects of these identities, documenting them in their diverse manifestations, before we can elaborate an interpretive framework capable of comprehending them. In this chapter, I hope to contribute to the realization of this empirical-theoretical task. In doing so, I recognize that an undertaking of this nature consists of multiple phases that piece together various fragments of a portrait that is both complex and in permanent flux.

I begin by exploring a concept—*lo transfronterizo* (transborderness)—that has been developed in order to capture the uniqueness of life on the border. *Lo transfronterizo* refers simultaneously to both the Mexican and U.S. sides of the border and, in general, is defined as a mode of life characterized by a continuous interaction among individuals and institutions belonging to two distinct socioeconomic structures (in this case, nations) in the region where they share a common border. *Lo transfronterizo* is reflect-

An earlier version of this chapter was published in 1992 in Spanish in *Frontera Norte* 4, no. 7: 103–130. Thanks are given to the publisher, El Colegio de la Frontera Norte, for granting permission to publish an English-language version of the article for inclusion in this book. Translated by David Spener.

ed in both material activities and ways of thinking. It is nothing new to people who inhabit the border region; in fact, it is ubiquitous. Shopping trips
across the border, for example, are facets of border society that sooner or
later involve many of the region's residents. Relatively little is known,
however, about what elements compose the transborder mode of life and
who are the social actors participating in it.

In this chapter, I discuss and present research findings on only one of
the many manifestations of *lo transfronterizo:* the temporary visits to Baja
California (Mexico) made by Mexican American and Mexican immigrant
residents of the south end of San Diego County, California (United States).
My purpose is to explore the character of these visits and examine the
extent to which familiarity with Mexican border space influences or motivates such visits. To do so, I divide the chapter into four parts. The first section begins with a conceptual and methodological discussion in which I
break the transborder concept down into several elements: practices, accumulation of knowledge, and the adjacency of different structures. Second, I
describe the research techniques used and present my categories of analysis. In the third section, I discuss San Diego–Tijuana as a specific case of *lo
transfronterizo* in order to contextualize the contemporary transborder relation in more concrete terms. I do this by describing visits made from San
Diego to Baja California, utilizing the concepts elaborated in the first section. Last, I present some general conclusions regarding cross-border visitors' patterns of behavior. It is important to emphasize that this analysis is
exploratory. My research is in an early stage, and the cases I have observed
are not statistically representative. This analysis serves only as a first step
toward addressing the broader question of how Mexican ethnic identities
are constructed on the U.S.-Mexico border.

Conceptual Framework

Practices

Lo transfronterizo results from the historical sedimentation of cultural practices: the physical, emotional, and mental activities that reside in particular
material conditions. Practices may be daily or occasional but in either case
are recurrent. On the border, they might refer, for example, to daily crossings to *el otro lado* (the other side, either the U.S. or the Mexican side of
the border, depending upon from which side one is speaking), as well as to
the choice exercised by some Tijuana women over the generations to cross
the border to give birth to a child on U.S. soil (an occasional practice). It is
the adjacency of the U.S. and Mexican socioeconomic structures that generates the part of *lo transfronterizo* that consists of cultural practices. Not

all transborder practices, however, are developed by every person and community along the border; nor are they expressed in the same manner among these people and communities. Not all pregnant women from Tijuana give birth to their children in San Diego. Moreover, even among those who do, there are some women who would be just as happy to have their children born on Mexican soil. A basic step in the analysis of *lo transfronterizo* is, therefore, to examine not only the practices themselves but also the selectivity of their adoption, that is, to examine the factors that promote the cultivation of one practice or another. Thus, in order to begin to understand the patterned social and spatial distribution of transborder cultural practices, we must look into the process of how such practices are adopted.

Accumulation of Knowledge

Practices are learned. This acquisition is a process of mediation that rests between "simple familiarization," in which the apprentice acquires the principles of the "art of living" experientially and, at the other extreme, the explicit and express transmission of knowledge by means of formal, prescriptive education (Bourdieu 1977). The learning of cultural practices begins at a very early point in people's lives and continues through adulthood. It occurs, for example, in the form of children's games and in the acquisition of language. Seen in another way, mastering practices involves the acquisition of knowledge from the existing material conditions in which people live, whether this learning occurs consciously and rationally or unconsciously and irrationally. In the context of the Mexico-U.S. border, the learning of practices consists of coming to think, feel, express, and conduct oneself within the possibilities and restrictions imposed by an area where two nations adjoin one another. Acquired practices form part of what Nigel Thrift (1996: 97) defines as stocks of knowledge: the accumulation of knowledge understood as the stockpiling of historical experience (on the part of individuals and social groups), which is available to generate, carry out, or change the particular cultural practices that are used in the present and the future.[1]

Although there are several types of knowledge, here I will discuss only two types drawn from Thrift's (1996) work, since they are most useful for analyzing the nature of cross-border visits. These two types are practical knowledge, which is experienced directly by the subject, and empirical knowledge, which is transmitted and acquired as information. The difference between the two lies in the way in which they are acquired. Practical knowledge is acquired by means of lived experience, implying personal participation in the activity that is being learned. Empirical knowledge, however, is acquired through a medium (an intervening link between the subject and the original source of the knowledge being transmitted) and a mediator (the agent who organizes the presentation of the knowledge being transmitted). An example of the first type is the knowledge that Tijuana residents acquire when they travel to San Diego. An example of the second type is the information that Tijuana residents receive about Los Angeles from travel agencies without ever having visited the city.

The learning of particular practices and the accumulation of knowledge, in turn, constitute two parts of a dialectical relationship that involves the individual acquisition and exercise of practices that form part of the social accumulation of stocks of knowledge. In other words, although the social accumulation of knowledge and the learning of practices occur at different levels, there is nonetheless a constant interaction between the two. This interaction presents itself in two main ways. First, the existence of accumulated stocks of knowledge tends to be self-reinforcing: knowing that there are desirable goods *en el otro lado* makes it more probable that a person goes to *el otro lado*. Second, practices generate new knowledge that can contribute to the accumulation of extant social knowledge. For example, crossing the border makes certain experiences possible for travelers (encounters with people and ideas, etc.), such that when they return home those experiences can contribute to social stocks of knowledge there.

Space

Although the processes of the creation of stocks of knowledge and the learning of practices are of a sociocultural and psychological nature, both processes occur in space; that is, they are located in concrete spaces and in the networks of social relations that are particular to them (Soja 1985). More specifically, they are socially dispersed in space. On the border, different social groups and classes and individuals that inhabit either side of the international boundary possess knowledge that derives from the relation they maintain with the diverse spaces that are found along it (e.g., living in or visiting a specific place along the border). In this sense, knowledge is unevenly distributed along the border.

Thus, space acquires a special significance in the context of this border. As Tito Alegría (1989) writes, the adjacency of different structures on the Mexico-U.S. border—the convergence of two distinct systems—has resulted simultaneously (and paradoxically) in an intense interaction between the two systems *and* the mutual isolation of their elements. On the one hand, structural difference promotes, for example, the flow of capital in search of profitable markets as well as the flow of persons in search of better salaries or merchandise prices. On the other hand, structural difference impedes cross-border integration of resources. This is manifested, for example, in the difficulty in crossing from one side of the border to the other without the necessary official documents.

The individual exercise of a given type or piece of knowledge (for example, visiting the other side of the border) depends upon (1) conditions that are propitious for putting such knowledge into practice (being able to cross) and (2) valuing that knowledge (wanting to cross). Not knowing means not being able to avail oneself of an opportunity. Nevertheless, the fact that knowledge is possessed does not guarantee that it will be put to use. Knowledge is taken advantage of or not depending on whether propitious conditions do, in fact, exist. On the border this means anything from having legal crossing documents to having access to a means of transportation that allows one to explore the possibilities offered by cities like Tijuana and San Diego (González-Aréchiga 1987). Putting a piece or type of knowledge into practice also implies that such knowledge is valued by its bearer. It is possible to know what is available to the visitor in Baja California but not to take advantage of it due to a general lack of interest in or attraction to Baja Californian society and its people. Knowing that there are forms of entertainment available in Tijuana such as movie houses and restaurants does not mean that they will be used if a person also believes them to be of poor quality. Thus I summarize the previous discussion in the form of a general theoretical premise: The daily and occasional practices exercised by individuals are learned in both conscious and unconscious ways throughout the life course. Such practices form part of a social group's historical set of accumulated experiences/knowledge. They are dispersed unevenly in border space due to its peculiar structure, which simultaneously blocks the flow of some types of knowledge and encourages the flow of others. Knowledge is transformed into individual practice when propitious conditions for its valorization exist. Starting from this premise, I now attempt to analyze the relationship between border space and the nature of cross-border visits.

Methodological Framework

My analysis of visits to Baja California made by U.S. residents of Mexican ancestry consists of (1) describing the visits made and (2) exploring the role that space plays, in terms of the location of different types of knowledge, in influencing the nature of different types of visits. In the description that follows, I present some numerical indicators of the different types of visitors and visits. My objective is to identify whether variation in the characteristics of visitors of Mexican ancestry (for example, their place of birth and their income) modifies the nature of the visits they make to Baja California. To do so, I explore three aspects of the visit: motive, frequency, and duration. Motive refers to the reason a person decides to visit Baja California. Here I divide visits into five categories:

1. Visits to family and friends
2. Border crossings made to shop or to use medical services
3. Tourist visits
4. Border crossings made for professional or employment reasons
5. Visits made for other reasons

With regard to frequency, I seek to identify whether persons think of their visits in terms of trips per week, per month, or per year. By duration, I mean the number of hours that are spent on each visit. Analyzing the length of visit implies a discussion of how the limitations of time determine the content of the visits made: What can and cannot be accomplished with shorter or longer periods of time? What types of purposes motivate visits of different lengths? What types of knowledge are implied by different types of visits? Finally, I reflect upon how the extent to which an individual values a given piece or type of spatially based knowledge determines his or her level of motivation to actually exploit specific border spaces.

In operational terms, I examine how the motive, frequency, and duration of visits vary with regard to changes in three characteristics of the visitors themselves. Two of these are of a spatial nature: the place of birth of the visitor and his or her interurban experience. The other factor is socioeconomic: the visitor's income level. With regard to place of birth, I distinguish between persons who were born in Mexico or became naturalized U.S. citizens (Mexicans) and those who were born in the United States (Mexican Americans).[2] Interurban experience refers to having resided in Baja California before establishing residence in San Diego County. Finally, I look at the effect of income level on the nature of the visits to Baja California, grouping subjects into three categories: (1) low-income (less than U.S.$12,000 in annual income for a household head, that is, persons living below the official U.S. poverty line at the time the research was conducted; (2) middle-income (U.S.$12,000 to $17,999 per year); and (3) higher-income (annual earnings of U.S.$18,000 or more).

My examination of cross-border visits is based on both survey data and in-depth interview transcripts. Most of the analysis I have conducted is based on the pilot study, Demographic and Inter-relatedness Survey at the United States–Mexico Border (DISB) (Colegio de la Frontera Norte and International Population Center 1989). This survey was carried out among 149 households in San Diego County in late 1988 and early 1989.[3] The results I present in this chapter are based on a subsample of 122 cases obtained from the total 149 households. The subsample is limited to persons who were household heads, made visits to Mexico, and were of Mexican ancestry. I supplement the survey's results with findings from in-depth interviews I conducted with twelve heads of households whose members made frequent visits to destinations in Baja California. In the analysis I also make reference to results from a survey titled Investigación Estadística del Turismo Fronterizo 1 (IETF1) (Colegio de la Frontera Norte 1988), which was carried out by the Colegio de la Frontera Norte. The purpose of this survey was to uncover some of the characteristics of tourists in the Tijuana-Rosarito-Ensenada corridor. It consisted of a sample of 1,462 questionnaires and was carried out in person at the international gate in San Ysidro, California, in the fall of 1987.

The decision to restrict the sample to persons of Mexican origin who resided in southern San Diego County was based on both substantive and practical factors. Substantively, this area is the site of intense cross-border interaction between Tijuana and San Diego, two of the most economically and sociodemographically dynamic cities on the U.S.-Mexico border. Practically speaking, data from the two surveys became available for analysis. It is important to signal that the two surveys were conducted with different purposes in mind and made use of different techniques and methods. As such, their results are not strictly comparable in a narrow statistical sense. Nevertheless, the results obtained from each illustrate important aspects of transborder reality, especially with regard to the cross-border trips made by U.S. residents of Mexican ancestry. In this chapter, I make use of the two surveys in a complementary fashion in order to explore the general picture of the nature of cross-border visits.

The San Diego–Baja California Relation

In general terms, the different types of visits made by Mexican immigrants and Mexican Americans to Baja California seemed to reflect differences in their respective spatial experiences on the border. In large measure, different types of visits were related to differences in individuals' knowledge of particular border spaces, which, in turn, allowed them to recognize the ways in which they might put such knowledge to use. In this section I present, in abbreviated form, some of the results of the two surveys and propose several hypotheses regarding the relation between the characteristics of the visits and the spatial distribution of knowledge along the border.[4] Before presenting the breakdown of results by place of birth, interurban experience, and income level, it is important to present a general overview of the characteristics of the group of persons whose activities constitute the raw material of *lo transfronterizo*.

Data from the DISB show that the mean age of the 122 Mexican-ancestry household heads who visited Baja California from the U.S. side of the border was forty-eight years. The majority of these household heads were women. Twenty percent were naturalized U.S. citizens, and another 20 percent had been born in the United States. A little over half the sample was married, and over half had gotten married in Mexico. The majority maintained Mexican citizenship, and about 25 percent had been born in the state of Baja California. Over half had entered the United States before 1969, and most of these had entered in the 1960s. Nearly half lived below the official U.S. poverty line, and the great majority (around 80 percent) had not completed high school or its Mexican equivalent. Around half reported that they spoke English poorly or not at all.

Thus, the "average" person in the sample, whether male or female, was a household head who lived in a precarious socioeconomic situation, at least by U.S. standards. Middle-aged, these border crossers had access to few resources; their income was low, they had completed little formal education, and they did not speak English well. Most were born in Mexico, and relatively few of these had become naturalized U.S. citizens. The women household heads were in an especially vulnerable situation, receiving a substantial portion of their incomes in the form of welfare payments from the state, while most of them supported at least one or two dependent children.

The majority of persons interviewed (65 percent) said that their principal motivation for crossing the border was to visit relatives and friends. This finding is supported by the IETF1 survey, in which 49 percent of those interviewed responded that they crossed in order to see relatives and friends. The other types of motivations for crossing the border trailed far behind this one. In order, they were shopping and use of medical services; tourism; work; and other unspecified activities. However, the in-depth interviews indicated that it is not always possible to neatly classify a cross-border trip according to the reasons for making it. Visits to friends and relations and shopping trips were not mutually exclusive; frequently a cross-border trip was designed to fulfill several missions. In other words, the household head, whether a man or a woman, would cross the border to see his or her siblings, for example, and also would visit stores or supermarkets to buy food and other articles that were unavailable or more expensive on the U.S. side.

Generally speaking, the Mexican-ancestry population made frequent cross-border visits. In a recent study of tourism in Tijuana, it was found that this group made up nearly 60 percent of the total number of U.S. tourists visiting the city (Bringas 1991). Although the frequency of visits ranged from every day to once a year, monthly visits were the most common. Furthermore, the majority of visits made were of short duration, averaging only four hours in length.

Results of both the DISB and the IETF1 show significant differences between the border-crossing practices of Mexicans and Mexican Americans. First, the great majority—around 80 percent—of those who crossed the border from San Diego County into Baja California were Mexican-born. Second, although the principal motive for crossing into Baja California for both Mexicans and Mexican Americans was to visit friends and relatives, the Mexican-born were more than twice as likely as U.S.-born Mexican Americans to shop and use services in Baja California (25 percent versus 11 percent, according to the DISB). In addition, according to the IETF1, Mexicans were much more likely to visit residential neighborhoods in Tijuana than were Mexican Americans, who tended to make most of their visits to the old downtown area. The Mexican-born were likely to visit Baja California more frequently than Mexican Americans, measuring their visits in terms of number per week (45 percent, versus only 27 percent for Mexican Americans), though the visits of the Mexican-born tend to be of somewhat shorter duration.

These survey findings were corroborated by the in-depth interviews I conducted. Several Mexican household heads said that they crossed in order to visit relatives (especially to participate in special events such as birthdays and weddings), and that in addition they shopped and used services on the Mexican side (for example, they bought food and took their car to the mechanic). Some shopped on the Mexican side for certain foods that were unavailable in San Diego. In the case of a family consisting of a male head, his wife, and their two-year-old daughter, trips to Tijuana almost always included the purchase of food that, in the words of his wife, "you probably could buy here [in San Diego], but it doesn't taste the same." In other cases the reason was mainly economic, as indicated by the words of a woman household head with a child to raise: "I just buy what is cheaper to buy there than here . . . since I make very little money, I have very little." Medical services in Tijuana were used in part for the same reason, although in some cases, there was also a preference for Mexican doctors or discomfort with the manner of U.S. doctors. This was the case with one family head who, after having had some bad experiences with U.S. doctors, decided to rely exclusively on Mexican doctors. The visits by Mexican Americans, in contrast, were typically restricted to getting together with family members in Tijuana, almost always with brothers or sisters.

It appears that there were a number of reasons that Mexicans residing in San Diego County crossed the border more frequently and for shorter periods of time than their Mexican American counterparts. The distinct visiting patterns of the two groups reflected their unequal knowledge about Baja California space. The differences in motives for trips indicate that Mexicans knew more about what Baja California had to offer and appreciated it more than did Mexican Americans.

First, visits by Mexicans were made for a wider range of reasons than among Mexican Americans. Mexicans, in addition to crossing the border to visit friends and relatives, also availed themselves of stores and services, carried out other unspecified activities, and participated in tourism. Related to the more diverse motives for their visits, Mexican immigrants were more likely than Mexican Americans to visit a wider variety of Baja California urban spaces, ranging from tourist areas (such as the Avenida de la Revolución and the Centro Cultural) to places known almost exclusively by people who resided on the Mexican side of the border (residential neighborhoods, the old city center). In addition, Mexicans not only visited a greater number of spaces in Baja California than did Mexican Americans, but their visits were also more evenly dispersed across the range of types of spaces. This reflected the Mexicans' greater familiarity with a greater number of Mexican spaces. In contrast, Mexican Americans concentrated their visits in just a few areas of Tijuana, especially Avenida de la Revolución, the Zona del Río, and parts of the historic city center.

Second, the differences in frequency and duration of visits suggest a difference in the extent to which each group valued its knowledge of Mexican spaces and had mastered the practices originating in those spaces. Mexicans crossed the border more frequently—several times per week or month. In contrast, the majority of Mexican Americans visited on a monthly or annual basis. If Mexicans crossed the border more frequently and for shorter durations of time per visit, it may well have been because their greater knowledge of Mexican space and Mexican practices permitted them to cross with less prior planning and accomplish the purposes of their visits in less time than Mexican Americans, whose knowledge of Mexican spaces and cultural practices was neither as broad nor as deep.

The differences in behavior between Mexicans and Mexican Americans discussed above were accentuated when I compared San Diego County residents who had lived previously in Baja California and those who had not. Nearly all of the fifty-eight persons in the DISB sample who had interurban experience were Mexican-born. Persons who had lived previously in Baja California were more likely than those who had not to cross the border more frequently, for a wider variety of reasons, and to visit a greater variety of types of Baja California spaces. Interestingly, the effects of interurban experience appear to erase the differences in crossing behavior according to place of birth: the behavior of Mexican Americans who had lived previously in Baja California was more likely to resemble that of Mexicans with a similar background than the behavior of those who had not had such experience.

It is arguably the case that heads of households with interurban experience had a high level of knowledge of Baja California in terms of what it offered and how to obtain it. Moreover, they valued this knowledge. In contrast, visits made by Mexican Americans (with the exception of those who had lived in Baja California) suggested a lower degree of knowledge of the Mexican side or an undervaluing of the knowledge they possessed or both. In other terms, the use of space reflected familiarity with and knowledge of Baja California and the concomitant mastery of practices that involved the use of Baja spaces. We may suppose that within the Mexican American population less was known about what existed in Baja California; few among this group had ever lived there. It is also possible that they did not know the Baja Californian side *adequately*. Knowing that there were foods that were cheaper on the Mexican side but not knowing where to find them would make them difficult to obtain. It may also be that they *did* know the Baja Californian side, but because they knew the San Diego side better it was simply quicker and easier to satisfy their wants and needs exclusively on the U.S. side.

At first glance, the low level of knowledge of Baja California on the part of Mexican Americans is surprising given the fact that their U.S. birth and citizenship made it easy for them to cross the border. Moreover, the physical proximity to Mexico afforded them the opportunity to easily find out what existed on the Baja side. In addition, it was quite common for a Mexican American person to participate in a network of social relations that included Mexicans and residents of Baja California. The fact that their trips were predominantly for recreational purposes raises the question of whether they simply did not see any other good reason to visit the Mexican side.

The apparent lack of interest in crossing the border on the part of Mexican Americans may be explained in several ways. It may reflect a preference for things "American" and a rejection or an undervaluing of goods and services available in Baja California, which implies, of course, the ability to acquire the same or similar goods and services in the United States. This might explain why Mexican Americans, especially those of higher income, were less likely to shop or use services on their trips to Baja California. Seen another way, if economic need provided the initial impulse to use Baja California as a resource, it may be that higher-income Mexican Americans substituted U.S. goods for Mexican goods. Ultimately, those with higher incomes both preferred and could afford to shop in the United States.

Nevertheless, it is difficult to separate the effects of a socioeconomic factor, such as income, from those of a sociocultural factor, such as the fact of being Mexican American, on one's willingness or unwillingness to cross the border. It is problematic because among interviewees there was a correlation between being Mexican American and enjoying a higher income. Therefore, the fact that people did not use stores and services on the Mexican side of the border may have been as much a reflection of the fact that they could *afford* U.S. goods and services as it was of a *preference* for them.

In terms of the relative value placed on Baja Californian spaces by each group of visitors, the question arises as to whether the difference in the nature of the visits made by Mexicans and Mexican Americans reflected differing relationships with the Mexican side within the Mexican-ancestry population residing in the United States. It may be that Mexican Americans no longer regarded "the other side" as a potential resource, but rather had come to regard it primarily as a place for rest and recreation. This generational change in value placed on Mexican knowledge and resources may have been reflected in the differences in the variety of spaces that were used by the two groups. Mexican Americans frequented places like Avenida de la Revolución and seldom visited others, such as the rest of the commercial center of the city, whereas the Mexican-born visited a much wider range of spaces in Baja California.

Several of the patterns already discussed were reproduced with respect to income variations. First, for all the income groups, the principal purpose for visiting Baja California remained seeing family and friends. Second, visits tended to be weekly or monthly. And third, visits tended to be short, lasting between three and four hours. Still, border-crossing behavior was differentiated by income level in two significant ways that do not parallel place of birth and interurban experience. With regard to the purpose of visit, higher-income Mexicans and Mexican Americans living in San Diego County were less likely to shop or use services and more likely to participate in tourist activities than were their lower-income counterparts. In addition, middle-income persons (those with annual incomes from U.S.$12,000 to $17,999) made the most frequent cross-border trips (nearly half calculated the number of trips they made in terms of number per week). In contrast, low-income respondents visited Baja California less frequently; this group was the least likely to talk of number of trips per *week,* and nearly one in five spoke of the number of trips they made per *year.* However, when I subdivide the low-income group into those who were or were not born in Mexico and those who had or had not had interurban experience, differences appear in the frequency of cross-border visits. Those with interurban experience were more likely to make at least one trip per week—48 percent of these did so, compared to 40 percent of all Mexicans and just 35 percent of all low-income respondents. Insofar as monetary income creates and limits the capacity for action, it influences the different types of visits that are made to Baja California. Low-income status limits dollar-based consumption, promoting the use of the Mexican side as a source of low-cost goods. Higher incomes permit increased dollar-denominated purchases, which by bringing more U.S. goods and services within the reach of the consumer may make the use of Baja Californian spaces less imperative.

Among the factors that motivated cross-border visits, income level was overridden by the two spatial factors: place of birth and interurban experience. This was clearly seen among low-income visitors, made up mainly (59 percent) of female heads of households. A large number of these women received government welfare assistance. Welfare funds made it possible for these women to satisfy some of their daily needs on the U.S.

side, thus reducing their incentive to cross the border. As one interviewee explained: "[The government] sends me food stamps so I can buy food, it pays my medical bills—why am I going to go to Tijuana where I have to pay the doctor myself?" However, among low-income persons in the sample, those who had interurban experience visited Baja California more often than those who did not. For these Mexican heads of household, Baja California represented practical ways to satisfy basic nutritional and health needs, even when these needs could be met on the U.S. side through the use of food stamps and the receipt of other types of government welfare assistance.

This was the case for a woman household head who was born in Tijuana and supported both herself and her two small children with welfare. Although a large portion of her basic needs was taken care of by the government, her mother and her sisters in Tijuana bought her food, clothing, and medicine, and when she crossed the border in order to avail herself of certain low-cost services in Tijuana, her family baby-sat her children. This woman and probably many others like her had developed strategies to take maximum advantage of the varying resources available on opposite sides of the border. The stark poverty of these household heads leads us to predict that they would have made many of their essential purchases in Baja California. In fact, an important proportion did cross frequently for a variety of reasons related to the maintenance of their households.

Conclusion

Visits to Baja California are facilitated by knowledge that is specific to particular spaces. Living on one side of the border means learning types of knowledge from that side but not necessarily from the other. The visits of Mexicans and of Mexican Americans are distinguished from one another in part because of the unequal knowledge each group has of Baja California. This helps explain why, in spite of the fact that it might be economically worthwhile to cross the border into Mexico, many individuals do not do so and thus fail to take advantage of much of what Mexican border space might offer them.

The unequal knowledge of both sides of the U.S.-Mexico border and the consequently unequal mastery of the cultural practices of each side can be understood if we take into account the border's unique structure. The border is a zone where two profoundly different socioeconomic and cultural systems converge. Although this difference generates an important part of the tremendous interaction that occurs between the two sides of the international boundary, it also prevents the homogenization of the communities living in this binational space. The existence of the international line impedes not only the movement of persons but also the transmission of knowledge. This makes it difficult and at times impossible for someone to learn what can be done on "the other side" or how one might live there. Those who *do* know most likely have experienced living on the Mexican side of the border, thereby accumulating knowledge of Mexican border space and mastering many of its cultural practices. Mexican-ancestry residents of San Diego County who have accumulated knowledge about Tijuana through the direct experience of having lived there are more likely to value that knowledge and put it to use, using "the other side" as an alternative source of physical, mental, and emotional resources.

The Mexican-ancestry population on the U.S. side of the border is both the subject and the product of a process of "social knowing" on the border, as demonstrated by their visits to Baja California. Their trips to shop in commercial districts and to visit relatives in residential areas reflect special geographical life experiences and the mastery of forms of life specific to those geographies. Furthermore, I suggest that their visits contain the potential to alter, subtly or radically, the processes of accumulation of social knowledge, in both its practical and empirical forms, that are particular to the spaces from which different groups within this population have come. In this relation between individual and social knowledge, we find one of the keys to understanding the many transborder ways of being.

These ways of being, in turn, constitute part of the ethnicity of the Mexican-ancestry population in the border region of the United States. Although it is risky to generalize about the nature of ethnicity from just one reduced aspect of its makeup, these findings nonetheless lend themselves to generating some tentative conclusions about the nature of Mexicans' cultural identity in the United States. In what remains of this chapter, I present three hypotheses about ethnic formation on the border based upon a brief discussion of the acquisition of cultural practices that are, at bottom, the very substance of ethnicity.

First, space plays a major role in determining the learning/mastery of ethnic practices. Living in one of the multiple local spaces that compose the wider field of border space is the surest way to know and gain access to what that particular space has to offer. White and black Americans who cross the border to spend a day in Tijuana will see Avenida de la Revolución and little else, unless they have lived in Tijuana at some time in the past or have friends who currently do. Mexican immigrants and, to a lesser extent, Mexican Americans are far more likely to have had such experiences or to maintain such contacts. Thus, Mexican ethnicity on the U.S.-Mexico border has a significant territorial underpinning.

Second, the importance of a practice to daily life or the life cycle varies according to whether or not it is locally learned. Those practices that form part of the accumulation of knowledge of other spaces are less important to getting along where one lives. Thus, there may be less community support for their learning and subsequent application. The person from Tijuana who visits San Diego may learn local social and cultural customs, ranging from food habits to how to drive an automobile in the United States. Nevertheless, this knowledge often does not become incorporated into daily life on the Mexican side of the border. Territoriality appears to operate in such a way that it is possible for people to learn how to make instrumental use of "foreign" ethnic spaces without continuing to use practices native to those spaces once their instrumental motivations decline.

Finally, the possibility exists that individuals and even social groups learn and develop dual practices that in a given moment add to the range of choices or opportunities open to them. The border's territoriality permits the integration of binational systems in which individuals may satisfy their multiple daily needs (eating, working, relaxing) in at least two sets of ways. Returning to the example of health services, the possibility of knowing the opinions of specialists on both sides of the border regarding a health problem means having options with regard to the diagnosis, prescribed treatment, doctor's bedside manner, and cost. Obtaining the two opinions also implies, however, the possibility of conflict arising between two different health care systems and two different visions regarding illness and its treatment. Hence, new dilemmas are posed by the availability of more than one alternative solution to a health problem. These sorts of dilemmas form an inherent element of *lo transfronterizo*. On the border, such dilemmas are routinely faced by those individuals and social groups who have learned and mastered multiple ethnic practices and, in so doing, have become bicultural in their daily lives.

Notes

1. Thrift implies a conscious use of this knowledge. Nonetheless, in reality this use can also be unconscious; such is the case with activities whose origins have been forgotten but that are continued as either habit or custom. Homes in San Diego, for example, are heated, owing not to the local climate but rather as a carry-over from experience in the eastern United States. One need only cross the border to verify that heating is unnecessary given the local climate: in Tijuana, even the homes of the well-off are not heated.

2. Here I note that there are a number of terms used to refer to persons of Mexican ancestry who reside in the United States. For the purposes of this chapter, I refer to the total group of subjects as "U.S. residents of Mexican ancestry." When it is useful to distinguish between those who were born in the United States and those who were born in Mexico, I employ "Mexicans" to refer to those who were born in Mexico and "Mexican Americans" to refer to those who were born in the United States.

3. The purpose of this survey was to collect preliminary information on trans-border demographic processes. It was carried out under the direction of El Colegio de la Frontera Norte and the International Population Center of San Diego State University. The communities covered in the sample included Chula Vista, Imperial Beach, and San Ysidro in the southern part of San Diego County that abuts the Mexican border.

4. For a more complete presentation of the statistical findings of this study, see Ruiz 1992 and 1995.

References

Alegría, Tito. 1989. "La ciudad y los procesos transfronterizos entre México y Estados Unidos." *Frontera Norte* 1, no. 2: 53–81.

Alvarez, Robert. 1987. *Familia, Migration, and Adaptation in Baja and Alta California, 1800–1975.* Berkeley: University of California Press.

Bourdieu, Pierre. 1977. *Outline of a Theory of Practice.* Cambridge, UK: Cambridge University Press.

Bringas, Nora L. 1991. "La participación de la población estadunidense de orígen mexicano y anglosajón en la composición de los grupos de visitantes hacia Tijuana." In *Grupos de visitantes y actividades turísticas en Tijuana,* Nora L. Bringas and Jorge Carrillo V., eds. Tijuana, B.C., Mexico: El Colegio de la Frontera Norte, 47–68.

Colegio de la Frontera Norte. 1988. "Investigación Estadística del Turismo Fronterizo 1 (IETF1)." Tijuana, B.C., David Spener.

Colegio de la Frontera Norte and International Population Center. 1989. "Demographic and Inter-relatedness Survey at the United States—Mexico Border (DISB)." San Diego: International Population Center, San Diego State University.

De Oliveira, Orlandina, and Vania Salles. 1988. "Reflexiones teóricas para el estudio de la reproducción de la fuerza de trabajo." *Argumentos,* Universidad Autónoma Metropolitana-Xochimilco, June.

El Colegio de la Frontera Norte–Fondo Nacional de Fomento al Turismo. 1990. *Caracterización del visitante extranjero al Corredor Tijuana-Ensenada.* Tijuana, B.C., Mexico: El Colegio de la Frontera Norte–Fondo Nacional de Fomento al Turismo.

González-Aréchiga, Bernardo. 1987. "Mexicanos indocumentados en la frontera: Su identidad y función en el desarrollo regional." Manuscript prepared for the Seminario de Investigación sobre México y las Relaciones México–Estados Unidos of the U.S.-Mexican Studies Center of the University of California–San Diego.

Ruiz, Olivia. 1991. "De regreso a la perfería." In *Grupos de visitantes y actividades turísticas en Tijuana,* Nora L. Bringas and Jorge Carrillo V., eds. Tijuana, B.C., Mexico: El Colegio de la Frontera Norte, 69–79.

———. 1992. "Visitando la matria: Los cruces transfronterizos de la población estadunidense de orígen mexicano." *Frontera Norte* 4, no. 7: 103–130.

———. 1995. "A Tijuana: Las visitas transfronterizas como estrategias femeninas de reproducción social." In *Mujeres, migración, y maquila en la frontera norte,* Soledad González Montes, Olivia Ruiz, Laura Velasco, and Ofelia Woo, eds. Tijuana, B.C., Mexico: El Colegio de México and the Colegio de la Frontera Norte, 113–130.

Soja, Edward. 1985. "The Spatiality of Social Life." In *Social Relations and Spatial Structures,* Derek Gregory and John Urry, eds. London: St. Martin's Press, 90–127.

Thrift, Nigel. 1996. *Spatial Formations.* London: Sage Publications.

Weeks, John. 1990. "Household Structure and Fertility at the U.S.-Mexico Border." Paper prepared for the Annual Meeting of the Association of Borderlands Scholars, February, Tijuana, B.C., Mexico.

6

Mexico Reflects on the United States: *Colonias*, Politics, and Public Services in Fragmented Federalism

*Kathleen Staudt, with Angélica Holguín
and Magda Alarcón*

Visualize this North American space at an international border that divides a so-called first world, rich country of the north from a third world, poor country of the south: Two large urban areas sit side by side. In a Latin American–style urban development pattern, unplanned settlements called *colonias* (neighborhoods) emerge at the urban peripheries in which people of Mexican heritage reside. One periphery settlement gets most public services within several years of settlement; the other waits for these services for more than two decades after settlement. Which is where: north, south? rich, poor? first, third?

The international border is the 2,000-mile-long territorial line that divides the United States and Mexico. The urban areas operate within federal systems of governance: the Municipality of Ciudad Juárez and the City and County of El Paso, across which cut several water and school districts. The *colonia* with public services is at the Juárez periphery, whereas the underserved *colonia* is outside the City of El Paso, in a veritable regulatory vacuum of El Paso County government.

In this chapter we ask why public services come quicker in northern Mexico than in the southern United States. The answers are found in political economy, with an emphasis on politics rather than economics. Local and state officials have little interest in political engagement with the residents of El Paso's *colonias*, for reasons we unravel in this chapter. To ground our analysis theoretically, we tap the seemingly curious reversal of "civic cultural" traditions in the United States and Mexico, along with the revival of concern about "political community" in the United States, or at least political community among men. At this border migratory crossroads, resident women invent and sustain political community, limited as it is.

The data for this chapter come from a 1992 study of informal economies at the U.S.-Mexico border in the largest urban conglomeration of the first and third worlds: Juárez and El Paso. This study targeted six neighborhoods, three on each side of the border, in spatially distinctive downtown and old and new peripheral neighborhoods. Random sampling was done in each neighborhood to choose interviewees, and face-to-face interviews were conducted using sixteen-page questionnaires (plus four-page supplements), rendering data on a total of 465 households, 2,031 individuals, and 131 self-employed workers/businesses. In addition, interviews were conducted with officials and activists in various targeted communities. From 1991 to 1995, we combed local newspapers—*Diario de Juárez, Norte de Ciudad Juárez,* and the *El Paso Times*—to maintain a clippings file on relevant topics. We focus particularly on two new peripheral neighborhoods. In the first part of this chapter we ground the analysis theoretically, subsequently drawing on civic culture, political community, and clientelism in the second part. After that we analyze settlement patterns in both *colonias* to ask, finally, whether political community existed as residents engaged with political authorities to secure services.

Theoretical Perspectives

More than thirty years ago, leading analysts in comparative politics celebrated the term *civic culture* in a five-country study. In a civic culture, citizens view institutions and policies as legitimate, tolerate plural interests, and feel politically competent (Almond and Verba 1963).[1] Political competency is measured and exercised in political participation, such as voting, contacting officials, and joining organizations and political parties.

The United States shone in Gabriel Almond and Sidney Verba's conception and measurement of civic culture. Mexico, on the other hand, acquired the derogatory label *parochial culture;* its citizen-official ties reeked of personalism. Citizens participated in rituals but expected and received few opportunities to express themselves. The civic culture study was not the first to note the importance of vertical ties, called *clientelism,* that connect politically engaged clients with either patrons or machine-style, nonideological party organizations in Mexico and many other countries (selections in Schmidt et al. 1977).

With the growing strength of independent organizations, Mexico has been lumped together with other Latin American countries as being in "transition to democracy." In such cases, horizontal ties between people thereby supplement the vertical dyads of clientelism (Foweraker and Craig 1990). But Mexico is "limping along" in this transition; Judith Hellman argues that the system is neither repressive nor democractic but "more Mexican than ever," by which she means a "manipulative interplay of persuasion and coercion" (1994: 125). Moreover, independent organizations, even the ideological organizations that occasionally get ensnarled in partisan politics (Vélez-Ibáñez 1983), reproduce some of the same clientelist ties.

Female citizenship deserves special comment, for it was only in 1953 that Mexico extended voting rights to women. Political parties developed stakes in mobilizing female voters with "feminine sectors," though women got few policy concessions, candidacies, or appointments in exchange (Venegas Aguilera 1995; Staudt and Aguilar 1992). Many grassroots organizations have a large female membership (Vélez-Ibáñez 1983; Craske 1993; Bennett 1995). As household managers, women have perhaps the largest concerns among residents regarding access to water, electricity, sewer, and other public services. As Alejandra Massolo puts it, "urban politics are women's politics" (cited in Craske 1993: 134). Using Maxine Molyneux's brilliant distinction between "practical" and "strategic" women's interests (the latter addressing female subordination) (1985), we understand women's urban politics to be an expression of practical interests. Yet women's very involvement creates a sense of citizenship, says Massolo (in Bennett 1995: 79).

One might have predicted that the United States would shine amid the 1960s subtle academic modeling of political modernity as a quintessential feature of U.S culture. Using a male yardstick, Almond and Verba's surveys found U.S. and British women more involved than women in the other three countries of the study, but women's voter turnout and contacting behavior was always "less than" men's. Almond and Verba (1963) did not look specifically at women's experiences and their stakes in all parts of the public sector, from education to prices, nor did they look at political channeling and narrow policy agendas for women and men. However, the strength of U.S. independent organizations had already acquired fame as far back as the mid-nineteenth century, with the writings of French observer Alexis de Tocqueville, in *Democracy in America.*

More recently, however, observers have bemoaned the U.S. swing away from community toward individualism. Robert Bellah et al. seek to revive civic society and renew a communitarian tradition (1985). In the latest of these iterations, Robert Putnam worries, as the title of his widely cited article suggests, that Americans are "bowling alone" (1995). Drawing on this mostly male sport symbol, he bemoans the declining membership of traditional civic groups. All this occurs in the context of U.S. public anxiety over the family and personal connections between people. Putnam's message to the United States is this: rebuild "social capital." In our analysis, we wonder if the Putnams of the world are looking in all spaces and places to find this capital, including communities of immigrants and women's networks.

Civic or parochial culture? Communalism or atomized individualism? Thirty years after the seeming pinnacles and depths of civic competency in both the United States and Mexico, we look in the new peripheral neighborhoods to examine political community (or the lack of it) at the border. Besides looking at border residents themselves, we look at the structure of political opportunity in the local governments of both countries. Unlike Bellah, Putnam, and others, we worry about the ways in which political energy is channeled and contained in an individualized electoral relationship between citizen and representative, wherein vital issues are absent from the campaign agenda and technicians handle important issues within the bureaucracy. This channeling has been well under way in the United States; it is currently in process under conservative party rule in Juárez.

Political Opportunity Channels at the Border

Our worry about political channeling stems from two issues on which we focus in this analysis: immigration and collective organization. First, focusing on the border puts the citizen-resident distinction under scrutiny. Borders are magnets for migrants. In Juárez, migrants come from the interior; half the city's residents were born outside the city, according to Mexico's 1990 census (Staudt 1998: 94; Instituto Nacional de Estadistica, Geografia e Informática 1993). Of course, they are all citizens in a government that watches voter "abstentionism" very carefully for signs of alienation.

According to the 1990 census, El Paso counts 98,902 residents as "foreign born Mexicans," and just 31 percent of those residents are U.S. citizens (Tomás Rivera Center 1995: 85). Drawing on de Tocqueville, immigration scholar Lawrence Fuchs argues that the nationality of immigrants has been constructed through exercising civil rights (1990: 3). Citizens, by birthright or naturalization, have the right to vote; legal permanent residents do not.

The 1986 Immigration Reform and Control Act granted amnesty and the opportunity to obtain naturalized citizenship to undocumented residents who had lived in the United States since 1982. Of 2.7 million amnesties, 2 million went to people of Mexican heritage (U.S. CIR: 1994). Many legal residents opt to maintain their Mexican citizenship or to seek naturalization after a longer period than immigrants from other parts of the world. Citing the lengthiest rates between arrival and naturalization, Alejandro Portes and Rubén Rumbault discuss the "notorious resistance among Mexican and Canadian immigrants to change flags" (1990: 124). For those in the borderlands, proximity to the homeland undoubtedly figures into these decisions. In his chapter of *The California-Mexico Connection,* Jorge Castañeda says, "Mexican immigration is contributing to the 'dedemocratization' of California society" (1993: 41; also see Pachón 1987 on U.S. Latino leadership perspectives).

The second issue on which we focus is collective organization, certainly part of the social capital or communalism that Bellah and Putnam cherish. Exercising civil rights involves more than voting. Collective organization adds value to voting and is particularly useful to politically marginal communities because it offsets the usual class bias of participation, at least in the United States (Verba and Nie 1972). Various Latino communities have adopted an organizational model, in which leaders mobilize members through institutions of social trust, such as churches, to seek local political accountability. In Los Angeles, Latinos work in United Neighborhood Organizations (UNOs); in San Antonio, in Communities Organized for Public Service (COPS); and in El Paso, in the El Paso Interreligious Sponsoring Organization (EPISO) (Villarreal 1988).

EPISO operates in a veritable party vacuum with weak, personalistic organization at the county level; city elections have been "professionalized" since 1957, when they became nonpartisan. Despite these problems, elections are still viewed as people's ultimate source of power. The Southwest Voter Registration Project buys into this model with its campaign, complete with shirts and hats: "Su voto es su voz" (your vote is your voice). Declining voter turnout nationally, even lower locally, sends another message.[2]

Mexico's machinelike dominant party, the Partido Revolucionario Institucional (PRI), affiliates various organizations under its wings at national, state, and local levels. In Ciudad Juárez, under two PRI-controlled municipal terms from 1986 to 1992, *colonia* leaders worked with block leaders, known as *jefes de manzana,* of approximately 200 neighborhoods. The local PRI has on-again, off-again coalitions—overt and covert—with the Comité de Defensa Popular (CDP) a radical organization that once claimed control over as many as thirty-one *colonias* where settlers occupied land through invasion.

What propels people to join organizations and sustain their commitments? One model differentiates between incentives: material, solidary (social- and status-related), and purposive (goal and ideologically oriented) (Wilson 1973). Although the early case study literature portrays as ideological those groups that work with neighborhoods to secure public services (selections in Gilbert 1989; Foweraker and Craig 1990), many members' incentives to sustain their involvement would likely evaporate once they achieved services (Pelayo 1993). So instead, leaders avoid seeking public services and instead promote "piracy" (pirating electrical and water lines) as an effective hook for organizational maintenance, much to the dismay of neighboring *colonias* that pay user fees and municipal agencies that depend on fee collections (on Monterrey, see also Bennett 1995). In one of the CDP's more important projects, leaders operate in the informal business world, protecting their members from official harassment (Lau 1992; Staudt 1996). Political parties have also adopted a top-down neighborhood-based organizational model in Juárez, but leaders and members adapt it to their own interests, as we show in later sections of this chapter.

Even with relatively dense, partisan-linked organizational nets, the PRI could not deliver the majority municipal vote amid a cynical citizenry. To little avail, the federal Solidarity Program (whose government three-color symbols matched those of the PRI's "tricolor" emblem) spent considerable sums for social programs in which the municipal government and beneficiaries shared financial and labor responsibilities. In 1992, the conservative opposition party, Partido Acción Nacional (PAN), won a three-year term on the city council, revisiting its triumph from 1983 to 1986, which initiated a more streamlined administration (Rodríguez and Ward 1992). PAN aims to individualize the relationship between citizen and government and, in so doing, to undermine the largely PRI-based neighborhood organizations. From 1992 to 1995, the chief of the municipality's Social Development Department, PAN political appointee Ramón Galindo, pursued a vigorous campaign to criminalize allegedly fraudulent leaders. The PAN administration also publicized a land regularization effort in former CDP-controlled *colonias* to sidestep the increasingly factionalized CDP. Finally, PAN reinstalled nearly 200 *comités de vecinos* (neighbor committees) in the *colonias* that blanket the city (Gobierno Municipal 1994: 25–27, 76).[3] Voters elected Galindo municipal president in 1995, and the PAN took a majority of *cabildo* (council) seats in proportion to the votes it received. The *regidores* (members of the municipal council) do not represent geographic districts, as in El Paso's city council and county board, reinforcing the need for neighborhood organization.

The very process of settlement is highly charged politically. After settlers "invade" land, publicly or privately owned, they negotiate to acquire land title deeds and public services. Although "invade" suggests confrontation, actual patterns are mixed and sometimes conciliatory, with support of or tolerance from the authorities. Once on the land, settlers construct and improve houses on small plots of land in high-density settlements. For government, this housing and settlement pattern is a cheap alternative to subsidized housing, and it keeps the political peace.

Most Juárez housing is constructed by settlers, with official estimates ranging from 55 to 65 percent (Programa de Vivienda para Cd. Juárez, cited in World Bank 1991). Only a tenth of homes get built by private contractors. Mexico also subsidizes home ownership for those who have paid into the National Institute to Promote Worker Housing (INFONAVIT), accounting for approximately a third of Juárez houses (World Bank 1991: 11). Data from both Mexico's 1990 census and from special studies at the Colegio de la Frontera Norte (COLEF) show that the vast majority of urban residents have access to public services such as electricity, piped water, and sewer lines.[4] COLEF categorized areas from Economic Strata I to III (privileged to marginal), documenting impressive coverage even in Strata III (Guillén 1990). Residents' anxieties occur over land title deeds, the gems around which leaders and officials organize for political opportunity.

Although Juárez has a single unit of municipal government, in which water and sewer public utilities are available, El Paso is divided into city and county governments plus water districts. A privately owned monopoly provides electricity in El Paso, whereas a federal agency manages this utility in Mexico. Inside El Paso's city limits, private contractors build houses, usually in large subdivisions, and city ordinance requires that water and sewer lines be laid. Outside the city limits, however, unplanned settlement occurs in areas called *colonias*. The Spanish word for neighborhoods thereby takes on an ominous tone, for reasons outlined below. In Pablo Vila's eloquent words, "Spanish is the language of poverty" at the border (forthcoming).

Beginning in the 1970s, adverse publicity began to circulate about *colonias* that hugged the border, especially in southern and western Texas. Approximately 73,000 residents live in 151 *colonias* in El Paso County (Larson 1995: 185–193). In these areas, residents are responsible for their own water and sewer facilities. To dispose of sewage, residents use septic tanks, outhouses, and cesspools. To get water, residents borrow or buy water or build their own wells, many of the wells too shallow to avoid contaminated groundwater. The result is an extensive public health risk, particularly for hepatitis and dysentery.

U.S. residents settle in *colonias* to buy relatively cheap land and to own their own homes. For better or worse, settlement has occurred with neither land-use zoning nor building codes; contracts for deed are not secure for legal land title until loans are fully paid (Larson 1995: 240). The City of El Paso has little material interest in annexing space with low property taxes and costly service needs (Towers 1991).

Numerous federal and state agencies in the U.S. system of fragmented federalism control much-sought-after funds, although federal austerity programs of the 1980s dried up many sources. It takes organization, resources, and commitment to acquire whatever funds remain. In 1986, the El Paso County Lower Valley Water District Authority was organized, initiating a long-term process to negotiate grants, loans, and groundwater exchanges with El Paso's water utility (the Public Service Board). However, low-density settlement increases the costs of providing services (Peterson 1993: 565).

We now turn to data on the actual new peripheral neighborhoods, drawing on the 1992 household interviews in more than eighty households in each neighborhood and on in-depth interviews with leaders. To understand neighborhood access to services in each case, it is crucial to analyze patterns of immigration and collective organization.

Colonias on Both Sides of the Border

Located just 20 miles apart, but separated by an international border, *colonia* residents pursue planned upward mobility strategies in areas that officials call "unplanned settlements." Their housing, land, work, and migration characteristics are relevant to our analysis.

Residents seek to own their own land and homes. Sizable numbers said they were buying or already owned their homes: 91 percent of households in Juárez and 77 percent in El Paso. A full 88 percent of household members in the Juárez *colonia* built their homes themselves, whereas 44 percent did so in the El Paso *colonia*. As might be predicted from the previous analysis, the acquisition of a land title deed is more uncertain in Juárez: only 48 percent have documentation, compared with 84 percent in El Paso.

Residents work tenuously at factory and service jobs, run small businesses, or perform service work.[5] The Juárez *colonia* is a bedroom community for nearby maquiladoras, or export-processing factories that are mostly U.S.-owned. As such, earners bring home per week what a minimum-wage U.S. worker might earn in one or two days ($30–$60, before the 1994–1995 devaluation reduced the peso's value by at least half).

Many *colonia* dwellers were born in areas far from their current residence, including outside the country; only ten of the adults surveyed were born in Juárez. Yet most had recently moved from nearby. In Juárez, the vast majority of residents came from nearby *colonias* in the municipality. In other words, most did not come directly from Mexico's interior, although members of thirteen households came directly from other cities and states in Mexico. Residents moved because they heard land was available for eventual purchase. "We came for the land" was the common phrase expressed in household interviews. Intriguingly, six individuals from the Juárez *colonia* were U.S. citizens (one of them a PRI *jefe de manzana!*).

In the El Paso *colonia,* residents' most recent moves were from a variety of places, from the City of El Paso to other U.S. states and to Mexico. Sizable numbers came from the downtown rental and tenement areas, an area from which *colonia* residence is clearly an upward mobility step. In twelve households, members had migrated directly from Mexico, during a period when the border was "leakier": the 1980s, including the amnesty, and the pre–border blockade period of 1993. (Officials subsequently renamed the blockade "Operation Hold the Line.") Many residents moved from nearby *colonias* or from areas recently annexed into the City of El Paso. Mexico was the birthplace of adult household members who moved from other U.S. states, mostly in the west such as California and Colorado. In only five households in the entire *colonia* sample were all adults born in the United States, although frequently their children were.

In both *colonias,* sizable numbers claim access to sewer, electricity, trash collection, and indoor toilets. Both state-owned (Mexico) and private monopoly providers (United States) quickly extend access to electricity. El Paso *colonia* residents' sewer facilities consist of privately installed septic tanks, which may contaminate nearby shallow wells. Paved roads are virtually nonexistent in both areas because they are costly to build and to maintain; however, dusty, unpaved roads have high public health costs due to respiratory problems.

The data illustrate some surprising achievements in Juárez compared to El Paso, in both water lines and street lighting. Given the wealth of "rich" countries like the United States and the public resource problems in "poor" countries like Mexico, the water problem seems particularly vexing. Moreover, the U.S. *colonia* has been settled more than two decades, versus just three years (at the time of the interviews) for Juárez. Politics helps explain why, a topic to which we now move in the next section.

Political Community in *Colonias*

In the section on theory, we discussed civic culture and communalism, neat and abstract terms unmuddied by everyday realities. In this section's analysis of collective organization, we show that many incentives motivate and sustain involvement, among them income generation, material benefits, and religion. We reconstruct brief histories and narratives about political community in both *colonias* from in-depth interviews.

The Juárez Colonia

We interviewed a variety of leaders: four *colonia* "leaders," eight *jefes de manzana,* and four members of the emergent *comité de vecinos.* We could use the feminine form in Spanish, *jefas,* for women predominant at block-level leadership. Yet men monopolize leadership at higher levels, in government, and even as chairs of the *comités de vecinos.*[6]

Both interviewees and residents used the generic term "leaders" to describe several activities. At one level, leaders represent communities or serve as brokers to convey demands and negotiate benefits. At another level, leaders control space and its occupants for a political party; such "control" may be a delusion, however, for this ostensible PRI *colonia* transformed itself to a PAN *colonia*. At yet another level, some leaders pursue an informal business; they collect fees for ends that are both legitimate (specific services, with labor-intensive requirements) and illegitimate (title deeds that they do not control).

The Juárez *colonia* was first settled in 1989, when the PRI controlled municipal government. The founding leader mobilized settlers, based initially on economic need and PRI political affiliation. At first, settlers constructed homes from wood and cardboard cartons, though people subsequently improved their shelters with cement blocks. Some of the land was privately owned, and the rest was under municipal and state control. Both PRI and later PAN officials negotiated with one private owner who was reluctant to sell at the price offered; the government land was already authorized for sale and land title deed registration. Former president Carlos Salinas de Gortari made a high-visibility visit to the area, an event at which some residents received title. From household interviews, we averaged payment prices to find a cost of U.S.$800 for a small plot of 33 by 57 feet (10 by 17 meters).

As the *colonia* grew, new leaders arrived, competing with the founder and mobilizing new settlers. One of the new leaders, who was loosely affiliated with the PRI, got started in the party's youth branch, and another claimed a revolutionary heritage. The other supported the PAN from 1983 to 1986 (its first municipal victory), after which he accepted a PRI appointment. New settlers came with an ability to pay, rather than the original criteria of need and PRI loyalty. Others arrived without leaders' blessings.

To secure water, sewer, and electrical lines, leaders circulated petitions and presented them to officials. These services blanketed the *colonia,* according to respondents in the household interviews. Respondents were required to pay installation charges (at wildly variant rates); they continue to pay user fees (the monthly bills) at modest rates compared to those in El Paso. Some residents complained about installation fee collection and rates; they said some collectors gave no receipts and others fled with the money.

Do leaders bring services along with their mobilizations and threats of protest? Or have officials routinized the extension of services in a high-density settlement, with cost recovery through installation and user fees in the extension package? Peter Ward's comparisons of two PRI administrations in Mexico City periodizes the change: a politically charged distribution of urban services and land regularization, accorded to those leaders who created the most disturbances, was replaced with a more efficient and streamlined allocation system, dependent upon residents' labor contributions and user fees (1991). PAN governance in Juárez reinforced streamlining, from 1983 to 1986 (Rodríguez and Ward 1992) and from 1992 onward.

Yet the threat of political disturbance and the power of low-income residents in urban settlements to determine electoral victory sustains officials' political interests in appeasing their constituencies. (In the Juárez sample, voter registration rates are a high 85 percent.) As one official remarked about his government's "zero tolerance of negotiation" policy, negotiations are made on the condition that negotiating leaders not inform their members (quoted in Staudt 1996). Thus, we believe services get delivered for both administrative and political reasons.

The *colonia* leaders respond to material incentives to sustain their work, just as members often responded in material ways to concrete benefits from participation. Some leaders received stipends from the municipal government under the PRI, whereas others spoke more vaguely about acquiring "support." One leader was inspired to become a land invasion leader because he had formerly been a *colono* (settler) who was duped into making payments to a leader who never produced land title deeds. Now he credits himself with leadership in eight *colonias*.

Residents' experiences with PRI leaders were not always happy ones, for once the services came, in irregular ways requiring unpredictable fees, little else was forthcoming. Under the PRI administration, *jefe/as de manzana* could neither receive discounts in their water bills nor nominate needy residents for discounts. Material incentives remained but were less significant motivators than before. Under the PAN administration, these PRI-affiliated leaders lost some of their membership base. Newspaper articles headlined this *colonia* in transition from a PRI to a PAN base, with much fanfare about its *comité de vecino* members who represented a whole new cast of characters.

In the 1992 household interviews, residents complained about paying weekly fees and also about compulsory attendance at Sunday meetings. Although a sizable group acquired title deeds, the majority has no such security, despite various payments they thought they made for the land. Several residents filed suits against three of the *colonia*'s four leaders. In interviews, leaders denied receiving money for land, but they blamed each other for fraud. They said they collected fees on a voluntary basis for services rendered.

Our interviews with the leaders suggest that the leaders were entrepreneurs. Three of the four *colonia* leader interviews took place in their homes, which serve as offices. (The fourth leader insisted that the interview take place at PRI headquarters.) Several leaders had homes in other *colonias* they helped found. One leader's home had a particularly striking atmosphere: His first room, the office, had a desk, chairs, and a couch. The desk was adorned with a goblet of candies; on a small table sat a bottle of brandy with other decorations. On walls, he hung newspaper articles about the *colonia* at different stages of development and pictures showing him shaking hands with other leaders and government officials.

Under fierce media competition in Juárez, a great deal of attention is being focused on *colonia* residents, legitimizing their struggles. In competitive media capitalism, ambitious newspapers also provide new leverage for public accountability. The two Juárez newspapers we reviewed both have daily one-page spreads focusing on public problems (garbage, potholes, etc.), along with pictures of urban eyesores. The oldest newspaper, *El Fronterizo,* folded in 1994.

Just as the media covers "invasions," so also do they cover elections and moves against allegedly corrupt leaders. Under the PAN administration, such moves became highly visible. In the *colonia,* the PAN administration appointed nine members of the *comité de vecinos,* and neighbors subsequently voted for members amid competition and choice. Under the previous PRI government, leaders had nominated *jefe/as* who subsequently secured signatures of support. The PAN portrays itself as a clean government, with transparent procedures. It forbids *comité de vecino* members from collecting fees and requiring meetings. (Of course, residents' cynicism might make such collection impossible anyway.) The PAN has even issued a directory and procedural manual for the neighbor committees, providing addresses and phone numbers for municipal offices.

Comité members, most of them women, seek funding for neighborhood improvement. They encourage residents to plant trees and clear fields for a possible park. To raise funds, they sponsor parties, bazaars, and raffles. In a more ambitious move, they sought resources for road paving but were ultimately unsuccessful in packaging Solidarity Program funds with municipal contributions and residents' labor. According to interviews with Juárez Social Development Department staff, negotiations broke down over the amount of PAN's municipal contribution, for Solidarity reneged on its initial promised funding amount. Solidarity is a mixed blessing for opposition governments, for the program creates the appearance of PRI beneficence. Although the PRI does not appear to squeeze opposition governments in formula-funded projects, some evidence suggests that PAN cannot pursue public-debt financing for high-cost, long-term public works projects (Ward 1995; Rodríguez 1995).

The El Paso Colonia

This U.S. *colonia* was settled over twenty years ago in a high desert region east of the city. In a common *colonia* development pattern, farmers and ranchers sold developers land that was no longer profitable for agricultural purposes. Many developers exercised political clout through their contacts with officials and campaign contributions—in fact, the long-term congressional incumbent decided not to run in 1995 after public scandals over developers' loans and campaign donations.

Settlers in this *colonia* purchased lots that ranged from one-quarter to one-half acre in size. Individual families moved in and out of this *colonia* at different times; leaders did not organize settlers, as in Juárez. Land prices have inflated in value over the years, but prices outside the city limits are a "good deal," largely because developers have done little but put in unpaved roads. This *colonia* has been without water for two decades.

For most residents, political engagement rests on the lowest common denominator: citizen voting. In the El Paso sample, only 38 percent of adults were registered to vote, compared to 85 percent in Juárez. But even those with the right participate infrequently. Of the 41 percent of adult *colonia* citizens who are eligible to register, less than half actually register. Of those registered, 35 percent voted in the last local elections and 20 percent in the last presidential election.

In the sample, respondents revealed little knowledge about political parties—their leaders or agendas. Of course, the political channels help little in this regard: many local elections are nonpartisan, and campaigns are frequently personalistic rather than policy-driven. Half of the respondents sympathized with a party. Of those, two-thirds supported the Democrats and one-eighth the Republicans. Others gave a presidential name or described their party of choice with phrases like "the ones for the poor," and a handful called themselves independent. Frequently, important decisions for the region are made through bureaucratic fiat, such as the U.S. Border Patrol's decision to install a blockade.

In a fragmented federal system, citizens have many representatives, but few know all their names and responsibilities. The county contains fourteen water districts and nine school board districts. One of four county commissioners represents this large area. In the bicameral state legislature, representatives decide for citizens, as do the U.S. congressional representatives and senators. Many representatives at the state and local level earn small salaries, so they depend on other jobs or pensions.

Perhaps more important, the technical complexities of government mean many rules, procedures, and standard-setting decisions are made by bureaucrats rather than representatives (or the people, of course). Lacking land-use and planning offices, Texas counties pursue only minimal control over *colonias* through county attorney offices. The Texas legislature has expanded county attorney authority in efforts to halt further *colonia* development (for legal details, see Larson 1995).

With few exceptions, the English-language El Paso newspapers report little about settlement and individual household struggles for services, compared to Juárez newspapers. No Spanish-language newspaper exists for residents of this and other Spanish-speaking *colonias*. The biggest exception to the news blackout on ordinary settlers involves EPISO, an advocacy organization that gives voice to residents' needs for water and sewer lines. It does so in occasionally confrontational accountability sessions with officials. Its founder was a woman.

Now in its second decade, EPISO mobilizes its members mostly through Catholic churches. In EPISO's early years, El Paso's political establishment treated leaders like radical outside agitators. Ironically, though, many leaders and members are socially conservative Catholics who organize partly within the moral space of religious institutions. Cause-friendly priests legitimize EPISO and its agenda from the pulpit. After the first few years of hard organizational work, EPISO became a power broker for large numbers of people, particularly in El Paso's lower valley where many *colonias* are located.

In our sample, a quarter of *colonia* households claimed affiliation with EPISO. EPISO leaders perceived similar levels of support from this *colonia,* according to our interviews. Sister Mary Beth Larkin, former leader of EPISO, networks with neighborhood leaders. In our interview, she expressed pride over high attendance at the 1993 convention in El Paso's Civic Center. She said support was built through 180 home meetings in the lower valley. EPISO leader, subleader, and member ranks contain many women. With the help of attention from the media and official studies, the existence of so-called third world *colonia* conditions prompted border congressional representatives to vow to pay more attention to water and sewage facilities (U.S. GAO 1990; Texas Department of Human Services 1988). Back in 1983, former Texas governor Mark White made public remarks about helping residents dig ditches for water lines; populist rhetorical lines work well in Texas. But extending water lines to low-density settlements is expensive, particularly with high regulatory standards.

EPISO worked at local and state levels to bring visibility to problems. It helped create a Lower Valley Water District in the mid-1980s, a turning point for many other *colonia* residents. It collaborated on grant proposals to get loans and grants for residents to extend lines from roads to their property. Yet water bills are double, sometimes triple the amounts those city dwellers pay, due to bond repayments for the costly lines in these low-density settlements (Peterson 1993: 569).

In the *colonia* of our study, loans and grants have finally begun to trickle down to residents, a quarter-century after the *colonia* was born. Without EPISO and related media coverage, officials would not have cared about this near-dormant resident population because its residents didn't matter politically.

Besides EPISO, our household interviews uncovered four more informal community organizations with which residents were affiliated. They connect people concerned about water use and food bank distribution, a type of public charity. Strong religiosity, reinforced by material needs, motivates people's affiliation in both formal and informal organizations. Religious-based organization is a safe space in which to connect, at a distance from the intimidation and government surveillance surrounding immigration control, which waxes and wanes for reasons beyond the control of ordinary people. A vibrant literary tradition is growing over border residents' experiences with the Border Patrol (Sáenz 1992; Nathan 1987). The tenuous, growing political community in the *colonia* of this study offers inspiration to those in the mainstream who bemoan the decline of social capital and communalism.

Conclusion

Colonia residents in Mexico acquired most public services soon after settlement. Their political organization, flawed as it obviously was, helped explain the need for services to the municipal administration. Both the PRI and the PAN are attentive to political constituencies. Campaigns in northern Mexico are highly competitive, and parties promise different approaches to solving municipal problems. They usually deliver on those promises, with the PAN offering an individualized, streamlined approach to good governance, rather than working through organizational brokers as do the PRI and CDP. PAN capitalizes on its image as less corrupt.

The United States has long offered an individualized, streamlined approach to governance, with citizens served by technically trained public administrators. In Texas, traditions of minimalist government—especially counties—remove many problems from public gaze. Parties have been weakened through professionalization. Amateur politicians who run personalistic campaigns have some potential to oversee government machinery, but they respond primarily to those with political clout. Noisy and hardworking organizations also force some response. Women are at the base and first-tier leadership positions of organizations in the United States, matching a growing tradition in Mexico, or perhaps making visible the female grassroots that was there all along (except in the eyes of mainstream political observers).

The technical wheels of expensive, high-standard modern bureaucracy move extraordinarily slowly in the United States. The vertical dyads of Mexican-style clientelism have clear drawbacks, but they offer more responsiveness than U.S. officials, who lack either responsibility for or incentives to respond to politically marginal people. For residents of the Juárez new peripheral *colonia,* their clout was limited to campaign periods, when they exercised some limited leverage, rather than in between elections, when they once again became pawns.

Public service delays occur at the expense of potential health and safety problems for residents who share the same water, air, and sewage drainage as citizens. Yet residents are virtually silenced in the official political channels. Residents are part of the North American Free Trade Agreement, which recognizes no community bonds outside of those linked to trade and commerce. Regional (much less global) citizenship seems to be beyond the comprehension of those who share an old-style civic (masculine?) culture, where tolerance and solidarity stop at both official national identity and the national border, despite the shared heritage, economies, and realities on both sides of the border.

Notes

This chapter was presented at the International Studies Association Meetings in Toronto, March 17–21, 1997. Parts are summarized and extracted from Staudt 1998. Thanks to the National Science Foundation (HRD: 9253027). A collaborative team of four faculty (Cheryl Howard, Alejandro Lugo, Gregory Rocha, and myself) and twelve students planned and implemented the 1992 household surveys. We promised not to name individuals or their neighborhoods because of the sensitivity of data about which we queried.

1. See chapter 6 in Staudt and Weaver (1997), where we review the political culture research through the contemporary period. Critiques continue to be necessary.

2. Turnout in El Paso varies according to whether elections are local, state, or national. Turnouts have been lower than 10 percent in some local elections. Of course, U.S. turnout rates in presidential elections range from 50 to 55 percent in recent years. The turnout in Texas tends to be lower.

3. Besides official propaganda, like that from Gobierno Municipal de Cd. Juárez, *A Mitad del Camino* (1994), we follow the newspapers carefully and conduct local research about neighborhood affiliations. Staudt (1996) lists the numerous interviews done with officials and activists.

4. The *quality* of water and sewer services is not discussed in the text. Although percentages are impressive, piped water into homes is untreated but probably safe for drinking. However, during heavy usage periods and seasons, water pressure drops, increasing risk. Sewage is emptied through collectors that deposit waste in the *aguas negras* (black waters) outside the city, contaminating groundwater and irrigation canals. Despite its huge size, Juárez has no wastewater treatment plant (interview with Nancy Lowery, Center for Environmental Resource Management, University of Texas–El Paso, 1995). Thanks also to environmental expert C. Richard Bath, of the University of Texas–El Paso, for many conversations about water and waste.

5. A feature of the study is its focus on the "informal economy," including self-employment. See Staudt (1998).

6. Juárez has never had a female municipal president (El Paso has had one female mayor). Currently, in 1997, three women sit on the *cabildo*. Two women sit on El Paso's City Council, but the county council is all male.

References

Almond, Gabriel, and Sidney Verba. 1963. *The Civic Culture.* Boston: Little, Brown.

Bellah, Robert N., Richard Madsen, William M. Sullivan, Ann Swidler, and Steven M. Tipton. 1985. *Habits of the Heart: Individualism and Commitment in American Life.* Berkeley: University of California Press.

Bennett, Vivienne. 1995. "Gender, Class, and Water: Women and the Politics of Water Services in Monterrey, Mexico." *Latin American Perspectives* 22: 2.

Castañeda, Jorge G. 1993. "Tolerance and Dedemocratization." In *The California-Mexico Connection,* Abraham Lowenthal, ed. Princeton: Princeton University Press, 34–47.

Craske, Nikki. 1993. "Women's Political Participation in *Colonias Populares* in Guadalajara, Mexico." In *Viva: Women and Popular Protest in Latin America,* Sarah A. Radcliffe and Sallie Westwood, eds. London: Routledge, 112–135.

Foweraker, Joe, and Anne L. Craig, eds. 1990. *Popular Movements and Political Change in Mexico.* Boulder: Lynne Rienner.

Fuchs, Lawrence H. 1990. *The American Kaleidoscope: Race, Ethnicity, and the Civic Culture.* Hanover: University Press of New England.

Gilbert, Alan, ed. 1989. *Housing and Land in Urban Mexico.* La Jolla: Center for U.S.-Mexico Studies, University of California–San Diego.

Gobierno Municipal de Cd. Juárez. 1994. *A Mitad del Camino.* Juárez: Gobierno Municipal.

Guillén, Tonatiuh. 1990. "Servicios Públicos y Marginalidad en la Frontera Norte." *Frontera Norte* 2, no. 4: 95–120.

Hellman, Judith. 1994. "Mexican Popular Movements, Clientelism, and the Process of Democratization." *Latin American Perspectives* 21: 2.

Instituto Nacional de Estadistica, Geografia e Informática. 1993. XI Censode población y vivienda. Agnascabrentes: Author.

Larson, Jane E. 1995. "Free Markets Deep in the Heart of Texas." *The Georgetown Law Journal* 84, no. 2: 179–260.

Lau, Ruben. 1991. "Historia Política del CDP." *Movimientos Populares en Chihuahua.* Juárez: Universidad Autónoma de Ciudad Juárez.

———. 1992. "Pólitica, economia informal y tenencia de la tierra: El caso de Ciudad Juárez." Unpublished. (Expanded from an earlier version, see Rubén Lau. 1991. "El Sector Informal y el CDP." *Nóesis* 6–7: 45–52.

Molyneux, Maxine. 1986. "Mobilization Without Emancipation?" In *Transition and Development,* Richard Fagen et al. New York: Monthly Review.

Nathan, Debbie. 1987. *Women and Other Aliens: Essays from the U.S.-Mexico Border.* El Paso: Cinco Puntos Press.

Pachón, Harry. 1987. "Naturalization: Determinants and Processes in the Hispanic Community." *International Migration Review* 21, no. 2: 299–310.

Pelayo, Alonso. 1993. "Self-Help Housing on Irregular Urban Settlements in Juárez: The Case of Lucio Cabañas Neighborhood." Unpublished manuscript.

Peterson, John Allen. 1993. "Whose History? Whose Place? A Cultural History of the Lower Rio Grande Valley of El Paso." Ph.D. diss., University of Texas–Austin.

Portes, Alejandro, and Rubén G. Rumbault. 1990. *Immigrant America: A Portrait.* Berkeley: University of California Press.

Putnam, Robert D. 1995. "Bowling Alone: America's Declining Social Capital." *Journal of Democracy* 6: 65–78.

Rodríguez, Victoria E. 1995. "Municipal Autonomy and the Politics of Intergovernmental Finance: Is It Different for the Opposition?" In *Opposition Government in Mexico,* Victoria Rodríguez and Peter M. Ward, eds. Albuquerque: University of New Mexico Press, 153–172.

Rodríguez, Victoria E., and Peter M. Ward. 1992. *Policymaking, Politics, and Urban Governance in Chihuahua.* Austin: Lyndon B. Johnson School of Public Affairs, U.S. Mexican Policy Report no. 3, University of Texas at Austin.

Sáenz, Benjamin. 1992. *Flowers for the Broken: Stories.* Seattle: Broken Moon Press.

Schmidt, Steffen W., James C. Scott, Carl Lande, and Laura Guasti, eds. 1977. *Friends, Followers, and Factions: A Reader in Political Clientelism.* Berkeley: University of California Press.

Shklar, Judith. 1991. *American Citizenship: The Quest for Inclusion.* Cambridge: Harvard University Press.

Staudt, Kathleen. 1996. "Struggles in Space: Street Vendors in El Paso and Ciudad Juárez." *Urban Affairs Review* 31, no. 4: 435–454.

———. 1998. *Free Trade? Informal Economies at the U.S.-Mexico Border.* Philadelphia: Temple University Press.

Staudt, Kathleen, and Carlota Aguilar. 1992. "Political Parties, Women Activists' Agendas, and Class: Elections on Mexico's Northern Frontier." *Mexican Studies/Estudios Mexicanos* 8, no. 1: 87–106.

Staudt, Kathleen, and William Weaver. 1997. *Political Science and Feminisms: Integration or Transformation?* New York: Twayne/Macmillan.

Texas, State of, Department of Human Services. 1988. *The Colonias Factbook: A Survey of Living Conditions in Rural Areas of South and West Texas Border Counties.* Austin: DHS.

Tomás Rivera Center. 1995. *Latinos in Texas: A Socio-Demographic Profile.* Claremont: Tomás Rivera Center.

Towers, George William. 1991. *Colonia Formation and Economic Restructuring in El Paso, Texas.* Ph.D. diss., University of Arizona–Tucson.

U.S. CIR (Commission on Immigration Reform). 1994. *U.S. Immigration Policy: Restoring Credibility.* Washington, D.C.: U.S. CIR Report to Congress.

U.S. GAO (General Accounting Office). 1990. *Problems and Progress of Colonia Subdivisions Near Mexico Border.* Washington, D.C.: U.S. GAO (GAO/RCED-91-37).

Vélez-Ibáñez, Carlos. 1983. *Rituals of Marginality: Politics, Process, and Culture Change in Central Mexico, 1969–74.* Berkeley: University of California Press.

Venegas Aguilera, Lilia. 1995. "Political Culture and Women of the Popular Sector in Ciudad Juárez, 1983–1986." In *Opposition Government in Mexico,* Victoria Rodríguez and Peter Ward, eds. Albuquerque: University of New Mexico Press, 97–112.

Verba, Sidney, and Norman Nie. 1972. *Participation in America.* New York: Harper and Row.

Vila, Pablo. Forthcoming. *Crossing Borders. Reinforcing Borders. Social Categories, Metaphors and Narrative Identities on the U.S.-Mexico Border.* Austin: University of Texas Press.

Villarreal, Roberto E. 1988. "EPISO and Political Empowerment: Organizational Politics in a Border City." *Journal of Borderlands Studies* 3, no. 2: 81–96.

Ward, Peter M. 1991. "Political Pressure for Urban Services: The Response of Two Mexico City Administrations." *Development and Change* 12, no. 3: 379–408.

————. 1995. "Policy Making and Policy Implementation Among Non-PRI Governments: The PAN in Cd. Juárez and in Chihuahua." In *Opposition Government in Mexico*, Victoria Rodríguez and Peter M. Ward, eds. Albuquerque: University of New Mexico Press, 135–152.

Wilson, James Q. 1973. *Political Organizations*. New York: Basic.

World Bank. 1991. *Juárez: Urban Issues Survey*. Washington, D.C.: World Bank.

Part 3

Bordered Identities

7

Globalizing Tenochtitlán?
Feminist Geo-Politics:
Mexico City as Borderland

Julie A. Murphy Erfani

Mexico City, 1650: The Conquerors and the Conquered

The family crest rears itself pompously in the ornamented iron over the gate, as if over an altar. The master of the house rolls up in a mahogany carriage. . . . Within someone stops playing the clavichord; rustlings of silks . . . are heard, voices of marriageable daughters. . . . This city of Mexico, city of palaces, is one of the largest in the world. Although it is very far from the sea, Spanish and Chinese ships bring their merchandise . . . here. The powerful Chamber of Commerce rivals that of Seville. . . . The Indians, who built this city for the conquerors on the ruins of their Tenochtitlán, bring food in canoes. They may work here during the day, but at nightfall they are removed on pain of the lash to their slums outside the walls. Some Indians wear stockings and shoes and speak Spanish in hope of being allowed to remain and thereby escape tribute and forced labor. (Galeano 1985: 236)

Feminist Geo-Politics: Bodies-Cities, Urban Borderlands

I knew that the capital city had become a borderland when I saw its tattoos: ubiquitous, Los Angeles–like graffiti inscribing symbols and cicatrices along the walls and buildings where power and resistance rage on a daily basis in the Ciudad de México. Mexico City is now as much a margin as a center of national state power: the city and its residents are part of a borderland whose contours range from U.S.-style globalization to indigenous Mesoamerican civilization. As such, the graffiti is a symptom of broader struggles over symbols, meanings, identities, and authority in an increasingly transnational and transcultural urban space. It is not that the U.S.-

Mexico border of Juárez–El Paso fame has been relocated to the capital but, instead, that yet another borderland has sprung up right in the heart of the country.

The architecture, streetscapes, and neighborhoods of Mexico City have become sites of intense geopolitical struggles over culture, identity, representation, and authority in the space of a megacity situated at the crossroads of the Americas. In the current era of the North American Free Trade Agreement (NAFTA), hemispheric free trade, and globalization, the physicality as well as the metaphorical and cultural character of the spaces of Mexico City are up for grabs. Also at stake are the relationships of the spaces of the city to time, memory, and the past. Like the socially constructed surface of bodies, Mexico City's culturally fluid and chaotic mix of architectural styles, its racially and class-charged streetscapes, its gendered buildings and politicized walls tell a story of corporeal inscription and subversion of power. Mexico City is a *frontera* (border): an in-between, fluid space neither overwhelmingly "alien" nor thoroughly "indigenous" (see also Anzaldúa 1987; Ortiz Monasterio 1995).

Why and how the capital of a country—home to the center of national state power—can become a borderland is difficult to explain from the vantage point of the center of the discipline of international relations. The discipline's dominant paradigm, neorealism, offers no explanation. Neorealism is wedded to the classical geopolitics of the territorial state, whose power is said to be maximized by national government. In this view, the capital city merely "houses" national government; it is not the center of crucial geopolitical struggles. Classical geopolitics teaches that space is and should be territorialized; that is, conquered, named, mapped, culturally homogenized, and controlled by national government in the interest of furthering national state power (Blunt and Rose 1994). The state's territorialization of space involves the enclosure, possession, fixity, and militarization of space as well as the housing of state power in the capital city. Geopolitical theorists and neorealist practitioners of spatial territorialization see geopolitics as the nation-state's control and mastering of enclosed space for the purpose of possessing and exploiting the natural and human resources located within a territory. Consequently, the power and influence of the nation-state rest with the production, control, and often the expansion of space as territory as well as the exploitation of resources within territorialized space. Relatedly, a country's capital city serves as the geographic-symbolic center of the amassed power, security, impenetrability, and authority of the territorial state.

Contrary to classical geopolitics, however, a feminist geo-politics understands the time-space dimensions of transnationalism and transculturation in theorizing space and time at the interstices of the physical and the metaphorical. Cartesian geopolitics does not permit such theory because the physical/material as experienced through the body and the mental/ metaphorical as perceived through the mind are conceived as binary opposites. In other words, space and time are viewed only as physical objects to be observed and manipulated by a detached, disembodied mind uniquely empowered by a reason deemed to be separate from the physical/material world. Following Gearóid Ó Tuathail (1996), I designate this unproblematized, logocentric conception of space and politics as *geopolitics* written with no hyphen. In contrast, by seeing and theorizing space and time in the interstices of the physical and the mental, feminist *geo-politics,* hyphenated, interrogates fixed notions of geopolitics to study globalization and resistance through methodologies of social construction and phenomenologies of embodiment. Feminist geo-politics theorizes both the commercial and resistance aspects of transnationalism and transculturation across the axes of time, space, the material, and the metaphorical.

The capital city of Mexico is as much on the margins of the nation-state as a home to the governmental center of territorial state power. My feminist geo-political reading of the architecture, streetscapes, and built environment of Mexico City sees the capital as a physical and cultural borderland. Physically, the city's urban space is divided, patrolled, and territorialized but is also fluid and uncontrollable in ways parallel to the spatial paradoxes of Juárez–El Paso. Culturally, the city is a metaphorical space of struggle and mixing between dominant and subordinate national, racial, classed, and gendered social forces. As a borderland in the heart of a territorial state, Mexico City and its architecture, streetscapes, and other spaces are key to understanding the theory and practice of an emergent urban geopolitics that is disembodying, reconfiguring, and obscuring the territorial state in the Americas.

To see and study the capital and center of a territorial state as a borderland subverts key claims of the center of the discipline of international relations. The theory and practice of classical geopolitics and neorealism elevate national government to the center of control of both domestic politics and foreign policy, virtually erasing cities and locales as decisive sites of contestation in a country's political and governmental landscape. This erasure is due, in part, to a Cartesian perspective that establishes a binary opposition between mind and body. Such binarism sets national government up as a rational mind controlling an irrational body politic. The Cartesian separation of mind from body establishes national government as a "rational," "scientific" observer said to be capable of an "objective" vision of a world of objects as seen via a detached, neutral, disembodied gaze (Massey 1994: 232–238; Ó Tuathail 1996: 23–24). The Cartesian perspective genders cities, like all the territory of the nation, as feminine and imagines them as feminine bodies to be controlled and cared for by the "rational mind" of national government within the confines of a territorial state.

Moreover, in the Cartesian geopolitical imagination, capital cities are distinguished from other urban centers by the special political-symbolic role they play as "home" to and "woman" of national government. In order to validate the centrality and prestige of national government and the associated power of the territorial state, capital cities of modern territorial states are imagined to be the feminine Other of national government. Thus, they symbolize and embody the essential character of the nation, the people, and the homogeneity, purity, and steadfastness of national culture. Like feminine bodies, capital cities are constructed as the homes, the housewives, the wombs that cradle and nurture the national government. Architecturally, capital cities give birth to the buildings that are the physical places of national government, though the cities themselves are deemed insignificant to decisionmaking within the national household exclusively presided over by national government. Minor and tedious housekeeping details of the city, such as garbage collection, are left to the housewife—municipal government—while national government directly controls budgets or other key aspects of those capital cities governed as federal districts.

Parallel to the social construction of feminine bodies, the feminine physical appearance, shape, adornment, and beauty of the capital city are imagined to be key to the capital's symbolic-political role. As the feminine Other of masculinist national government, the capital's feminine appearance/aesthetic is all-important and often reflects a blending of what dominant Western culture defines as stately, alluring, exotic, familiar, delicate, secured, and well-tended. As a symbol of national pride, the capital city should be unblemished, opulent, and expansive in a controlled way and eminently presentable in an exterior, superficial way: its facades and exterior matter most. The capital city should always appear attractive on the outside in spite of any interior problems not visible on the surface. From a Cartesian geopolitical perspective, the capital city is a feminine object whose surface appearance and feminine aesthetic are of symbolic-political importance to the power of the state. By imagining and seeing the capital city as a prized bride and maternal home to national government, neorealist practitioners of international relations make the capital city irrelevant to the most important aspects of the politics of global space and authority, especially in foreign affairs. Just as women's bodies are often constructed as surface-only objects of masculine pride, so too cities as crucial sites of political, cultural, and spatial struggles are of secondary importance to the political and governmental landscape.

In contrast to Cartesian perspectivism, a feminist geo-politics based upon corporeal feminist philosophy can render cities, like bodies, visible again as crucial sites of struggle over international relations, politics, space, identity, and authority (see Enloe 1989 and Pettman 1996). Feminist geo-politics as delineated here is first and foremost about new ways of seeing, theorizing, and practicing the connections between space and politics and between nature and culture. Instead of positing a neutral mind detached from the body and observing space "objectively," feminist geo-politics theorizes ways of seeing and knowing about space and politics at the interstices or spaces fusing mind and body. That space or borderland where knowing occurs is the realm of experience of the corporeal subject (Grosz 1994: 94–95).

In locating epistemology in the experience of the embodied subject, corporeal feminism points to a feminist geo-politics that theorizes the local as an integral site for understanding politics and activating the possibilities for its transformation. The local—such as cities, neighborhoods, streets, homes, bodies, selves—consists of many places where the knowing, corporeal subject might resist and transform the politics of modern, territorial states. Rather than producing space as vast territory to be conquered, enclosed, mapped, named, controlled, and exploited, feminist geo-politics seeks to see and produce space as many local places that are spatially open and fluid; culturally heterogeneous; and grounded in memory, history, and a sense of place without perpetuating the oppressions of the past (see Blunt and Rose 1994; see also McDowell 1996). Rather than seeing and producing space as purely physical and territorial, feminist geo-politics sees and produces spaces and places as metaphorical and physical sites of cultural reconstruction and political resistance and struggle (Massey 1994: 1–13; see also Duncan 1996).

In this regard, feminist geo-politics sees cities as decisive sites of contestation and struggle over space, culture, politics, and economics, especially in an era of globalization and time-space compression. Drawing on both phenomenology and social constructionism, corporeal feminism theorizes bodies-cities together as mutually constitutive. Elizabeth Grosz, a key philosopher of corporeal feminism, sees cities and bodies interfaced in a two-way linkage (Grosz 1992). In several respects, Grosz's vision of bodies-cities advances what I refer to here as feminist geo-political reformulations of the relations between space and politics and nature and culture. First, her corporeal feminism implies that as cities undergo processes of globalization, the mutually constitutive relations between bodies and cities mean that globalization's effects on cities must be studied in tandem with its effects on bodies. Second, bodies and cities are not just sites of inscription but also of subversion of power. Consequently, Grosz's corporeal feminism suggests that as bodies shape cities and vice versa, bodies-cities will be key sites of both inscription and subversion of the socioeconomic and cultural values and effects associated with globalization. In other words, feminist geo-politics can use corporeal feminist philosophy to critique globalization and study resistance to it by describing the specific ways in which bodies-cities transform globalization as much as they are inscribed by it. Given the urban character of most globalization, Grosz's work implicitly suggests that we cannot adequately study globalization and resistance to it unless we study bodies-cities.

An example will be instructive. Feminist geo-politics as posited here theorizes hybridity in a Latin American world city as a borderland mingling four dimensions: the axes of time, space, physicality, and metaphor. The metaphorical and physical hybridities of and in Mexico City reflect a montage-like borderland of the four intersecting axes. Consider, for example, a private security guard of Maya descent and rural, campesino origins standing in front of a Citibank building in downtown Mexico City. Culturally, he crosses metaphorical borders between Mexican and U.S. culture as well as temporal borders between indigenous, Mesoamerican conceptions of time and ultramodernity. Physically, his job and his homelife locate him in a material/spatial borderland reaching from the privatized, U.S. territory of the ultramodern Citibank building he physically guards to the top of the deteriorating high-rise apartment building on whose roof he cultivates food and livestock in simulated, rural Maya fashion (see Bonfil Batalla 1996 and García Canclini 1995a).

Architecturally, the apartment building rooftop, the openness and fluidity of its space, poised as it is in the middle of a megacity, plays a role in enabling him to resist some aspects of modern urbanization and urban globalization. In spite of living in the center of a globalizing city and working for Citibank, he retains the agricultural subsistence practices that are key elements of a Mesoamerican cultural heritage (Bonfil Batalla 1996). As a corporeal subject in a globalizing megacity, he is Mayan as well as Citibankesque; he embodies transculturation and transnationalism in temporal, spatial, physical, and mental ways. He embodies and himself constructs globalization and resistance to it. In turn, the buildings and the city that help construct his hybrid, corporeal subjectivity are key physical and symbolic places where he lives out a transcultural and transnational life. In a similar vein, anthropologist Néstor García Canclini argues that indigenous residents in Mexico City reconstruct the capital within their own ethnic frameworks as they eat, build their houses, cure their ailments, and build community networks. In fact, García Canclini questions what it means to be *chilango*—one identified with Mexico City—when half the capital's inhabitants have been born in other regions of Mexico and when 263,000 indigenous people and several million more citydwellers come from predominantly indigenous regions, such as Oaxaca, Guerrero, and Michoacán (García Canclini 1995a: 81).

The notion that one can be a Mayan campesino and a loyal Citibank employee without living in the countryside or ever having been in the United States implies a new cultural cartography. This new cartography identifies and locates major cultural borders within a single, urban corporeal subject who, in relation to various architectures within the city, crosses cultural borders as he or she crosses in and out of different buildings and zones of the city. Such cultural cartography reorients and relocates cultural geography in the in-between cultural spaces of urban buildings, facades, rooftops, streetscapes, neighborhoods, and bodies. This then disrupts the national cultural homogeneities and unified subjectivities and identities theorized and advocated by the conventional geopolitics of territorial states.

The example of the Maya-Citibank security guard illustrates as well that spatial transnationalism occurs not just when bodies migrate across national territorial borders established by states. Spatial transnationalism also occurs when urban bodies, for instance, cross territorial boundaries established by foreign transnational banks and corporations that privatize, nationalize, and territorialize space within and around the commercial buildings from which they operate within a globalizing city. The U.S. investor–owned and operated corporate or financial building itself constitutes a simultaneously public-private, U.S. territorial space within the heart of Mexico City. As a form of reterritorialization of U.S. state and society within Mexico, the corporate building is patrolled by a private security force that exercises a mix of public-private sovereignty over the activities and actors who enter and do business in the building. The sovereign authority exercised in the building is public to the extent, for instance, that it relies upon Canadian, Mexican, and U.S. state sovereignty for many of the laws, regulations, and trade agreements (e.g., NAFTA) that govern and legally protect the commercial operations undertaken in the building. The sovereign authority exercised within the building is private to the extent that it relies upon privately funded security forces and private investor decisions about the commercial activities undertaken in the territorialized space encompassed by the building. (See Sassen 1996 for a similar argument about the privatization of sovereignty in New York City.) In other words, spatial transnationalism—or territorial border crossing—occurs not just across the borders dividing national states but also across and among the buildings and streets of a world city.

In the section that follows, I read the contemporary urban geopolitics of the capital city's architecture through a corporeal feminist lens. I argue that this allows me to see a Mexico City different from that represented in modern maps of the city and of the country. Located precariously on the edge and at the center of Mexico, the city is a space of many times and places. Within that urban space where indigenous Mesoamerica intersects with ultramodernity, the clash of globalization and resistance is building a postmodern Mesoamerican city. As resilient as it is conquered, a Tenochtitlán consisting of Mesoamerican street vendors and reflective glass temples of a global commercial elite is displacing key parts of what has been modern Mexico City. At once Mesoamerican and neoliberal, this reconstructed Tenochtitlán is being built over the ruins of an unfinished modernity whose exclusions began with Hernán Cortés and accelerated once again with Carlos Salinas de Gortari. Thus, it is to the urban architecture of a resilient yet globalizing Tenochtitlán that I now turn.

Mexico City as Borderland: Urban Architecture as Geo-Politics

There's an order to Mexico City's architectural chaos. Buildings speak vastly different architectural languages, although they manage to communicate enough to arrange the spaces of the city. In many respects, buildings and other structures practice geopolitics on a daily basis as they play out the politics of border space in the capital. In a megacity like Mexico City so infused with transnational flows of capital, culture, goods, and people, buildings and streetscapes define and control space more than formal government. It is not that government, governance, and the state cease to exist. Rather, as Ian R. Douglas argues, "globalization is perhaps the last visible form of governance, that holds in its very essence, the technologies of disappearance to be employed by the state" (Douglas 1997; also Douglas forthcoming). In fact, the seeming disappearance of the state even in a city serving as center to national government is key to understanding the capital city's emergence as a borderland.

As in the Juárez–El Paso borderlands, the state in Mexico City is not absent or entirely failed. Rather, transnational flows and transculturation have so intermingled government and social forces in both Mexico City and Juárez–El Paso that the state is as invisible in daily life as it is stridently visible in patrolling borders. The changing geopolitics of globalization are most evident in these borderland spaces precisely because of the stark visual paradoxes associated with governance. Physical borders are visibly patrolled by the state only to be rendered entirely invisible by the obvious mixing that results from subversion of the border by migrants, products, and culture. In the urban borderland of Mexico City, there is a stark visual presence of the state because the city is the capital of national government, but the visual, aural, and respiratory chaos of the city makes formal governmental presence and effectiveness seem to blur and fade.

The city's architectural chaos adds to the illusion of the disappearance of the formal regulatory authority of government. However, this visual disorder is itself part of a transnational and transcultural order whereby the state and globalization as well as resistance to them become embedded in the city's built environment. Architectural chaos is part of a contested geopolitical order in which the urban built environment is as much a revised form of governance and globalization as a forum of resistance to governance and globalization. In effect, the city's built environment is geopolitics, and architecture becomes a geopolitical act within the context of a changing global political economy that intertwines the local and global. More than just a political act affecting identities, urban architecture is a geopolitical act affecting the symbolic representation of space and the material conditions of the quality of life, both of which affect and are modified by urban bodies. As such, buildings, structures, and streetscapes are visual representations of space and sites of discipline and resistance, both of which are simultaneously engendered by transnationalism and transculturation. The new World Trade Center (WTC) Mexico City and the vendor kiosks of the city's informal economy illustrate the geopolitics of ordered disorder evident in the city's architectural chaos. These two architectural phenomena share a parallel history of having been constructed, both literally and figuratively, over the ruins of Mexico's unfinished modernity. Each speaks a vastly different architectural language, although both are linked as part of the transnationalization and transculturation of the city and its residents.

Like NAFTA, both the World Trade Center and the recently expanded street vendor kiosks were built over the ruins of Mexico's ever-unfinished, modern economy. After the import substitution industrialization underpinning Mexico's modern economic growth hopelessly stagnated in the late 1970s and 1980s, the governments of Miguel de la Madrid Hurtado and Carlos Salinas de Gortari sought to rebuild Mexico's economy by opening it up to global and regional market forces. As the principal architect of NAFTA, Salinas sought to reconstruct Mexico's inefficient and unfinished modern economy by entering into a free trade agreement with the United States and Canada. By formalizing free trade in North America, NAFTA was supposed to attract greater foreign capital and investment and stimulate global market competitiveness in industry as Mexico's closed national economy became increasingly open to regional and global capital and competition. As a method of regionally based economic restructuring, NAFTA was conceived as a form of neoliberal economic architecture intended to gut and then redesign Mexico's modern economy, which was clearly in ruins by the end of the lost decade of foreign debt of the 1980s. In other words, NAFTA was a project to globalize and thereby redefine and redesign, not restore, the ruins of the modern economy (Erfani 1995: 127–182).

Parallel to NAFTA, the World Trade Center, Mexico City, was built over the ruins of an unfinished and deteriorating modern skyscraper in order to redefine, redesign, and thereby globalize the form and function of economic modernity in Mexico. Just as Salinas endeavored through NAFTA to change and globalize the image of the ruined edifice of the Mexican economy, so too the architect and developers of the WTC wished to alter the image of the abandoned, half-finished modern skyscraper that they acquired for conversion to the WTC. Spurred by Salinas's NAFTA initiative in 1989, developer Juan Diego Gutiérrez Cortina of Grupo Gutsa began construction of the WTC over the abandoned shell of a building originally conceived as the Hotel de México. The hotel was to be the skyscraper centerpiece of an architectural project undertaken in the mid-1960s in anticipation of the Olympic Games in Mexico City in 1968. As its name suggests, the Hotel de México was conceived as *the* major tourist hotel and convention center in the country at a time of economic nationalist ferment. Buoyed up by optimism about an expanding modern economy, Mexico's president at the time, Gustavo Díaz Ordaz, persuaded the developer, Manuel Suárez y Suárez, to build the hotel complex in the heart of the capital city instead of in Cuernavaca (interview, Pedro R. Dupeyron V., World Trade Center Mexico City, April 1997).

Much like the indebted modernization of Mexico's national economy, the modern Hotel de México was never completed once the developer ran short of funds in 1964. As a result, the uncompleted shell of the skyscraper stood abandoned, in the ruins shown in Figure 7.1, for about twenty years until the World Trade Center was completed in 1994. In effect, the enormous, dilapidated shell of the building stood for two decades as a monument to the incomplete, indebted, and failed modernization of the Mexican economy. In a parallel fashion, the national process of import substitution industrialization, the state's strategy for stimulating growth in the modern economy, began to stagnate by the late 1960s and then entirely unravel during the 1970s and 1980s (Erfani 1995). These were precisely the years of the skyscraper's abandonment and decline.

Thus, the abandoned skyscraper of the Hotel de México served as both a metaphor and a material gauge of the decline of Mexico's modern economy from the late 1960s until the early 1990s, when NAFTA was formulated. The building stood in ruins from 1964 until WTC construction commenced in 1990, approximately the same time that NAFTA was proposed. Successive presidents of Mexico tried unsuccessfully to convince Suárez to sell the abandoned hotel and complex for redevelopment (interview, Pedro R. Dupeyron V., World Trade Center Mexico City, April 1997). Suárez, however, refused, and it was not until after his death that his heirs sold the property, a very imposing ruin towering over the intensely traveled, major north-south artery, the Avenida Insurgentes Sur, along a highly visible, commercial stretch of the avenue. Given repeated presidential attempts to persuade Suárez to sell, successive Mexican governments apparently judged the ruin's damage to the capital city's aesthetic to be substantial,

Figure 7.1   The incomplete shell of the Hotel de México, Mexico City

infringing as it did on capital dwellers' sense of national pride and faith in economic modernization. As a vertically massive skyscraper ruin, the deteriorating shell of the Hotel de México disturbed the capital city aesthetic of exterior opulence, well-tended elegance, and feminine physical beauty. Although the national government proved powerless over the situation, Mexican presidents acted as if it were a matter of national pride to intercede on behalf of the country to do something about the ruins. The building was an obvious blemish on the city's gendered aesthetic, whose primary duty was to confirm through a feminine otherness the power and prestige of the national government and modern economy.

Unlike the architectural text of economic nationalism of the Hotel de México, the World Trade Center building is a hybrid, public-private show of transnational commercial force. As with NAFTA, the commercial

transnationalism embedded in the building's aesthetic, function, and operation is dedicated to the paradoxical task of eliminating borders as obstacles
to global commerce while reinventing borders as restraints on average people. The entrance to the WTC as shown in Figure 7.2 evokes the public,
intergovernmental image of the United Nations with colorful flags of multiple countries seeming to welcome the world to come in to do business. The
enormous white archway speaks a language of global good intentions associated with building worldwide free trade as means of creating a borderless
world. In approaching the building, one quickly learns, however, that the
invitation to enter this borderless utopia favors a specific type of businesspeople whose movements and activities in the building are themselves
strictly controlled and patrolled. Indeed, the structure of the building, its
army of private security, and its aesthetic all reinvent a series of borders of
national, classed, raced, and gendered orientation.

Aesthetically, for instance, the building's obvious modern skyscraper
style immediately seems to tell observers that they are in a major city in the
United States, not in the capital of Mexico. In fact, a key intent behind the
aesthetic seems to be to convince foreign investors that they are in the
United States, even while they are in Mexico. Indeed, the culturally
homogenizing, globalist orientation of all world trade centers around the
world provides an Americanized set of business services and linkages all
generally standardized to U.S. business practices and norms (Nedkov

Figure 7.2   The entrance to the World Trade Center building in Mexico City

1996). Geopolitically, the U.S.-style aesthetic and U.S.-oriented commercial purpose of the building construct a national border around the building such that the structure becomes a territorialized space resembling and functioning as if it were in the United States. Reminiscent of classical geopolitics, the army of private security further demarcates, patrols, and militarizes the space of the skyscraper such that the building serves as a privately constructed piece of simulated-U.S. territory situated within the heart of Mexico City.

Although the building is formally 100 percent privately Mexican-owned, in fact the political sovereignty exercised within the building is a subtle mix of private and public authority. Privately, Grupo Gutsa funds and controls the building's security force. Grupo Gutsa also privately determines to a certain extent the range, types, and conduct of the commercial activities and services that go on in the building. Embedded in and disguised in this privatized sovereign, territorial skyscraper-space, however, are key elements of public authority and state sovereignty as well as public, intergovernmental agreements and agencies, especially those governing trade and commerce, such as the General Agreement on Tariffs and Trade (GATT), its new incarnation, the World Trade Organization (WTO), and NAFTA. To the extent that the building is dedicated to facilitating hemispheric and worldwide free trade and commerce, the commercial activities that it promotes are reliant upon, as well as governed by, key aspects of these public, interstate trade agreements. In the case of NAFTA, key elements of U.S., Mexican, and Canadian state sovereignty also help govern the commercial activities within the building. In this regard, the World Trade Center exemplifies how urban architecture reflects the globalization of political-economic relations to facilitate the seeming disappearance of states. Although government and governance are still quite operative and important, their formal institutional arrangements are increasingly disembodied as public authority becomes embedded in the public-private, territorialized spaces of the neocolonial architecture of the city.

The cultural borders of race, class, gender, and nation perpetuated and reinvented by the neoliberal geopolitics of the World Trade Center are quite daunting. As a form of neocolonial architecture, the WTC geopolitically constructs a cultural and territorial presence of the north in the south through a mixture of public-private authority centered in a privately owned commercial building. As state authority is embedded in private architecture, the disembodiment of the state facilitates the private sector's use of architecture to reinforce and reinvent cultural borders of race, class, gender, and nation. In constructing a physical and material presence of the north in the south, neocolonial architecture accentuates a whole cultural set of binary oppositions whose borders are consolidated by and within the buildings themselves. In terms of race and class, for instance, the spatial politics of

the WTC reinforces a binary opposition between white and mestizo men,
between the privileged, middle- and upper-class managers overseeing commercial activities in the building and the primarily indigenous, working-
class, private security guards relegated to standing around on all floors to
guard the space dominated by the managers and visiting white businesspeople.

As much as it is raced and classed, the space of the WTC building is
also clearly gendered, with white and mestiza women populating the secre-
tarial staff that serves the white and mestizo male managers throughout the
building. Moreover, the United Nations aesthetic of the WTC interfaced
with its verticality render "natural" an implicit humanism and phallocentrism operative throughout the architecture and neoliberal trade activities of
the building. As Elizabeth Grosz (1992) argues: "Phallocentrism is . . . not
so much the dominance of the phallus as the pervasive unacknowledged
use of the male or masculine to represent the human. The problem, then, is
not so much to eliminate as to reveal the masculinity inherent in the notion
of the universal, the generic human." The appearance of the building
speaks a universalist-humanist language suggesting that the World Trade
Center serves a worldwide common human interest in free trade. This universalist humanism disguises the fact that neoliberal free trade privileges
certain elite, classed, raced, gendered, and national interests while subordinating many others. Such disguised dominance, privilege, and hierarchy are
rendered "natural" by being embedded in the architecture of the building.
In appropriating the universalist language and aesthetic of the UN and
attaching it to private, neoliberal economic operations, WTC architecture
represents privatized, transnational commercial space as egalitarian and
culturally generic, beneficial to all nations and all humans. This representation of space is an unacknowledged use of masculinist, Anglo theories and
practices of neoliberal economics to represent the human (see Tickner
1992). This humanism serves to naturalize and legitimize the privilege,
dominance, and hierarchy represented by and practiced through the verticality of the building and its neoliberal commercial operations. The higher
a manager is in the building, the more privileged, powerful, and dominant
he is within the corporate hierarchy and the better his office view as well as
his "vision," presumably, of the city's role in neoliberal world trade and
commerce. Like the Cartesian perspective of classical geopolitics, top
WTC managers aspire to "see" the city with a mind's-eye gaze in order to
control and exploit its resources.

Perhaps the most startling neocolonial cultural effect of the World
Trade Center on all its various employees across the gender, race, and class
divisions perpetuated within the building is the creation of a work space
where everyone operates according to the neoliberal economic precepts of
businesspeople in the advanced industrial West. The indigenous security

guards, some of the lowest-paid workers in the building, display loyalty, efficiency, and commitment to neoliberalism as they stand guard over the office spaces of the highest-paid, white and mestizo corporate managers in the "Corona," the crown that houses the corporate managerial elite on the very top of the building. In fact, one such indigenous guard was so avid about doing his job that he would not permit me, as I was waiting to interview his boss, to photograph the views of the city from the Corona. While I shot a few photos through the window of the lobby, the guard commanded me to stop until his criollo boss arrived and granted me permission. It became clear in the interview with the guard's boss that the corporate managers in the Corona covet the stunning city views from their offices (interview, Ismael González, World Trade Center Mexico City, April 1997). The WTC building is, as its developers boast, the tallest building in Mexico City. Congruent with a Cartesian geopolitical perspective, to see the city from that height is deemed a key first step to possessing and exploiting it. This is quite parallel to global business managers' drive for "global vision": to see the globe as a whole is the key to commanding it and global markets. In my particular photographic episode in the WTC, the security guard seemed convinced that his boss's view of the city was a piece of private property under the exclusive command and possession of WTC managers. As such, it was the guard's job to patrol and secure that sovereign possession. Indeed, "Corona," the architectural name of "crown" given to the top of the building, evokes the notion of the absolutist sovereignty of kings. In accord with the metaphor of royalty, the security guard performed his colonized role as military defender of the sovereign domain of the crown. In effect, this incident demonstrates the neocolonial cultural effects of commercial transnationalism at its worst.

Like the commercial transnationalism of which it is an integral part, the WTC building excludes and, in part, denies, anything about the local that is deemed to be less than modern, efficient, profit-generating, or Western. In the name of promoting global neoliberal efficiency, the architecture of free trade and of its ultramodern towers culturally and materially excludes that which is indigenous, Mesoamerican, subsistence-oriented, non-Western, and often even that which is national. In urban architecture, such exclusions are achieved by, among other things, the use of modernist and ultramodernist aesthetics, the territorialization and militarization of the space of corporate and global financial buildings, the use of security checkpoints to register and monitor all visitors, and the imposition of identification (ID) tags and procedures for all residents and visitors to buildings. These IDs serve as the passports and visas that determine who may enter and circulate in the territory of corporate and financial buildings. In the name of building a borderless world where goods and commerce flow freely, the WTC and the Cartesian geopolitics informing its architecture and commercial activities reinvent borders within a territorialized space more tightly controlled than was ever possible within the confines of most nation-states. As shown in Figure 7.3, it is this type of neocolonial architecture of territorialized, northern space that is being reproduced throughout the city in the financial and corporate reflective glass towers of globalization.

Embedded within the architectural chaos of Mexico City is a resistance architecture often juxtaposed to the city's proliferating neoliberal glass towers. Reflective of a geo-politics of resistance, neovernacular structures with indigenous, Mesoamerican elements, colonial-era and faux-Spanish colonial buildings, as well as aesthetically hybrid architectures in many ways dispute the neoliberal logic, spatial politics, and cultural homogeniza-

© 1998 Julie A. Murphy Erfani

Figure 7.3   Example of neocolonial
architecture in downtown Mexico City

tion of economic globalization. Although often entangled with globalization and world commerce, the resistance transnationalism of such architecture is also embedded in Mexico City's built environment. Architecturally, this alternative built environment is often located right next to, bordering on, and mixed up with the architecture of commercial transnationalism. The resistance evident in such architecture is cultural and spatial: its aesthetics and spatial politics subvert and defy physical and cultural borders. This border-subversion includes both the metaphorical as well as the physical borders constructed by modernity and reconstructed by neocolonial globalization. By differing so fundamentally in an aesthetic-visual sense, this alternative architecture constructs the urban built environment as a forum of cultural resistance to the homogeneity of the city's ultramodern towers. Moreover, the self-built, popular varieties of such alternative architecture physically reclaim and reconstruct vast portions of urban space, often overflowing all over the streets and sidewalks of the city, as is the case with the vendor kiosks of the informal economy. With their popular-canvas aesthetic and horizontal rather than vertical physical immensity, this alternative commercial space of kiosks not only reclaims the physical spaces of the city but also rebuilds its cultural spaces.

Through its physical proximity and juxtaposition to the city's neoliberal architecture, alternative architecture of various neovernacular, colonial, faux-colonial, and hybrid styles speaks a language of spatial resistance and cultural difference. In other words, by sharing borders with the ultramodern glass towers of globalization, alternative architecture subverts the perfectly ultramodern aesthetics of neoliberal architecture by upsetting the cultural homogeneity of neoliberal streetscapes. The cultural impact of such architectural juxtapositions is parallel to the adjacent socioeconomic differences so visible along the U.S.-Mexico border. The presence of northern Mexico's poverty along a shared 2,000-mile border with the United States disrupts the otherwise ultramodern, advanced industrial image of North America. Moreover, alternative architecture's presence and persistence next to and in the face of the increasing dominance of ultramodern, neoliberal buildings in key commercial zones of Mexico City undermines some of the latter's powers of denial and exclusion of the local.

Although neoliberal buildings may effectively exclude or deny much of what is local in the interior of corporate and financial buildings, the persistence of neovernacular and Spanish-colonial architecture subverts the exclusion and denial of the local and the past on streets. For instance, the historic colonial building wedged in between two ultramodern glass towers in Figure 7.4 speaks a language of persistence and resistance to the homogenizing, place-denying visual effects of neoliberal architecture. Even while each glass tower viewed in isolation seems to say that one is in the United States, the historic colonial building in between triggers memory and a

Figure 7.4   An example of a historic colonial building wedged between
two ultramodern glass towers

sense of the past that help one recover a sense of place in Mexico City. This
particular streetscape on Paseo de la Reforma is a borderland in the heart of
the capital. Although the two neoliberal skyscrapers tower over and hem in
the historic building on both sides, the old building subverts the two neocolonial buildings' construction of a perfectly ultramodern, culturally
homogeneous streetscape. To the extent that "space contains compressed
time," as Gaston Bachelard writes, a citydweller walking this particular
stretch of Reforma can, in certain transcultural respects, walk from the
ultramodern to the colonial by simply traversing the few steps separating
these three buildings (Bachelard 1969: 8).

In visually confronting the neoliberal and geographically mingling
with it, alternative architecture plays out a geo-politics of resistance that
assures that, as George Yúdice argues, modernity in Mexico City becomes
"more a question of establishing new relationships with tradition than of
surpassing it" (Yúdice 1992: 21). In the street vendor kiosks of Mexico
City's informal economy, for instance, elements of economic neoliberalism
commingle with indigenous Mesoamerican market traditions to produce a
vast, alternative commercial space throughout the city. Unlike the World
Trade Center building, which attempts to surpass tradition by denying its
existence, the vendorscapes of kiosks simultaneously embody neoliberalism and Mesoamerican culture. Rather than denying the past, the kiosks

make the past contemporary by mixing the market traditions of Mesoamerica with the products of post-Fordist global production and neoliberal free trade. Through such indigenous-ultramodern hybridity, vendor kiosks make the global local by creating employment and income through the construction of alternative commercial space for average people. Unlike the WTC, the self-built kiosks of vendorscapes include average, poor, and indigenous people by design. The informal, street vendor economy resists and transforms the global by embracing it. Street vendors take neoliberalism and free trade with their fiscal instabilities and socioeconomic hardships and translate globalization's economic dislocations into vendor employment.

Vendorscapes embed resistance to globalization into the built environment of the city. They build a resistance transnationalism derivative of commercial transnationalism but also transformative of it. Street vendors embrace commercial transnationalism to the extent that they deal in the products of post-Fordist global production. However, by selling often pirated products that violate commercial private property rights and infringe on patents, street vendors also subvert key principles of neoliberal free trade for the purpose of local profitability and economic survival. In these economic as well as cultural ways, street vendors and their built environment transform the global into the local. The hybrid aesthetics of some vendor products often reflect a mix of local cultural content and imported culture. Moreover, the aesthetics of vendorscapes reflect a transcultural mix of U.S.-style ultramodernity and the indigenous vernacular. As shown in Figure 7.5, most vendor kiosks are a mix of open and enclosed space; they employ modern canvas covers to shield products from the elements but are primarily open-air forms of vending that tend to flow out of control, filling sidewalks and swelling streets. Occupying vast amounts of urban sidewalk space, such vendorscapes extend further horizontally along sidewalks than the modern commercial space of the Torre Latinoamericana, shown in the background, extends vertically into the skyline of the city. In their makeshift, temporary character, vendorscapes disturb the feminine aesthetic of opulence and elegance of the capital city. In fact, in many ways the kiosk conglomeration in Figure 7.5 resembles the vendorscapes of Tijuana on the Mexico-U.S. border.

The resistance geo-politics of this vendor architecture stands in stark contrast to the Cartesian geopolitics of the city's neoliberal tower architecture. In terms of building materials, the canvas tops and temporary wooden tables of vendorscapes evoke a kind of tentlike nomadism suggestive of fluidity and shift rather than fixed conceptions of space (see Deleuze and Guattari 1977). In contrast, the concrete, steel, and glass of the World Trade Center make the building seem permanently planted, fixed in space, stable, and more durable than other urban architecture. The seeming durability of

Figure 7.5   Vendor kiosks

the building belies the devastating fiscal instability of capital markets
brought home by the drastic 1994 peso devaluation, the hardships of which
the vendorscapes testify to. As much as the architect and developers of the
WTC would have us believe in the durability and stability of the building
and of NAFTA, the kiosks and their architects are testimony to how flimsy,
unstable, and unreliable neoliberal economics and transnational capital
flows can be. Moreover, in conceiving space as temporary and shifting, the
kiosks minimize notions of the permanent possession and control of territory, especially since they are often unlicensed. In forgoing individual ownership of land as territory and private property, most vendorscapes mirror
indigenous, Mesoamerican notions of communally held land (see Bonfil
Batalla 1996: 19–40). As neoliberal towers dominate the city's skyline vertically and project managerial elites and their offices high into the sky, vendorscapes reclaim and fill horizontal spaces of the city with average people.
As Figure 7.6 suggests, vendorscapes have taken over the sidewalks of
some zones of the city in its historic center, as indicated in this crowded
sidewalk scene visible when exiting the Juárez metro stop near Alameda
Park. It is this historic center where the Templo Mayor of the original
Tenochtitlán was located and is now being excavated, in more ways than
one.

    Parallel to the World Trade Center, many vendorscapes were construct-

© 1998 Julie A. Murphy Erfani

Figure 7.6   Vendorscapes

ed, literally and figuratively, in the shadow of an unfinished modernity whose deficiencies, exclusions, and failures were alarmingly exposed by the earthquake of 1985. During the earthquake, many modern buildings that had been built shoddily or under code collapsed or sustained irreparable damage. In fact, many of the buildings that collapsed were built by Grupo Gutsa, the very same construction firm that developed the World Trade Center (Poniatowska 1995: 241). Today, many contemporary vendorscapes are built in the vacant lots adjoining the condemned modern buildings damaged by the earthquake. As shown in Figure 7.7, kiosks have sprung up in the shadows of these abandoned and condemned buildings. Vendorscapes represent self-built forms of economic survival for average people seeking to weather the economic dislocations of a modern economy constantly in ruins. Geo-politically, what is embedded in the spaces and culture of these

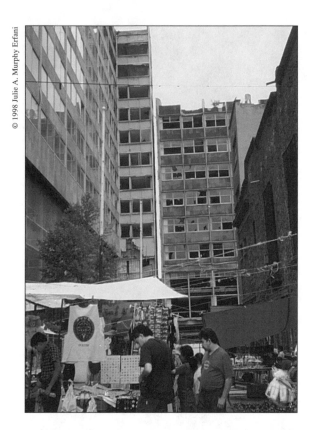

Figure 7.7   Kiosks among condemned modern buildings

vendorscapes is a hybrid mix of public–private sector modern economic failure and private vendor resilience vis-à-vis the failures of the formal economy.

Vendorscapes contribute to the seeming disappearance of the state by overflowing all over the central city's sidewalks beyond government's ability to control or dismantle. In sidestepping state regulations of the formal economy, vendors render the state's taxation capabilities irrelevant. They are visibly and physically beyond the control of the state even while they cover for the state's and the national economy's failures, thereby internalizing and embodying certain governance functions. As vendorscapes disembody the state's presence, they themselves reflect the state's implication in and support for neoliberal economics and free trade. The vendors, their kiosks, and architectural vendorscapes embody a cultural and physical borderland between a commercial and a resistance transnationalism. As neoliberal towers and corporate managers of global commerce are building a conquered Tenochtitlán, the city's street vendors are rebuilding a resilient Tenochtitlán. Like the last Aztec emperor's name Cuauhtémoc, "eagle that falls," and the new mayor who also bears that name, the city embodied continues to rise up and resist colonization even while it falls.

Conclusion

Feminist geo-political studies of urban transnationalism, transculturation, and hybridity constitute new ways of seeing and thus new ways of mapping contemporary relations between politics and space. This chapter illustrated this by viewing Mexico City as a borderland. Transnationalism—the crossing of national borders—is shown to occur in both territorial and cultural terms within the spaces of Mexico City and within the cultural spaces of the corporeal subjects who are its residents. Transculturation—the crossing of cultural borders of race, class, gender, ethnicity, and nationality—also occurs within the cultural spaces of the city and within urban corporeal subjects. Both transnationalism and transculturation involve temporal as well as spatial border crossing in the realms of identity and subjectivity. In Mexico City, transcultural and transnational identities and subjectivities involve cultural border crossing between nations and often between vast time spans, from ancient to modern. By looking at the city's architecture and streetscapes, I show how transnationalism and transculturation occur within and across one and the same city, neighborhood, street, building, or body. This kind of optics begins to destabilize and remap classical geopolitical visions of the relations between space, politics, culture, and time.

Geo-politically, the capital is a culturally heterogeneous, intensely transnationalized site of highly contested urban struggles over space, identity, symbols, meanings, and authority. The city is spatially and culturally fluid, permeable, and uncertain even while it is territorially fixed, mapped, enclosed, and militarily secure. Geographically and demographically, the city flows and overflows all the time. Mexico City is out of control even while it is home to the center of control of the territorial state by national government. Even as the neoliberal architecture of globalization reconstructs cultural hierarchies and borders within the city, a geo-politics of resistance of ordinary people on the streets often contests such borders and hierarchies. In other words, neoliberal buildings embody some of the conventional geopolitics of nation-states; however, the geo-politics of everyday life on the streets often contests the very borders and hierarchies reincarnated by neoliberalism. As such, territorial borders between nations are constructed and crossed every day without one ever having to leave the capital city. This implies a new political cartography locating national-terri-torial borders and border crossing within and across the bodies and built environment of Mexico City itself.

In sum, this chapter began to refocus the study of political and cultural geography from territorial states to the city in general, and to streetscapes, buildings, and urban residents in particular. Like the bodies residing there, Mexico City's architecture and streetscapes speak a chaotic array of visual-cultural languages, including neoliberal globalization, Mesoamerican ver-nacular, U.S.-style modernity, Spanish colonialism, and multiple postmod-ern hybridities. However, the city's built environment is not an integrated, architectonic expression of some kind of biologically hybrid body. Contrary to biological and essentialist arguments and imagery, the hybridi-ties and chaotic diversities of the city's architecture and corporeal subjects constitute socially constructed borderlands. Because the globalization of cities and bodies entails social inscription of power and resistance, bodies, buildings, and cities constitute a borderland of contestation and mixing between the urban practice of classical and resistance geo-politics. For this reason, the paradoxes of fluidity and enclosure characteristic of the Juárez–El Paso borderlands also appear in the urban borderland of Mexico City, even though the city is in the modern geographic heart of the country.

Note

I owe a special thanks to Ian R. Douglas, Jeffrey Edwards, Darryl Hattenhauer, Jennifer Hyndman, Andrew Kirby, and Kath Weston for invaluable comments on earlier drafts of this chapter. I am also indebted to the work of author Gloria Anzaldúa and photographer Pablo Ortiz Monasterio, who inspired this conception of the city as borderland.

References

Allen, Stan, and Kyong Park, eds. 1997. *Sites and Stations: Provisional Utopias: Architecture and Utopia in the Contemporary City.* New York: Lusitania Press.
Anzaldúa, Gloria. 1987. *Borderlands/La Frontera: The New Mestiza.* San Francisco: Spinsters/Aunt Lute Press.
Bachelard, Gaston. 1969. *The Poetics of Space.* Maria Jolas, trans. Boston: Beacon Press, p. 8.
Blunt, Alison, and Gillian Rose, eds. 1994. *Writing Women and Space: Colonial and Postcolonial Geographies.* New York: Guilford Press.
Bonfil Batalla, Guillermo. 1996. *México Profundo: Reclaiming a Civilization.* Austin: University of Texas Press.
Borden, Iain. 1996. "Thick Edge: Architectural Boundaries and Spatial Flows." *Architectural Design* 66, nos. 11–12: 84–87.

Colas, Santiago. 1994. *Postmodernity in Latin America.* Durham: Duke University Press.

Dalby, Simon, and Gearóid Ó Tuathail. 1996. "Critical Geopolitics." *Political Geography* 15, nos. 6–7 (special issue): 451–665.

Deleuze, Gilles, and Felix Guattari. 1977. *The Anti-Oedipus.* New York: Viking.

Douglas, Ian R. 1997. "Forget Globalization."
Available @ http://www.powerfoundation.org
———. Forthcoming."Globalization *as* Governance: Toward an Archaeology of Contemporary Political Reason." In *Globalization and Governance,* J. Hart and A. Prakash. eds. London: Routledge.

Duncan, Nancy, ed. 1996. *Bodyspace: Destabilizing Geographies of Gender and Sexuality.* London: Routledge.

Enloe, Cynthia. 1989. *Bananas, Beaches, and Bases: Making Feminist Sense of International Politics.* Berkeley: University of California Press.

Erfani, Julie. 1995. *The Paradox of the Mexican State: Rereading Sovereignty from Independence to NAFTA.* Boulder: Lynne Rienner.

Galeano, Eduardo. 1985. *Memory of Fire, I. Genesis.* New York: Pantheon Books.

García Canclini, Néstor. 1995a. *Consumidores y ciudadanos: Conflictos multiculturales de la globalización.* Mexico City: Editorial Grijalbo.
———. 1995b. *Hybrid Cultures: Strategies for Entering and Leaving Modernity.* Minneapolis: University of Minnesota Press.

García Canclini, Néstor, Alejandro Castellanos, and Ana Rosas Mantecón. 1996. *La ciudad de los viajeros: Travesías e imaginarios urbanos: México, 1940–2000.* Mexico City: Editorial Grijalbo.

Grosz, Elizabeth. 1992. "Bodies-Cities." In *Sexuality and Space,* B. Colomina, ed. New York: Princeton Architectural Press.
———. 1994. *Volatile Bodies: Toward a Corporeal Feminism.* Bloomington: Indiana University Press.

Jameson, Fredric. 1991. *Postmodernism, or the Cultural Logic of Late Capitalism.* Durham: Duke University Press.

Kirby, Andrew. 1993. *Power/Resistance: Local Politics and the Chaotic State.* Bloomington: Indiana University Press.

Massey, Doreen. 1994. *Space, Place, and Gender.* Minneapolis: University of Minnesota Press.

McDowell, Linda. 1996. "Spatializing Feminism: Geographic Perspectives." In *Bodyspace*, Nancy Duncan, ed. London: Routledge.

Meskimmon, Marsha, ed. 1997. *Engendering the City: Women Artists and Urban Space.* London: Scarlet Press.

Miyoshi, M. 1996. "A Borderless World? From Colonialism to Transnationalism and the Decline of the Nation-State." In *Global/Local: Cultural Production and the Transnational Imaginary*, Rob Wilson and Wimal Dissanayake, eds. Durham: Duke University Press.

Nash, Catherine. 1994. "Remapping the Body/Land: New Cartographies of Identity, Gender, and Landscape in Ireland." In *Writing Women and Space,* Alison Blunt and Gillian Rose, eds. New York: Guilford Press, pp. 227–250.

Nedkov, Louisa, ed. 1996. *World Trade Centers Association Directory.* Toronto: Trade Winds Publications.

Olalquiaga, Celeste. 1992. *Megalopolis.* Minneapolis: University of Minnesota Press.

Ortiz Monasterio, Pablo. 1995. *The Last City.* Santa Fe: Twin Palm Publishers.

Ó Tuathail, Gearóid. 1996. *Critical Geopolitics: The Politics of Writing Global Space*. Minneapolis: University of Minnesota Press.

Pettman, Jan Jindy. 1996. *Worlding Women: A Feminist International Politics*. London: Routledge.

Poniatowska, Elena. 1995. *Nothing, Nobody: The Voices of the Mexico City Earthquake*. Philadelphia: Temple University Press.

Pratt, Mary Louise. 1992. *Imperial Eyes: Travel Writing and Transculturation*. London: Routledge.

Rose, Gillian. 1993. *Feminism and Geography: The Limits of Geographical Knowledge*. Minneapolis: University of Minnesota Press.

Sassen, Saskia. 1996a. "Identity in the Global City: Economic and Cultural Encasements." In *The Geography of Identity*, Patricia Yaeger, ed. Ann Arbor: University of Michigan Press, pp. 131–151.

———. 1996b. *Losing Control? Sovereignty in an Age of Globalization*. New York: Columbia University Press.

Tickner, J. Ann. 1992. *Gender in International Relations*. New York: Columbia University Press.

Ward, Peter. 1990. *Mexico City: The Production and Reproduction of an Urban Environment*. London: Belhaven Press.

Westwood, Sally, and John Williams. 1997. *Imagining Cities: Scripts, Signs, Memories*. London: Routledge.

Wilson, Elizabeth. 1991. *The Sphinx in the City*. London: Virago.

Yúdice, George. 1992. *On Edge: The Crisis of Contemporary Latin American Culture*. Minneapolis: University of Minnesota Press.

———. 1995. "Civil Society, Consumption, and Governmentality in an Age of Global Restructuring: An Introduction." *Social Text* 14, no. 4 (winter 1995): 1–25.

8

Border Signs:
Graffiti, Contested Identities, and
Everyday Resistance in Los Angeles

Bradley J. Macdonald

Despite the great cultural mirage sponsored by the people in power, everywhere we look we find pluralism, crisis, and non-synchronicity. The so-called dominant culture is no longer dominant. Dominant culture is a meta-reality that only exists in the virtual space of the mainstream media and spaces of the monocultural institutions.

Today, if there is a dominant culture, it is border culture. And those who still haven't crossed a border will do it very soon. (Gómez-Peña 1993; 46–47)

The Borderlands are physically present wherever two or more cultures edge each other, where people of different races occupy the same territory, where under, lower, middle and upper classes touch, where the space between two individuals shrinks with intimacy. (Anzaldúa 1987)

As do all urban places, Los Angeles presents a number of disparate images. From the vantage point above the teeming metropolis (especially at night, when the geometry of Los Angeles appears in its most clear form), one perceives harsh lines of demarcation, grids of stability, intersecting pathways whose clarity intimate order and control. The vertigo produced by the immensity of Los Angeles as a space is seemingly alleviated by this abstract geometry of boundaries, eliciting a sense of representational capture and clarity.

On the ground, and in the street, we confront a different series of images. There, we take in the relative chaos of urban life, the vortex of movement and travel, the actions of passersby that do not necessarily follow set pathways defined by those in authority but that perambulate in unique vectors and countermoves. These images do not have the totalizing clarity of the bird's-eye, but rather are more mundane, localized, disparate, and limited.

To articulate these different representations separately is not to set up a hierarchy between the two, in which the bird's-eye or street-level is given priority as more "real." Both of these images correspond respectively to what Michel de Certeau characterizes as the practices of "strategies" and "tactics" and are intricately interwoven into the fabric of urban life. "Strategies" are those spatial practices that articulate the lines of power, the spaces of the "proper" (and of *proper*ty), the boundaries of control, whereas "tactics" are the multiplicity of ways that inhabitants subvert and reappropriate urban space in defiance of power and control (de Certeau 1984: 34–39). Politically, they represent the contradictory practices of control and resistance, of real oppression and longings for liberation. Taken together, they make up the constitutive matrix of this city on the "border."

For the diverse cultures and communities in Los Angeles, monocultural institutions and discourses define a strategic space that is replete with binarisms and oppositions in which the dominant Anglo culture is situated as a privileged term, reinforcing the urban socioeconomic separations that already exist while also engendering ideological practices that subtly, and not so subtly, attempt to redefine and appropriate marginal cultures. But inevitably, even with such continual attempts to define the borders of monocultural space clearly—to police the incursions of everyday coyotes—the lived space of Los Angeles is fractured and indeterminable, a true kaleidoscope of tactical ploys and contesting identities that work within the borders of power, only to transgress and subvert the lines of its containment.

For Latino communities, these tactical and contestatory practices are intimately involved in the everyday reality of their diverse members: in language, dress, music, murals. Arguing that the 22 million Latinos in the United States constitute a unique ethnic group (in that nearly 80 percent speak Spanish at home) whose growth as a sociocultural group in the United States has been coexistent with the relatively new political realities associated with the welfare state, Juan Flores and George Yúdice state that it is best to see Latino identity formation in terms of "new social movements" theory. From this perspective, identity and struggle are not solely reducible to class but involve a resolute interrogation of power in all of its forms, revolving around areas of everyday life that have been traditionally considered "private" (art, language, family) (Flores and Yúdice 1990: 58–59). Drawing upon the notion of the United States as a "living border," a polyglot and intercultural space in which participants continually negotiate its boundaries, they argue that Latinos continually practice "border culture" as "their cultural politics." "As such," Flores and Yúdice continue, "Latino aesthetics do not pretend to be separate from the everyday practices but rather an integral part of an ethos which seeks to be politicized as a means to validation and self-determination" (Flores and Yúdice 1990: 60–61).

Although Flores and Yúdice focus primarily upon linguistic "transcreations" within everyday language, popular culture, literature, and poetry, I think that one can apply similar tropes to other symbolic practices occurring within Los Angeles. Of particular note, the 1980s witnessed an unprecedented explosion in graffiti, whose ubiquitous presence now adorns many facades in L.A. Although graffiti writing is no longer unique to Latino communities, L.A.'s first graffiti crew (L.A. Bomb Squad) came out of the barrios of Pico-Union and East L.A., an area with a long history of graffiti writing by Latino gangs and an established practice of community murals that flowered most spectacularly in the 1960s and 1970s. Moreover, some of the most important writers today are Latino youth. Although the dominant culture may see graffiti as terrifying signs of urban decay and rampant vandalism, there are other issues involved in this ongoing symbolic process: graffiti provides a glimpse into the continual attempt by oftentimes excluded groups to gain a sense of identity and community in the concrete streets of L.A. Moreover, implicated in these many "unreadable" scrawls, marks, and images—from "tags" to "throw ups" to "pieces"—is a critique of everyday relations of power that define Los Angeles and the intimation of the political ideal of creating a horizon of meaning and efficacy. More specifically, graffiti can be seen as "border signs," symbolic practices that continually contest the everyday repressions, lost horizons, and entrenched divisions that constitute urban space in Los Angeles, in the process providing an intimation of a utopian project of reconciliation (a true multicultural process) and human fulfillment. In interpreting graffiti in this way, we do not wish to glorify its existence: it is neither a defining cultural practice of Latino communities nor a necessary harbinger for much-needed political change. Yet, it *is* a cultural practice whose hidden politics elucidates the dilemmas facing marginalized cultures in an urban space that all too often denies them human dignity and self-legitimation.

Defining the Borders: The Politics of Urban Space

Sharp-eyed locals felt something bad coming over the town long before riots broke out on April 29. The writing was literally on the wall. (Wilson 1992)

Los Angeles has increasingly become the object of intense debate among urban theorists and commentators. Not only is there beginning to develop a significant amount of literature on the character of this urban space (which has engendered ample perspectives in itself), but there is a growing

realization that urban development in Los Angeles—especially its economic and sociopolitical characteristics—offers a glimpse into the character of all urban spaces (Soja 1989: 191) or provides a foreshadowing of the
coming fate of those cities "on the bad edge of postmodernity" (Davis
1991: 224). Moreover, Los Angeles is home to the largest Latino urban
population outside of Mexico City, creating a border culture that is symp-
tomatic of larger cultural trends in the United States. As Guillermo
Gómez-Peña argues, this convergence of cultures creates new intercultural
practices:

> Cities like Tijuana and Los Angeles, once socio-urban aberrations, are
> becoming models of a new hybrid culture, full of uncertainty and vitality.
> And border youth—the fearsome "cholo-punks," children of the chasm
> that is opening between the "First" and the "Third" worlds, become the
> indisputable heirs to a new mestizaje. . . .
>   In this context, concepts like "high culture," "ethnic purity," "cultural
> identity," "beauty," and "fine arts" are absurdities and anachronisms. Like
> it or not, we are attending the funeral of modernity and the birth of a new
> culture. (Gómez-Peña 1993: 39)

The recent eruption of the urban uprising within the city only confirms
L.A.'s premonitory status. Although ostensibly a reaction to the Rodney
King verdict and to the injustice of police brutality in L.A., the roots of this
urban explosion lie much deeper within the socioeconomic soil of U.S. life
during the 1980s and 1990s—the continued curtailment of urban programs;
the further deindustrialization and economic marginalization of African
American and Latino communities; and, of course, the continued virulence
of racism. As Mike Davis recently put it: "the nation's first multiracial riot
was as much about empty bellies and broken hearts as it was about police
batons and Rodney King" (Davis 1992: 743). Like Watts in 1965, Los
Angeles in 1992 was a crystal ball elucidating issues and tensions facing all
urban minority communities within the United States.

If the recent uprising in L.A. stands as a barometer of urban political-
economic devastation, it also indicates the precarious balance between
"strategies" and "tactics" in urban space. The increasing internationalization of Los Angeles throughout the 1980s engendered the strengthening of
an "intolerable political-economic order" for African American and Latino
communities, producing "devastating poverty for those weak in skill and
resources" (Davis 1992: 746). The riots were a clear form of resistance
against this increasing marginalization. As with most urban uprisings,
though, there were signs of resistance building much earlier, in seemingly
insignificant tactical engagements executed in the everyday practices of citizens. Learning from Los Angeles, we see that urban rebellions do not arise
directly from one single horizon but from a multitude of political and cul-

tural practices that condense around a particular issue (in the case of L.A., police brutality and its subsequent condoning by the judicial system), discursively producing a horizon of conflict (an irresolvable gulf between "us" and "them") that motivates people to take to the streets in defiance of the strategic order. Moreover, such overt collective resistance is oftentimes nurtured by the "hidden transcripts" of marginalized and oppressed groups, subterranean practices that skate the border of public life and provide arenas for oppositional identities and contestation (Scott 1990: 183–201).

As a strategic space, L.A. exhibits a number of different layers of power relations that affect its inhabitants. The first layer is related to *political-economic* conditions: the very (re)structuring of space in Los Angeles is intertwined with potent forces of domestic capitalist accumulation, international capital, and international labor migration. All of these processes taken together—what may be termed *post-Fordism*—produce a number of consequences that help us understand the spatial processes of power: for instance, the dual influx of international financial capital with low-wage immigrant labor has created a "third world, second city" within the space of a thriving first world capitalist city, engendering a spatial frontier of social contradiction in the downtown area (Davis 1987: 75–77); also, the same processes have furthered the economic marginalization of Latino and African American communities, creating massive pockets of unemployment and crime, which, in turn, ultimately reinforce gang activity (Davis 1989: 48–49; 1991: 306).

A second layer of spatial power lies in its *disciplinary* nature, a character that relates to the way in which all cities control and restrictively organize their inhabitants. It differs from the previous perspective in that it assumes that relations of power are not necessarily tied to capitalist economic forces and consequent class oppression but are also part of relatively autonomous practices of control and surveillance (Foucault 1979). This power is implied when Paul Virilio argues that the city emplaces the control and containment of "the fundamental anthropological side of revolution, of proletarianization: the migratory phenomenon" (1986: 6).

Los Angeles continues to be a not-so-intermittent stopover for the migratory dreams of the world. As a metaphor for our dreams, its draw has not diminished, still engendering a utopian image of a better life, not only for people in other parts of the country but also for many individuals around the world. Yet, this utopian longing is ultimately consumed by the ever-present relations of power that entangle its inhabitants. For the growing Latino immigrant population, this utopian space increasingly acts as a dystopian black hole that draws its all-too-willing participants into monocultural discourses and institutions that refuse to allow the light of human dignity to escape its imploding gravity: newly arriving Latinos are increasingly sequestered into blighted barrios, encounter a continual climate of official harassment, and are forced by necessity to either labor within sweatshops in the burgeoning underground economy or at low-wage service jobs in the surface economy. Moreover, these communities, like other marginalized lower-class groups, experience the ever-increasing spread of "new repressions in space and movement," all adding up to a "militarization of city life so grimly visible at the street level" (Davis 1991: 223). From the urban renaissance of the central city that has created massive architectural complexes of professional work spaces and corporate interests all impenetrable by the masses of "criminalized poor" in surrounding areas, to the ground and sky control of homeless and lower class public space by the Los Angeles Police Department (LAPD), Los Angeles, Davis argues, is increasingly becoming a "Fortress L.A." for its affluent citizens and a carceral terrain for its lower-class and minority passersby.

As exhibited in the work of Davis, some of the most interesting work on the politics of Los Angeles has consistently emphasized what de Certeau has argued is the "strategic" side of its practices—Los Angeles becomes a terrain of political and economic logics that emplace relations of power, distribute space, and ultimately contain and organize its inhabitants. Indeed, when these authors do attempt to locate lines of resistance, they are left either with a sense of the "cacophonous silence" of these potential forces (Soja 1989: 219); with a tentative hopefulness at emerging forms of third world cultures and the repoliticization of the criminalized gang cultures (Davis 1987: 77–78; 1991: 293–300); or, as one recent participant in this debate has claimed, a longing for a political struggle by Los Angeles's "internationalized working classes" (Keil 1990: 126).

The despair or utopian longing so evident in these types of narratives is directly related to the overemphasis on the strategic element of urban life. Although we do not want to ignore the strength of these forces, we also need to see that Los Angeles is not only a spatialized scene from film noir but is constituted by a very precarious tension between emplacing logics (of the political-economic and disciplinary kind) and their continual subversion. Thus we need to look to a third layer—the *hegemonic* articulation of urban space. From this level, we recognize that there is no necessary social teleology that encloses the inhabitants of this city, but rather only partial attempts to suture the ever-present contingent nature of urban space. As Ernesto Laclau and Chantal Mouffe argue: "the presence of the contingent in the necessary is what we [call] *subversion,* and it manifests itself as symbolization, metaphorization, paradox, which deform and question the literal character of every necessity" (Laclau and Mouffe 1985: 114).

If we were to follow the insights of Laclau and Mouffe into our area of concern, we would recognize that all attempts to enclose urban space within the "necessity" of functional space are always confronted by the "contingency" of urban life itself, the individualized horizons of refusal engendered by its very own inhabitants. This is what de Certeau ultimately means by his observation that urban space is constituted by the dual practices of "strategies" and "tactics." Moreover, to represent urban space as a hegemonic construction allows one to see it as a product of the diverse cultural voices that make up its inhabitants, a vision implied in the very notion of "border culture." Undoubtedly, the diverse cultural spaces of L.A.'s urban life are continually overlaid by the soundtrack of monocultural discourses, imposing a totalizing ethos that attempts to determine the fate of each disparate scene and ensuring that the lived space of its non-Anglo communities will always be experienced as a denial of a unique cultural identity. But to stay solely on that level is to miss how the lived experiences of these communities always enters into this strategic space, adding—at times imperceptibly and in coded cultural practices, although at other times in clear acts of defiance and collective action—a sense of its own right to live on other terms.

Thus, although urban space is a functional totality organized by socio-economic, disciplinary, and monocultural practices, its closure is continually subverted by the micro- and macropractices of its inhabitants. And although these tactical lines of resistance may never be able to completely liberate its inhabitants from this politicized space, they nonetheless provide a potential point d'appui for such a project. As Derek Gregory argues, urban "tactics," representing a fleeting, guerrilla-like appropriation of urban space, "are nonetheless effective in forging cultures of consolation, and on occasion, cultures of resistance" (Gregory 1990: 77). To understand the politics of urban space in this respect is to also be willing to recognize the importance of diverse forms of cultural and social resistance, from graffiti to urban insurrection, and to see them not as exceptional acts in urban life but as constitutive moments in the production of urban politics.

Chaking L.A.: Wild Signs and Contested Identities

I am the famous Chaka!

On November 28, 1990, Daniel Bernardo Ramos, a.k.a. "Chaka," was apprehended by police for writing his *placa,* or tag, on a street light in Lincoln Heights. Having just turned eighteen and thus now a legal adult, he was subsequently arrested for vandalism (whereupon he innocently exclaimed, "I am the famous Chaka!"), jailed, and eventually sentenced to 1,560 hours of community service and three years probation, in which he was admonished neither to tag nor to carry implements that could be used in such activities (Shanagan 1991: B1, 4). This ended the "spectacular" career of one of L.A.'s most prolific graffiti writers, who is claimed to have scrawled his tag on various facades throughout California over 10,000 times. Subsequently, after having his probation revoked for scrawling his tag in a court elevator during a visit to his probation officer and in turn serving more time, Ramos has now given up his life as a tagger and has embarked on a career as an artist. "I used to be Chaka," Ramos notes, "but now I'm Daniel Ramos, the artist" (quoted in Martin 1992: B3, 6). Not only are gallery owners interested in his work, but he has also been approached about putting his Chaka logo on t-shirts (Martin 1992: B1, 5).

Ramos's fate is both indicative of and unique in the recent history of tagging in Los Angeles. Increasingly, inner-city youth have turned to graffiti writing as a way to escape the harsh world of gangs and drugs that all too often marks their communities. Indeed, many inner-city youth are left with the choice of either joining gangs or joining one of the burgeoning number of tagging crews. Reflecting upon his career as L.A.'s most notorious tagger, Ramos notes that he "just wanted to get out of the Aliso Village housing projects, the ghetto life, the flying bullets and the drugs" (quoted in Martin 1992: B3). With increased public concern over graffiti and in turn harsher penalties for its practitioners (since 1993, taggers are now levied $1,000 fines for each tag), taggers are increasingly encountering the surveillance and police apparatuses that have been part of more "criminalized" gang cultures for years. Unlike most apprehended taggers, though, Ramos has been offered the chance to actually practice his craft in "legitimate" ways and even to get money for his efforts.

If in the Reagan era Los Angeles was becoming the stage on which the capitalist world would play its drama, it was also a period in which graffiti began to work its way onto diverse surfaces throughout Los Angeles's urban space. Although graffiti was confined originally to neighborhoods riven by gang conflict and activity and served as territorial markers, gang rosters, and hit lists, it now appears in almost every area, irrespective of the "genteel" and proper character of its space. In this period, we encounter the emergence of L.A.'s "graffiti subculture," whose participants engage in a form of symbolic violence by disseminating their insignia, or "tag," throughout the urban landscape. Although most of these tags are simple marks, quickly inscribed on the intended surface (buses, trains, billboards, fences, walls), others are more elaborate in their design and color. The latter works are known within the graffiti movement as "pieces" and are considered the highest form of the craft (this is due not only to their more "aesthetic" style but also to the risks incurred by spending so much time in their creation). Yet from the most basic tag to the most intricate "piece," the subject is almost always the same: the tagger's nom de guerre. Their monickers are invented and striking, having some personal significance to the tagger and representing clear statements of bravado and defiance: "Never,"

"Fana," "Razor," "Vector," "Empire," "Sin," "Hex," "Omega," "Felony," "Frameone," "Pearl."

Within the graffiti movement, writing becomes a ritual of competition, with each tag or piece representing a statement of personal victory and one-upmanship. Although this is usually an individual competition, many writers are linked up with larger groups called crews, and thus graffiti writing becomes also a way to gain notoriety and status for the group (some of the more famous graffiti crews in L.A. include "Key to Success," "Kill to Succeed—Second to None," "West Coast Artists," "Criminally Minded Artists," "Back Together Again," "Create to Devastate," "Loyal to None," and "Kids Gone Bad"). Moreover, a "well-done" tag (which would imply one that is well-placed in public view as well as unique and interesting) is not necessarily the goal; rather, it is the repetition of such a tag across a diverse range of environs, ensuring the continual social visibility of its form.

Graffiti writing has become a ubiquitous practice that is done increasingly by youth from all class and ethnic backgrounds, but it has a particular lure for inner-city youth whose lives, though replete with desires of status and fame, are limited by the harsh realities of their communities. Ultimately, the escalation of the practice of graffiti writing and the movement of Los Angeles into its status as a Pacific Rim capitalist center are not coincidental. As L.A.'s premier "graffiti buster" in the 1980s, Jay Besnick has clearly seen some connection between these events:

> When I started out in '76, mainly we were fighting gang stuff. It's what we now call "cultural graffiti." But after 1984, when the Olympics came, the whole scene changed. We got the taggers, people who want to get personal fame through graffiti. The taggers roughly doubled the size of the problem in LA. (quoted in Jones 1989: A3)

Besnick estimates that at least 1,000 tags go up nightly in metropolitan Los Angeles. Ultimately, he sees the growth of "tag culture" as a consequence of sponsorship of "the painting of murals on many freeway walls [during the Olympics], thereby demonstrating the potential of walls as sites of personal statements" (quoted in Jones 1989: A3). Yet, it may be better to attribute such a symbolic explosion to the larger urban practices that are implied in the singular event of the 1984 Olympics: the growing internationalization of Los Angeles's regional political economy engendered a growing sense of crisis on the level of the everyday, further producing at once the terror of personal disintegration and the increased marginalization, both economically and culturally, of L.A.'s non-Anglo cultures. In such conditions, I would argue, graffiti writing has a rather complicated role in identity formation.

Undoubtedly, as with other youth subcultures, graffiti crews provide a
sense of belonging for the taggers involved. As the thirteen-year-old Latino
tagger, Creator, notes: "It's like a family to belong to a crew. They watch
your back, you watch theirs. You kick it every day with them. . . . You get
friendship, love, supplies, everything" (Creator 1993: E1, 6). But the very
act of replicating their pseudonyms across the urban landscape raises other
interesting issues in community and identity formation. As a semiotics of
consolation, tagging is an example of the processes in which the very alienation of the individual becomes the expression of community, the proliferation of one's own fleeting tag on diverse surfaces providing the solace of
lasting company. In a monocultural space that blocks the formation of
autonomous identities, the continual repetition of one's name is an act of
self-legitimation. In this respect, Latino taggers engage in the same
processes that Flores and Yúdice argue are associated with other cultural
practices:

> Contrary to the monocultural dictates of the official public sphere, the
> border claims that it is "not nowhere." [The] first gestus of Latino cultural
> practice thus involves an emphatic self-legitimation, a negation of the
> hegemonic denial articulated as the rejection of anonymity. (Flores and
> Yúdice 1990: 60)

In terms of urban space, the "not nowhere" of border culture becomes
the "everywhere" of the many surfaces taggers and graffiti writers mark
with their signatures. Armed with spray paint and a Thomas's street guide,
the practice of "emphatic self-legitimation" is unlimited and wide-ranging.
But, as in all tactical engagements, such a practice borrows heavily from
the very territory it is resisting. This leads to a number of contradictory elements in the practice itself: graffiti attempts to stamp the public with the
personal and in that way strives to escape the anonymity experienced by its
practitioners by way of the seemingly "anonymous" tag. As Ramos so pre-
sciently notes, although "Chaka" could gain fame and status in the streets,
"Daniel Ramos, the artist" would have to come forward after such
escapades (Martin 1992: B1). There is inscribed in this admission a sense
in which taggers and graffiti artists must deny their real self-legitimation in
the process of establishing it in other terms, a practice that happens all too
often for marginalized cultures in monocultural discourses. Indeed, the use
of the "trademark" name to gain fame on the streets recalls our commodity
culture and the Hollywood status machine, institutions that thrive on name
recognition. As a filmmaker who recently chronicled the life of L.A.'s tag
subculture, Gary Glaser, noted: "This is hype town Number one. The kids
can't get on television, so they tag" (quoted in Martínez 1993: 120).

Unlike "political graffiti," whose message is intended to convince and
cajole the unsuspecting urban stroller and in that sense is intended to com-

municate some meaning, graffiti writing seems ultimately uncommunicative. Indeed, it is intentionally done in such a way that it cannot be deciphered by those who are not participants. As one former tagger notes about the meaning of graffiti: "it gives them a sense of belonging, of being somebody." But, it also is something more: "Graffiti is like a newspaper. . . . It's something to be read. But it's also a prank. You get a real rush when you do it, and it eventually becomes addictive. Some people say it's our way of getting back at society" (quoted in Citron 1988: 29).

If it is a "newspaper," it is one intended for a particular audience of initiates: "The fact that many outsiders cannot decipher the graffiti is irrelevant," one L.A. tagger notes. "The participants are only interested in communicating with each other" (quoted in Citron 1988: 29). We thus see one of the paradoxes associated with graffiti writing: it draws upon the ideal of name recognition only to displace its actualization, obscuring its meaning for the outside culture that promotes the name as fame. This semiotic dissonance undoubtedly allows one to understand the terror it elicits for those in areas supposedly sequestered from the urban troubles, in which it conjures up the spectacle that "Lotusland harbors a vandal force that authority cannot control" (Wilson 1992: 4). Yet, as a dialectical image, the terror graffiti writing (particularly, tagging) engenders is not only that there are groups willing to transgress the sanctity of secure middle- and upper-class communities—to deface the facades of their everyday life—but also that in fact such defacement goes on already, not only materially in the blighted neighborhoods many taggers and graffiti writers come from but continually throughout the urban environment. As Chaz Bojórquez and Luis Ituarte—two L.A. graffiti writers turned "organic intellectuals"—argue:

> We are all vandalizing in one way or another—pollution, political demagoguery, corporate irresponsibility, religious manipulation of spiritual dogma, education deficiency, and social and racial limitations. Graffiti represents all of this. The destruction comes from having no respect for the icons that represent them. In the graffiti movement the object is not destruction but re-building a new definition of the city. Graffiti lives in the failure of social responsibility. (Bojórquez and Ituarte 1993: 2)

In this respect, the "war" continually being waged in L.A. between commercial billboards and tags raises an interesting issue: although the "outdoor advertising industry" bemoans the onslaught of graffiti on its billboards, taggers are only reappropriating commercial advertisement as personal advertisement. Moreover, when graffiti adorns our billboards, it calls into question the very dissemination of power in our society: by disrupting our everyday landscape, it brings to our attention the way in which our lives are always "vandalized" by signs enjoining us to act in certain ways.

Writing Political Change:
Graffiti as Resistance and Utopian Figuration

Ultimately, graffiti writing is a form of border writing in that it attempts to constitute identities through the intermingling of cultures and spaces in urban life. Drawing lessons from mainstream culture, Latino youth who "write" their signatures for fame reappropriate monocultural spaces as signs of their anger and repressed desires. As Bojórquez and Ituarte (1993: 3) argue, graffiti writers "come from pain and anger, needing self-fulfillment, with an obsessive burning desire to validate their self-esteem. Through graffiti, our youth are not destroying the city, but deforming its walls to expose its social faults." Not only do graffiti writers deform public space to show the "social faults" in which they must survive, but in the process they constitute themselves as active subjects in the making of city life, a process that is too often denied in other ways. Self-formation, as Flores and Yúdice remind us,

> is constituted by everyday aesthetic practices such as the creative linguistic practices of Latinos which in the current historical juncture do not amount to subalternity, but rather to a way of prying open the larger culture, by making its physical, institutional and metaphorical borders indeterminate, precisely what the dominant culture fears. (Flores and Yúdice 1990: 73–74)

What is also important for our concerns here is the very process of creating graffiti, the practice that causes what one graffiti writer called the "real rush" of excitement and transgression (Citron 1988: 29). This is not necessarily related to a narcissistic glee at one's name. Rather, it arises from doing something against the dictates of those in authority (it is against the law to deface public property and another's private property), from transgressing the spaces of the proper, from jarring what Guy Debord calls the "visible freezing of life" that clings to capitalist urban landscapes (Debord 1983: 170). Indeed, these conscious attempts at transgression and play (what one writer calls doing a "prank" [Citron 1988: 29]) bear close resemblance to the radical proposals of a small group of avant-garde theorists and artists who roamed the urban landscapes of Paris in the 1950s and 1960s. These "revolutionary" passersby—who included Guy Debord, Michele Bernstein, Asger Jorn, Raoul Vaneigem, all of whom would become important members of the Situationist International—proposed what they call "unitary urbanism" to combat the extensive repressions of everyday life in the spaces of the city. For the situationists,[1] urban space had been captured by the processes of capitalist production, remaking "the totality of space into its own setting" (Debord 1983: 169). This has led to the rise of the "spectacle" (a lived practice of alienation, passivity, reification), in which the inhabitants are trapped in an extensive and intensive process of "banalization." The situationists proposed a conscious attempt at creating "situations" and zones of play within the spaces of the city: "the minimum action of unitary urbanism is to extend the terrain of play" (Debord 1981: 57). As the situationists argued:

> The main achievement of contemporary city planning is to have made people blind to the possibility of what we call unitary urbanism, namely a living critique, fueled by all the tensions of daily life, of this manipulation of cities and their inhabitants. Living critique means the setting up of bases for an experimental life, the coming together of those creating their own lives on terrains equipped to their ends. (Vaneigem and Kotanyi 1981: 66)

Although graffiti writers are rarely armed with such a theoretical insight into their activities, they do attempt to appropriate urban life for their own fun and play, and in so doing they liberate fleeting "bases for an experimental life." What is then represented in their intricate insignias is not only the attempt to gain a sense of identity but also the creation of areas of individual expression, a revitalization of everyday life. This is particularly the case for those writers who engage in creating "pieces," which represent more or less elaborate forays in expressive creativity. In so doing, graffiti articulates the possibility of transforming the urban environment for the expression of human needs (for instance, the creation of one's own life) and in turn represents a practice that is implicitly linked to a larger vision of political and social transformation. As Bojórquez and Ituarte argue: "We truly believe that creativity is a cornerstone of good citizenship. Even now, graffiti is preparing the social arena for the redemption of humanity" (1993: 3). Yet, as any graffiti writer knows, such a liberating practice is always brief and momentary. The walls will be scrubbed, and the authorities will be in pursuit. Having to work on a "canvas" that is already occupied by authority, graffiti writers must take any opportunity they can in their "bombing" missions. When de Certeau described what he meant by a tactic, he could not have described better the way graffiti poses its political subversion:

> It operates in isolated actions, blow by blow. It takes advantage of "opportunities" and depends on them, being without any base where it could stockpile its winnings, build up its own position, and plan raids. What it wins it cannot keep. . . . It must vigilantly make use of the cracks that particular conjunctions open in the surveillance of the proprietary powers. It poaches within them. It creates surprises in them. It can be where it is least expected. (de Certeau 1984: 37)

To discuss graffiti in such terms is not to romanticize the possibilities that it opens for large-scale political struggles—it is a displaced form of resistance and liberation that is not only contradictory in its appropriation of the dominant culture's code but also easily demonized given its transgressive quality. In terms of this latter issue, graffiti writers have been labeled as "gang-wannabes," "villains," and purveyors of urban decline, all of which help to reinforce the threat that citizens feel when confronting these strange writings. With the creation of such programs as Operation Clean Sweep (which coordinates much of Los Angeles's graffiti eradication efforts), increased expenditures on removal, a more highly organized police effort, and harsher penalties, the city has increased its energies to stop the spread of these urban scrawls (Stolberg 1992: A1, 12–13). Yet, such attempts to eradicate graffiti by "criminalizing" the practice—a modus operandi that is increasingly used by political authorities to deal with the panoply of social and urban problems facing the United States—do not get at the hidden politics that is implied in graffiti writing: it is the sublimated expression of the desire to live one's life with human dignity and to be part of a radical democratic practice of constituting life in the United States.

More constructive responses have come from various community groups in their attempts to provide outlets—mural walls, storefronts, community centers—for graffiti writing. At the very least, such actions recognize the validity of graffiti as a form of community art. Moreover, graffiti has increasingly become recognized as a viable art form, moving out of the street and into the galleries. In this respect, its subversive character is transformed into a culturally accepted aesthetic practice. Since the late 1980s there have been many exhibitions that have displayed the work of prominent graffiti taggers and piecers. For the participants, these exhibits provide a legitimation of their project. "People don't think of this as art," one graffiti writer on display avers. "They just see it as vandalism. But I want to be accepted as an artist, not as a hoodlum or vandal" (Marina 1989: 128). Gallery space thus helps to reaffirm the importance of their craft in light of the dominant culture. However, this is not just a case of finally recognizing talent that was first misinterpreted as vandalism, no matter how comforting that thought may seem to the graffiti writers themselves. For the writer, such a showing helps to legitimize his or her craft inside, as well as *outside,* the gallery. For the dominant culture, of course, what is important is to keep graffiti within the space of its sanctioned institutions. Indeed, in the public arena, without the blessings and incentives of the cultural establishment, it is still an unwanted transgression—a sign of "vandalism."

It is very clear that many writers see themselves as "artists," spending long hours with sketch books preparing their complex pieces and taking pride in the completion of their elaborate works. Yet, graffiti may never be fully incorporated into the sanctioned cultural art spaces because its practices are so intertwined with the transgressive desire of the "prank" and because its hidden politics speaks to issues beyond the white walls of the museum. As an attempt to actively construct urban life and gain a sense of self-legitimation, graffiti may, ironically, be too "avant-garde" for the art establishment. As Gómez-Peña argues:

> To be avant garde means to be able to cross the border; to go back and forth between art and politically significant territory. . . . To be avant garde means to perform and exhibit in the both artistic and non-artistic contexts: to operate in the world, not just the art world. (Gómez-Peña 1993: 49)

Notes

I would like to thank Gerry Riposa, Gustavo Leclerc, and Kathy Staudt for their support at various stages of my thinking and writing about graffiti. Gerry offered me a chance to take a first stab at conceptualizing the politics of graffiti, the result of which was published as "Citti Politti: Cultural Politics in Los Angeles," in *City of Angels,* G. Riposa and C. Dersch, eds. (Dubuque, Iowa: Kendall/Hunt Publishing, 1992), 16–30. This chapter was engendered by a request from Gustavo Leclerc to write a piece on Latino graffiti writers, a much shortened version of which appeared as "Writings on the Border: The Hidden Politics of Graffiti," in *Saber es Poder/Interventions* (Los Angeles: ADOBE-LA, 1994). This collection of writings coincided with, and intervened in, the "Urban Revisions: Current Projects for the Public Realm" exhibition at the Museum of Contemporary Art in Los Angeles, May 15–July 24, 1994. Upon reading the full-length version, Kathy supported its inclusion in the present collection, for which I am very grateful.

1. For a critical discussion of situationist theory and practice, see MacDonald 1995.

References

Anzaldúa, Gloria. 1987. *Borderlands/La Frontera: The New Mestiza.* San Francisco: Spinsters/Aunt Lute Press.

Barnett, Alan. 1984. *Community Murals: The People's Art.* Philadelphia: Arts Alliance Press.

Bojórquez, Chaz, and Luis Ituarte. 1993. "Social Abstraction: The Phenomenon of Graffiti." Unpublished manuscript, SPARC archives, Los Angeles.

Citron, Alan. 1988. "Upscale Youths Making Own Marks with Graffiti." *Los Angeles Times,* April 24, p. 29.

Creator. 1993. "War of the Walls." *Los Angeles Times,* July 14, pp. E1, 6.

Davis, Mike. 1987. "Chinatown, Part Two: The 'Internationalization' of Downtown Los Angeles." *New Left Review* 164.

———. 1989. "Los Angeles: Civil Liberties Between the Hammer and the Rock." *New Left Review* 170: 48–49.

———. 1991. *City of Quartz: Evacuating the Future in Los Angeles.* London: Verso, 306.

————. 1992. "In L. A., Burning All Illusions," *Nation* (June 1), 743.

de Certeau, Michael. 1984. *Practice of Everyday Life*. Berkeley: University of California Press.

Debord, Guy. 1981. "Situationist Theses on Traffic." In *Situationist International Anthology*, Ken Knabb, ed. Berkeley: Bureau of Public Secrets, 57.

————. 1983. *Society of the Spectacle*. Detroit: Black and Red Press.

Flores, Juan, and George Yúdice. 1990. "Living Borders/Buscando America: Languages of Latino Self-Formation," *Social Text* 24: 58–59.

Foucault, Michel. 1979. *Discipline and Punish: The Birth of the Prison*, Alan Sheridan, trans. New York: Random House.

Gómez-Peña, Guillermo. 1993. "The Multicultural Paradigm." In Guillermo Gómez-Peña, *Warrior for Gringostroika*. St. Paul: Graywolf Press.

Gregory, Derek. 1990. "Chinatown, Part Three? Soja and the Missing Spaces of Social Theory." *Strategies* 3: 77.

Jones, Robert. 1989. "Wall of Names Lists Winners in a Game of Tag." *Los Angeles Times*, November 28, p. A3.

Keil, Roger. 1990. "The Urban Future Revisited: Politics and the Restructuring of L. A. After Fordism." *Strategies* 3: 126.

Laclau, Ernesto, and Chantal Mouffe. 1985. *Hegemony and Socialist Strategy: Towards a Radical Democratic Politics*. London: Verso.

Macdonald, Bradley J. 1995. "From the Spectacle to Unitary Urbanism: Reassessing Situationist Theory." *Rethinking Marxism* 8, no. 2: 89–111.

Marina, Victor. 1989. "Graffiti 'Artists' Get a Serious Showcase." *Los Angeles Times*, August 20, p. I28.

Martin, Hugo. 1992. "Tagger Chaka Is Going Hollywood." *Los Angeles Times*, April 19, pp. B1, 5.

Martínez, Ruben. 1993. "Going Up in LA." In Ruben Martínez, *The Other Side: Notes from the New L.A., Mexico City, and Beyond*. New York: Vintage Press.

Scott, James C. 1990. *Domination and the Arts of Resistance*. New Haven: Yale University Press.

Shanagan, Louis. 1991. "Tagger 'Chaka' Agrees to Clean Up Graffiti." *Los Angeles Times*, April 24, pp. B1, 4.

Soja, Edward. 1989. *Postmodern Geographies: The Reassertion of Space in Critical Social Theory*. London: Verso.

Stolberg, Sheryl. 1992. "Engulfed in a Sea of Paint." *Los Angeles Times*, January 8, pp. A1, 12–13.

Vaneigem, Raoul, and Attila Kotanyi. 1981. "Elementary Program of the Bureau of Unitary Urbanism." In Ken Knabb, ed., *Situationist International Anthology*. Berkeley: Bureau of Public Secrets.

Virilio, Paul. 1986. *Speed and Politics*, Mark Polizzotti, trans. New York: Semiotext(e).

Wilson, William. 1992. "A Look at the Real American Graffiti." *Los Angeles Times*, May 27, pp. F1, 4.

9

The Competing Meanings
of the Label "Chicano" in El Paso

Pablo Vila

Nearly 70 percent of El Paso's population is of Mexican origin. A significant number of these residents have arrived in the United States within the last twenty years. It is thus easy to assume that people living on both sides of the border constitute a homogeneous population. Despite their common origins and regardless of the side on which they live, border residents do not think of themselves in this way. On the contrary, Mexican Americans and Mexican nationals feel that they are quite different from each other. Additionally, not only do Mexican nationals and Mexican Americans not consider themselves to be the "same," but also Mexican Americans display interethnic distinctions among themselves. Long-established Mexican Americans use those distinctions to distinguish themselves from new immigrants (Vila 1997).[1] This fact is reflected, for instance, in the way people of Mexican descent identify themselves. Thus, in a study conducted in El Paso in the early 1990s, interviewees used at least seven different labels to describe themselves. Mexican/Mexicano was the label chosen by most people, whereas only 1 percent of that population referred to itself as "Chicano" (Staudt 1998: 47). Twenty-four percent of those interviewed identified themselves as Mexicano; 18 percent as Mexican; 21 percent as Hispanic; 10 percent as Hispano; 8 percent as Mexican American; and 4 percent as Other Latino.[2] My own experience with students in my "Chicanos in the Southwest" and "Chicanos and American Society" courses at the University of Texas–El Paso shows the same trend: very few of my students use the label "Chicano" in public, although some of them use the term in private. Data from the 1979 National Chicano Survey show that El Pasoans are not much different in this regard from other people of Mexican descent who reside elsewhere in the United States (Hurtado and Arce 1986).

The goal of this chapter is to explain why so few individuals of Mexican descent in El Paso refer to themselves as Chicano in spite of the promotion of the term by the Chicano movement as a declaration of ethnic pride and resistance to Anglo hegemony.[3] My main hypothesis is that the label "Chicano" does not have a consistent meaning in the area, where many different variants of its usage are currently competing among each other to acquire the status of "common sense" (Gramsci 1975). Due to this ongoing symbolic competition, the label is, at most, imprecise, and at worst, loaded with very negative connotations. In this context, the positive connotation proposed by the Chicano movement is only one among several and, additionally, not the dominant one.

In order to explain why the label "Chicano" is not popular in El Paso, I will rely on some of the formulations advanced by poststructuralists to understand the relationship between discourse and identity. Poststructuralists argue that because experience is discursively created, there is an ongoing struggle among discourses for the shaping of that experience. According to this approach each social position a given actor occupies—including his or her ethnic position—is the site of a struggle about the meaning of such a position. In other words, each position is intersected by a variety of discourses that are trying to make sense of this position. With regard to ethnic positions, the outcome of this discursive struggle is that the ethnic labels at stake enter the realm of common sense with the connotations assigned to them by the winners of the battle for meaning. As Avtar Brah (1992: 131) points out:

> The usage of "black," "Indian" or "Asian" is determined not so much by the nature of its referent as by its semiotic function within different discourses. These various meanings signal differing political strategies and outcomes. They mobilize different sets of cultural or political identities, and set limits to where the boundaries of a "community" are established.

Thus, the poststructural approach maintains that the social construction of ethnic identity involves a struggle over the ways in which meanings get "fixed." My hypothesis is that such a struggle, in the case of the label "Chicano," is still open. Consequently, the meaning of "Chicano" is not yet fixed. On the contrary, there are several connotations that still compete with one another to win the battle of acquiring the equivalence between language and reality that characterizes hegemony. In my fieldwork I have identified several such connotations in addition to the meaning given to the term by the Chicano movement: Chicanos are militants who want to preserve their Mexican heritage. In addition to the Chicano movement's use of the term, in this chapter I will analyze various other connotations "Chicano" has come to take in El Paso: Chicanos as any person of Mexican descent living in the United States, as poor Mexican Americans, as *cholos*,[4] as those Mexican Americans who are losing their Mexican roots, as those uprooted Mexican Americans who are neither Mexican nor American, and so on. My analysis suggests not only that the meaning of "Chicano" proposed by the Chicano movement is just one of several meanings given the term by El Pasoans, but that it is not the most prevalent meaning, either.

Chicanos: Labels and Narrative Identities

In their article "Mexicans, Chicanos, Mexican Americans, or Pochos . . . ¿Qué somos? The Impact of Nativity on Ethnic Labeling," Aída Hurtado and Carlos Arce advance a series of hypotheses about why people of Mexican descent in the United States use so many different labels to refer to themselves. According to these authors, U.S.-born people of Mexican descent and Mexican-born immigrants do not perceive themselves as being the same. Additionally, differences in self-perception are also salient among the native born, and those self-perceptions vary "not only according to nativity and language, but also according to circumstances" (1986: 109).

In order to investigate why people of Mexican descent use such a diversity of labels to refer to themselves, Hurtado and Arce used data from the 1979 National Chicano Survey conducted by the Survey Research Center at the University of Michigan. In that survey, people were asked several questions. One of them inquired which label interviewees preferred to use in family settings. The overwhelming reply was the label "Mexican," either in Spanish or English. Nevertheless, U.S.-born individuals whose preferred language was English were less likely to select such a label when speaking about people of Mexican descent among family members. With regard to the label "Chicano," however, English-speakers were the ones who were most likely to use the term (17 percent of interviewees), whereas less than 5 percent of Mexican immigrants and U.S.-born Spanish-speakers chose that label as an in-group referent (Hurtado and Arce 1986).

In this sense, El Pasoans are not so different from people of Mexican descent in other parts of the United States. At the national level, "Chicano" is not widely used as a self-referential term in in-group settings, either. It is worth pointing out, however, that the 5 to 17 percent of the Mexican-origin population nationwide who identify themselves as Chicanos is still substantially higher than the 1 percent who do so in El Paso.

Because situational variation exists in choices of ethnic labels, the National Chicano Survey also had a question about *public* ethnic reference. That question asked people, "Which one [label] do you use most with people who are *not* of Mexican descent?" Here, again, "Mexican" was the label used most frequently (Hurtado and Arce 1986). The authors also note that there is a noticeable decline in [the use of Chicano] from the within-family frequencies. The frequencies for the more neutral labels, American, American of Mexican descent, Latin, and Hispanic, are the highest when compared to in-group labeling. The entire sample appears to be sensitive to the potential reaction of outsiders to the use of strong ethnic terms and respondents accommodate to this expectation to a certain extent. (Hurtado and Arce 1986: 119)

Interestingly, the group that was most likely to use "Chicano" as a self-referent in family settings—U.S. born interviewees whose preferred language was English—was the group *least* likely (less than 10 percent) to use "Chicano" self-referentially when speaking with people who were not of Mexican descent. In their conclusion, Hurtado and Arce (1986) recognize that the label "Chicano" is used by relatively few people of Mexican descent in the United States regardless of nativity and language preference, but they predict that the use of the label could increase in the future:

It is especially significant that 17 percent of the United States–born English speaking, working-class respondents choose the supposedly taboo label of Chicano when speaking to their families. As Moscovici and Nemeth indicate, whenever there is a radical change in culture, it is usually initiated by a small, educated elite. As the process of politicization increases, so does the adoption of the cultural change by the masses. Or as the Chuco in Miguel Méndez-M.'s novel states, "me empieza a cuadrar que me llamen 'chicano,' bato; me caí a toda madre, carnal; siquiera ya es uno algo, no cualquier greaser o pocho." (Hurtado and Arce 1986: 124)[5]

Such adoption has not occurred, however, at least not in El Paso.

José Limón (1981) takes a performative approach toward trying to understand why the label "Chicano" was not widely accepted by people of Mexican descent living in Texas. According to Limón, part of the rejection of the label "Chicano" by the larger Texas-Mexican community stems from the community's sense of the performance contexts in which it is appropriate to use this essentially folkloric term. Thus, Limón argues that the folk performance of "Chicano" is governed by certain cultural rules of restriction, where, ideally, an appropriate performance occurs in a Spanish-language-dominant, private, in-group situation. This performance context stands in sharp contrast to the public, intergroup, English-language discursive settings in which the term is used ideologically by the Chicano movement. In this interpretation, people of Mexican descent in Texas reject the label as it is proposed by the Chicano movement in part because such usage breaks the rules of performance that apply to in-group labels such as "Chicano" among Mexican Americans, "nigger" among African Americans, and "meskin" among Muslims. Limón's prognosis about the future of the word in the United States is exactly the opposite of that of Hurtado and Arce (1986), who speculated that its use would grow. On this basis, Limón suggests that "it is quite possible that because of the Chicano movement's public appropriation of the term, the larger community may use 'Chicano' less and less in the expressive interactions of everyday group life" (Limón 1981: 223).

Although I agree with Limón about the importance of performance in the acceptance or rejection of a folkloric term, we must bear in mind that a term also gains acceptance or rejection in relation to the ongoing symbolic struggle over its connotation. It is my contention that there are various meanings of the label "Chicano" that are currently competing to become fixed as the commonsense connotation of the term, as it reflects a particular interpretation of the experience of being a Mexican living in the United States. If, as poststructuralism suggests, experience lacks inherent essential meaning, "it may be given meaning in language through a range of discursive systems of meaning, which are often contradictory and constitute conflicting versions of social reality" (Weedon 1989: 34). Thus, experience is not something that language reflects: insofar as it is meaningful, experience is constituted in language. We may therefore view the symbolic struggle around the label "Chicano" as part of a broader struggle to define a particular experience, that of people of Mexican descent living in the United States.

In taking a poststructuralist approach, I argue that experience is discursively created and that there is an ongoing struggle among discourses for the shaping of that experience. In this sense, most discourses aspire to being socially recognized as "truth." To acquire the status of truth, a discourse has to discredit all alternative and oppositional versions of meaning and become common sense, that is, a "truth" that is not typically contested. One encounters here Gramsci's shadow behind the poststructuralist approach: the relations in which social actors participate are multiple, including relations of production as well as racial, national, sexual, gender, familial, and age relations. All these relationships have the potential of being, for the same actor, spaces of identities. In addition, each social position the actor occupies is the site of a struggle over the meaning of such a position. In other words, each position is intersected by different discourses that are trying to make sense of it. Ethnic identities and positions do not escape this discursive destiny.

Thus, my theoretical position is that ethnic identity is based on an ongoing discursive struggle about the meanings that define ethnic relationships and positions in society. The outcome of this discursive struggle is that the particular labels at stake enter the realm of common sense (Gramsci 1975), with the connotation proposed by the winners of the battle for meaning. This is so because uni-accentuality involves a practice of closure, namely, the establishment of an achieved system of equivalence between language and reality (Volosinov 1973). However, closure is always a conditional stage in this kind of approach because meanings that have been effectively coupled can also be uncoupled. In this sense, the political struggle about the meaning of a particular ethnic identity or subject position is never completely closed. The subjectivity of a given social agent is always precariously and provisionally fixed, even in cases where it remains fixed over a long period of time. In other words, ethnic identity and subjectivity are always precarious, contradictory, and in process, and the individual is always the site of conflicting forms of subjectivity (Laclau and Mouffe 1985; Laclau 1991). The multiplicity of labels people of Mexican descent apply to themselves in the United States and the different connotations of those labels for different individuals are good examples of how precarious and open ethnic identity is nowadays.

The different subject positions that converge to form what appears as a unified and unique self are cultural constructions created by discourses (understanding as discourse the linguistic and nonlinguistic practices that carry and convey meaning in a field characterized by the play of power relationships) (Laclau and Mouffe 1987). It is in the realm of culture that the struggle over the meaning of different subject positions and ethnic identities is fought, for in this realm people encounter the discourses that intersect such positions.

Of course, not all cultural options have the same weight, and here the problem of hegemony appears (Gramsci 1971). In this sense, the construction of hegemony is, above all, the proposal to the different actors in society of certain determined subject positions (subject positions defined in a way that is functional to the interest of the hegemonic group) and the acceptance by these actors (through a complex process of embracing, negotiation, and rejection) of the basic subject positions offered by the hegemonic group (Mouffe 1985; Laclau and Mouffe 1985). In the U.S. case the label "Hispanic" is the hegemonic label those in power propose to address people of Mexican (and other Latin American) descent, and "Chicano" is the counterhegemonic label the most important Mexican American social movement opposes to such a hegemonic definition (or "Latino," for those who want to encompass other people from Latin America rather than Mexicans alone). Here is where classification systems and the struggle for hegemony converge with narrative identities.

In *The Order of Things,* Michel Foucault, quoting Jorge Luis Borges, describes "'a certain Chinese encyclopedia' in which it is written that 'animals are divided into: a) belonging to the Emperor, b) embalmed, c) tame, d) suckling pigs, e) sirens, f) fabulous, g) stray dogs, h) included in the present classification, i) frenzied, j) innumerable, k) drawn with a very fine camel hair brush, l) et cetera, m) having just broken the water pitcher, n) that from a long way off looks like flies'" (1970: xv). The transparent absurdity of this classification system calls our attention to the arbitrary nature of such taxonomies. At the same time, it makes evident that the viability of a given system of classification depends neither on its "fit" with reality nor on its internal consistency but on the field of forces within which the struggle over its meaning takes place. What Foucault basically asks us to think about is what kind of self-definitions the organization of language allows us and how labeling works to channel possible accounts of the self into the forms acceptable to society. He points out that although what counts as true knowledge is defined by the individual, what is permitted to count is defined by discourse. What is spoken and who may speak are issues of power (Parker 1989).

In this way, our commonsense ideas about ourselves and the Others constantly use a variety of classifications and labels: age, gender, race, place of birth, occupation, and class. All these classifications appear to us so fixed that we consider them part of the natural world: our experience of everyday life is structured by classification systems whose credibility and connection with reality are never questioned. The very possibility of common sense is built upon this premise. If we believe, like Foucault does, that the knowledge that circulates in discourse is employed in everyday interactions in relations of submission and domination, then it becomes clear that classifications are not neutral identifications. On the contrary, they are loaded with meaning, and with meaning linked to the construction of hegemony in a particular historical time and place. Thus, each label in our classification systems comes with "information" about the occupants of that position, an information that we take for granted and that shapes our encounter with them as the Other. This is because social interaction always is, among other things, an interaction with the Other as a particular category. We can only know the Other through description and thus through the narratives and classificatory systems that, being part of the battle for meaning, are available within a particular cultural context.

It is through this complex construction of meaning that the names of the different social actors are being shaped and given content in classificatory systems we use to order and to comprehend the realities that surround us. Thus, we encounter in diverse cultural artifacts the different names we use to interpellate Others (or that Others use to interpellate us) (Althusser 1971), names and connotations that refer to the different subject positions we occupy in society: family, labor, class, age, gender, and ethnic positions. The different labels people of Mexican descent use to address themselves and their Others form part of those names that struggle to make sense of the ethnic experience of this population.

The label "Chicano" is a prominent label in this struggle because it is the name that the most important Mexican American social movement has adopted to address its constituency. However, the label not only has not gained widespread acceptance in El Paso, but also the connotation proposed by the Chicano movement is not the one most widely used by those who address themselves and others as Chicanos. I believe this is so because the Chicano movement has not yet won its symbolic struggle to fix the meaning of the term around its preferred connotation: "Chicano" as a person of Mexican descent who is proud of his or her Mexican origin and struggles against Anglo discrimination.[6] Instead, the label has several competing meanings, depending not only upon who is employing the term but also upon the various circumstances in which the same person finds it appropriate to employ it in a particular way. This is not happening with the other labels at stake: "Mexican," "Mexican American," "American of Mexican descent," and "Hispanic," which are not as polysemous as the "Chicano" label in everyday conversations in El Paso. I believe that the meaning of the term "Chicano" is less fixed than that of other terms because the symbolic struggle over this particular label is still being waged. In the remainder of this chapter, I discuss some of the different meanings the label "Chicano" currently takes in the region around El Paso.

Narratives and the Symbolic Struggle
over the Meaning of "Chicano" in El Paso

The term "Chicano" was not invented by the Chicano movement in the 1960s. It had already been used by the Mexican American community at least since the beginning of this century. According to Limón, the label was used in at least two different ways, first as an ethnic-class slur, that is, a derogatory term that referred to the poorer, more recent immigrants from Mexico. The term was used as such by middle- and upper-class U.S.-born Americans of Mexican descent. It seems that, over the years, the term was extended to refer to all poor Mexicans in the United States regardless of their date of arrival (Limón 1981). However, the term also had a second, more positive connotation, used to express closeness and group solidarity when it was performed within the in-group (Limón 1981).

My research confirms some of Limón's findings and adds other connotations of the label that are also working in El Paso and competing among each other to fix the meaning of the term. At the same time, to add complexity to an already complicated panorama, the use of the term is not consistent among the same interviewees either, some of whom use different connotations of the label to address different things. The interviews that are analyzed in this chapter flowed from discussions about various sets of photographs (300 photographs divided in three packages shown on three different occasions) that were taken in the border area and that portray various everyday activities in Juárez and El Paso (public interactions, family life, religion, leisure, work, etc.). Because I wanted to map differences in the process of identity construction, I interviewed both men and women, of different ages, class backgrounds, ethnicity, religion, nationality, region, education, and migration experiences. The interviews were structured as follows: People were first asked to look at the package of photographs to be discussed that day and then to select out those photographs they wanted to talk about with the group. After the entire group looked at the photos and chose the shots they felt deserved comment, the first participant was asked to tell the group why he or she decided to keep a particular photograph. When the interviewee had finished speaking, the others were asked if they had additional comments and if they agreed or disagreed with their companion. Usually, a discussion followed in which almost all participants expressed opinions about the photo or the issue it addressed. The interviews were taped and then transcribed to analyze their content.

"Chicano" as an In-Group Identifier

One of Limón's proposals is that the term "Chicano" is accepted in the in-group but rejected as a public way to address people of Mexican descent living in the United States. Some of the El Paso Mexican Americans we interviewed expressed attitudes consistent with this proposal. Other interviewees, additionally, were fully aware of how the label works as a slur when used in public and as an ethnic connection when it is used in an in-group situation:

Ramón: It depends, I guess, it all depends who calls you, huh?

Bob: If you're a wh, a white man calling you a Chicano you get offended. But if it's someone else, like a Chicano telling you, you know . . . you're not offended by it.

Ramón: I think when other Mexicans call another one Chicano it's kind of like . . .

Mary: Connection.

Bob: Connection, yea.

Ramón: . . . yea, family, Chicanos were . . .

Mike: But that goes with every race, 'cause like ah, for example, the black people, they, they like to call each other . . . niggers . . . but if *you* call them a nigger . . .

Ramón: Yea . . . then, we're Chicanos, they're niggers. You know, and if somebody calls them like that, they're gonna feel upset.

The second argument Limón proposes and that I also found in El Paso is
that the label has changed since the emergence of the Chicano movement in
the 1960s.[7] Oscar describes its evolution:

> When I was a kid and I was in the Navy, you know, the first thing when
> you saw . . . un morenito or whatever, ¿eres Chicano? [are you Chicano]
> . . . that was our communication, ¿eres chicano?, simon', verda [right?].
> ¿De onde eres? [where are you from] De Phoenix, de Denver, San
> Antonio, San Angelo, and those, we didn't go into this, I guess it came
> later, you know, we were involved in it in a small way, pero, at that time,
> it was . . . just a means of identification . . . ¿eres Chicano? ¿de 'onde
> eres? Del Chuco . . . el Chuco was El Paso . . . later on, of course, we had
> Cesar Chavez, and all this, and, uh, and we had our, whatever, you know,
> the Chicanos and the activists in the sixties, uh, . . . I don't know where
> we're at right now with that word . . .

Oscar's testimony not only confirms Limón's findings but also introduces
us to my main argument: the Chicano label has so many conflicting interpretations that most people in El Paso, for one reason or another, prefer not
to use "Chicano" as a public way to address their ethnic identity: "I don't
know where we're at right now with that word." In my fieldwork I have
encountered other, and sometimes contradictory, ways people understand
the label "Chicano."

"Chicano" as a Generic Term for
Mexicans Living in the United States

Some El Paso interviewees used "Chicano" as a generic term to describe
people of Mexican descent living on the United States, regardless of nativity. In this peculiar usage the term stands for *all* Mexicans regardless of
their relationship to their heritage, their stance regarding discrimination,
and so on. Without the qualifications I will introduce later, this particular
usage could be understood as an important victory for the Chicano movement, that is, that the movement had established a correspondence between
the entire population of Mexicans living in the United States and the connotation the movement was promoting. However, we will see that the connotation of the term is so contested that such a correspondence may be
largely illusory.

Among those using "Chicano" to intend a general meaning of the term
were a group of middle-class African American interviewees who are in the
military:

Bessie: I've always thought the word Chicano meant Mexico,
           Mexican.
Author: A synonym of Mexican?

Bessie:	Yea, ah-hum.
Billie:	That's good 'cause I was, I was, kind of, thinking . . . maybe it was Puerto Rican or something.

Here the connotation of "Chicano" is so general that it encompasses all Mexicans (putting together Mexican immigrants and Mexican Americans), but also it is so confusing that the other interviewee thought it applied to Puerto Ricans!

"Chicano" as a Term for U.S.-Born Mexicans

In addition to hearing "Chicano" used as a term for *any* Mexican in the United States, I also heard it used in a more restricted sense in El Paso: a Chicano was someone of Mexican descent who was born and raised in the United States. This was the meaning used by some middle-class Mexican American interviewees, including Saúl:

> I think Chicano . . . that's us . . . Mexican Americans, O.K.? We can't say, or go to Mexico and say that we are Mexican, because . . . Mexicans don't consider us Mexicans. And here, we have the same problem . . . "American," and no, they say to us, "You are Mexican." So, as far as I'm concerned, we are Chicano . . . both Mexican and American. (author's translation of original Spanish)

This statement expresses quite graphically the feeling of many of our interviewees that people of Mexican descent living in the United States get caught in a no one's land, where neither Mexican nationals nor Anglo Americans consider them "one of their own kind." In this type of usage, Chicanos are all those individuals who, regardless of their awareness, are objectively in between two different heritages.

The same general use was present in a group of working-class young people I interviewed in El Paso. For Ramón, one of these interviewees, the term "Chicano" applies to all people of Mexican descent who were born and live in the United States:

> Some people don't like to be called, ah, let's say they were born here and they don't like to be called Mexicans. . . . And, I know they're not *white!* [laughs] . . . So I guess they have to be Chicanos whether they like it or not.

In this sense, Ramón, who is a Mexican immigrant, does not consider himself a Chicano because he was not born in the United States. Nevertheless, his brother Alvaro considers himself a Chicano because he actually was born in the United States:

Ramón: I was born in Mexico; I call myself Mexican.
Mary: So, if somebody asks you, they ask you what are you,
         you're going to tell them . . .
Ramón: I'm a Mexican.
Mary: . . . Mexican?
Ramón: Yea, because I was born in Mexico.
Author: But what about your, your brother, that was born here?
Ramón: What are you?
Alvaro: Chicano.

In discussing a photograph depicting the Centro Chicano in the Segundo Barrio, another group of young working-class Mexican Americans who were the children of Mexican immigrants could not understand the need to have such a center in El Paso, where more than 70 percent of the population is of Mexican origin:

Author: Why did you choose this picture?
Susie: Why? . . . Because I think . . . "Centro Chicano," I mean
         . . . Chicano . . . you know, we're in El Paso, why
         "Centro Chicano"? Because Mexicans live there or
         what? I thought it was weird. . . . Why not "Centro
         Americano"? Why "Chicano"? If we are all just
         Mexican Americans in El Paso . . . all can go there!
         (author's translation of original Spanish)

"Chicano" as a Term of Ethnic Pride and Resistance

Against the two previous, very general meanings, the Chicano movement has proposed as its privileged meaning for the label a more narrow connotation: Chicanos as those people of Mexican descent who want to preserve their Mexican (and Indian) heritage and who struggle against discrimination in the United States. In this sense, the Chicano movement has tried to extend the label "Chicano" to address everyone of Mexican descent living in the United States, but at the same time its struggle against discrimination has identified the label with those who share that particular struggle, although, of course, not all Mexican Americans do.[8] For instance, César, a Vietnam veteran born in El Paso who works in a federal government warehouse, stressed not only his awareness of discrimination and his close relationship to Mexico, but also the mestizo character of his Mexican identity:

I was born here in Chihuahuita . . . but my grandmother . . . she was a descendant of the Yaquis Indians . . . and I am proud of that Indian heritage. . . . I took from her Indian blood, and there are people who are ashamed of that. . . . And to me . . . on the contrary! I am very proud of that!

Here they treat us as . . . because today there are so many Cubans, Puerto Ricans, and people from South America . . . they call us "Hispanic." Before they never called us "Hispanics," they called us "those Mexicans." . . . They put us together in the same group. . . . I do not consider myself a Hispanic. . . . I know that in Mexico they would call me *pocho,* but first of all . . . if they want to put a label on me, I would call myself Chicano. . . . I am Chicano. . . . Well, the label is not very common nowadays. . . . I am very proud of my Indian blood. . . . I could call myself "mestizo," too, because that is what I am. . . . It is the most correct label. . . . But, if they wanted to put a label on me, I would better call myself Chicano . . . Chicano-mestizo, but not Hispanic. . . . Hispanic means to be already grouped. . . . Anglos have grouped us that way. (author's translation of original Spanish)

Evidently, César is quite aware of the Chicano movement ideology and conscious of how Anglos label people like himself. But who are the "Others"? Basically, the "Others" are the Anglos who use what he considers politically loaded labels that contribute to the maintenance of power in their hands. Thus, in his reference to Anglos, what he is doing is describing how Anglos, the intellectual authors of the U.S. classification system, have acquired the rare privilege of not being referred to as an ethnicity, whereas all the other groups in the taxonomy are described as ethnic groups. César is extremely clear in his argument: the Hispanic label is an imposition originating from the power Anglos have "to label" others: "here *they* treat us . . .; *they* call us . . . ; *they* put us together in the same group." According to his argument, to accept the label "Hispanic" is to accept being named by the Others in power and in this way to reproduce one of the sources of their power: the ability to name, to classify what kind of people are going to be considered "the same"; to mark off the boundaries between those who can address the others and those who have to accept the label they receive; to offer for commonsense appropriation the starting point for an equivalence between name, attitude, and behavior, which forms the basis of negative images and racism. Of course, he does not feel represented by the label, and he prefers the term "Chicano" instead. What César is also referring to is his awareness of the weakness of the Chicano movement in El Paso today: "[the word Chicano] is not very common nowadays . . . "

Another thing César understands in relation to his use of the term "Chicano" is the movement's emphasis on Anglo discrimination as the major cause of Mexican American backwardness:

When I was in junior high school, in the '60s . . . there were . . . almost 50 percent of the students were Mexicans and the others were Americans

or Anglo Saxons, and now there aren't any more Anglos in San Elizario
[a small, historic town outside of El Paso that nowadays is almost completely Mexican American]. Now there are only Mexicans. Then where
are the Anglos now? . . . They started moving because . . . because what
we call *la raza* started moving in, and they . . . want to separate themselves . . . they separated to. . . . (author's translation of original
Spanish)

His reference to *la raza* here is quite significant. On the one hand, it is part
of his Chicano credo, the acknowledgment of the brotherhood that supposedly exists between Mexicans and Mexican Americans. On the other hand,
it is also the recognition of who the Other is in racial terms: the Anglos or
Americans who are not mestizos.

Another interview in which the militant connotation of the "Chicano"
label appeared was one I conducted with Gustavo and Pedro. Gustavo, a
lawyer who is in his forties, migrated to El Paso from Delicias, Chihuahua,
when he was an adolescent. Pedro is from Juárez; he is twenty-eight years
old and works as a technician. In their interview the major themes of the
Chicano ideology emerged again: discrimination and Mexican traditions.
Gustavo puts it this way:

It is strange that . . . whenever you say something . . . something that says
Chicano, right away we say because of discrimination . . . rather than saying because these people are trying to keep our culture up there. And are
trying to give us a sense of what we should be and what we should be
proud of. It's a connotation that I get right away: "Chicano. Ah, discrimination," . . . I'm a Chicano . . . that's *my* motto when I go out there and I
go fighting with people. I'm gonna call myself a Chicano and see what
comes out of it. . . . If you call yourself a Chicano, a lot of times instead of
proudly saying, "I'm a Chicano," you say it angrily, like saying: "So, what
are you gonna do about it?"

The other central theme of the Chicano movement that also emerged in
this interview was how Chicanos seem to really dislike the term "Hispanic"
and consider it as a label created by their political opponents. Here it is
important to point out that when interviewers question people about their
ethnic identity, they usually neglect to ask about the label people *do not
want* others to use to describe them (such a question was not part of the
1979 National Chicano Survey). I consider this question to be as important
as the others, because knowing which labels people dislike can shed some
light as to which kinds of identity labels these individuals resist most vigor-
ously. In my fieldwork in El Paso I have found that just as people of
Mexican descent chose a variety of ethnic labels to refer to themselves,
they strongly rejected certain labels as well. Usually these labels were the
ones used by those people interviewees consider to be the paradigmatic
Others. Thus, I have found that when asked which label they reject the

most, those interviewees who called themselves "Chicanos" (in the militant sense of the term, as used by César, Pedro, and Gustavo above) usually rejected the "Hispanic" label. They claimed such a label denies the specificities of the experience of being a person of Mexican descent living in the United States because it ignores the struggles the Chicano movement underwent defending Mexicans and Mexican culture in the United States.[9]

It is not by chance, then, that the "Hispanic" label was under attack once more in Pedro and Gustavo's interview:

> Pedro: People bring up Hispanic . . . but when the English language refers to Hispanic they're referring to *South America*, Central America, Mexico, all of the people speaking Spanish. . . . That's like saying that all Koreans are Chinese or, 'cause they're all Oriental and yet they're different peoples, different cultures . . .
>
> Gustavo: . . . that's a very good example . . . a woman asked me the other day that question. She says, "What is ah, what's a Hispanic and a Chicano? What's the definition to you?". . . And I say, "Well, as I've heard it before, a Hispanic is someone that is of Spanish origin that comes to the United States to look for the pot of gold and the Chicano is someone that's already been here, that has seen that *that* pot of gold is not available to him as easily as it is to somebody else, so he says, 'I'm a Chicano, I'm not a Hispanic.'"

"Chicano" as a Term Whose Moment Has Passed

César, Gustavo, and Pedro currently consider themselves Chicanos and use all the political connotations the Chicano movement has advanced. Other interviewees, however, accept that they *were* Chicanos in the previously defined political sense when they were younger, but that they are not Chicanos anymore. This was true of Rolando, a forty-year-old real estate manager and native El Pasoan: "Before . . . when I was going to college, I was a Chicano . . . because of the . . . the political connotation. . . . Ah, political activist. Now, I'm *apolitical* . . . for personal reasons."[10]

Rolando's testimony introduces us to another connotation of the label "Chicano": as something referring to the past. In this version, Chicano is an old word referring to some political movement that existed thirty years ago but does not exist anymore. According to this type of argument, the widespread use of the label "Chicano" would have disappeared along with the movement that proposed it as a way of ethnic identification. That kind of connotation was present in the interview I conducted with some

University of Texas–El Paso (UTEP) students in their twenties, also native
El Pasoans:

Antonio: When did the Chicano movement start?
Author: The '60s.
Antonio: It seems to be more of a, towards the Hispanics, more of
           a negative, negative word. Just the emphasis it seems
           like you wanna be a rebel. Like, I'm a Chicano. Do you
           like it or not? You know, What are you gonna do? You
           know, it just seems to be a rebellic [*sic*] word. So that's
           how I view, I look at the word. I don't know the history
           behind it, but that's how I look at it. Mexican, Hispanic,
           Latin American, you know, "I'm a Latin." But once you
           say Chicano, you are trying to define yourself like
           you're in a movement. And maybe at that time there was
           a movement where I would be proud to say "I'm a
           Chicano." You know, move on, take care of business.
           But now it's a word that has, we're in the '90s.
Ricardo: I've never heard it around here. I've never, or even in
           my neighborhood. Chicano. We just read it off, or read it
           off labels. But I've never heard anyone say, "Hey, are
           you Chicano?" or something. It's really, to me, I don't
           know about you or the rest, but I've never heard it. Or
           I've heard it, I've read it in books and so forth, but I've
           never used it with my friends.

It is not coincidental that Ricardo and Antonio, who did not want to be
called Chicanos, called themselves Hispanics. As we can see, their choice
of "label I like/label I dislike" is consistent with what happened with César,
Pedro, and Gustavo, but in the opposite direction: Ricardo and Antonio like
being called Hispanics but dislike being called Chicanos:

Ricardo: Chicano. When I hear that word I really don't know
           what that word defines. 'Cause I consider myself as a
           Hispanic not as a Chicano. So if I had to say in an exam
           and it would ask "Define Chicano" and it's not in the
           books or anything, I really wouldn't be able to define it
           'cause I don't see myself, I don't define myself, I don't
           categorize myself, label myself as a Chicano. I see
           myself as a Hispanic. And a Chicano . . . truth, I really
           don't know what a Chicano is, really. I really don't. I
           really don't. I should. Chicano. But I just can't. I just
           can't! 'Cause I see myself as a Hispanic. When I fill out

one of those tests, "What's your race?" Hispanic.
Sometimes it says Chicano, but I don't put Chicano, I
put Hispanic.

Disdain for Chicanos

Although the testimonies presented thus far reflect relatively positive connotations of the label "Chicano" in line with the meaning preferred by the
Chicano movement (Chicanos as militant people struggling to preserve
Mexican culture and combating discrimination), we have found interviewees who, understanding the word in that way, do not like its meaning. This
happened in our interview with Albert, a twenty-eight-year-old third-gener-
ation Mexican American born in Chihuahuita, one of El Paso's poorest
neighborhoods. Today, Albert is a professional with a college degree who
holds a managerial position at a maquiladora in Juárez. He currently lives
in an expensive home in an upper-middle-class neighborhood on the west
side of town:

> Those Chicanos are the bad guys in my opinion, those guys who find it
> very easy to blame someone else and don't have any initiative to better
> themselves! . . . Those are the guys who sit and complain day after day,
> night after night and then go home and have a fix or a six-pack of beer,
> then wake up the next morning, the next night and start all over again!

Albert perceived Chicanos as crying discrimination in order to avoid confronting their personal failures. For him, they are the sort of people who
build a political argument in order to hide their true identities as laggards
and drunks who are unwilling to work hard (as he did) in order to succeed.
The *barrio* as a way of life—with all its connotations of preserving traditions from Mexico such as big families, free time, leisure, and friends—is
part of the past, and it is the culture of the kind of people who do not want
real progress in their lives. The barrio is also *his* past, and in his narrative
identity Albert constantly addressed how far he is from that past and how
his future is going to be still farther away. According to Albert, to accomplish something in U.S. society, getting out of the ethnic ghetto is a *must*.
Thus, people who remain in Chihuahuita are, according to Albert, people
who have done nothing with their lives.

Author: Do you think that people who live there are going to live
         there all their lives or do you . . . ?
Albert: Yes! (curtly) I would say that a good 40 or 50 percent
         have no aspirations of leaving. I have a cousin, believe it
         or not, who here it is thirty-four years later who still for

some reason finds it necessary to stay in that damn corner there. I don't know what his purpose in life is, you
know. He's grown up and now he has little boys who are
fifteen, sixteen. . . . And this guy who is probably thirty-
five and still has a reason, I don't know what the hell his
reason is, but he still finds it necessary to stand at that
corner, you know, on Friday nights. I, shit, I don't know.
We all have priorities. I guess I have different priorities,
but . . .

Because for him the ethnic barrio reflects a backward past, Albert does
not regard Chicanos as an ethnic "vanguard." On the contrary, he sees them
as mired in the past. He sees them in this way, first, because Chicanos stand
for those Mexican Americans who want to hide inside traditional ethnic
boundaries—who are afraid to go out into the "real world" outside the barrio in which they encounter and compete with Anglos. Second, Chicanos
are also representatives of the past because, in not taking responsibility for
their individual destinies, they behave like children: "*No crecen*! They
refuse to grow up and assume responsibilities! It's a, it's a way to live in
the past and kind of forget all your problems and, yeah!, forget the responsibilities you should have as a father or a mother or, you know . . ."

In a sense, Albert thinks the Chicano movement and ideology ("I've
read the literature . . .") offer an easy escape ("a lot of people find the easy
way out . . .") from everyday life responsibilities that, for him, above all,
are individual. Therefore, Albert cannot understand how some people
decide freely to live in the barrio instead of moving to a more middle-class
Anglo environment: "Some people refused to leave, refused to let go, grow
up. You know, there's a whole world out there, just, people don't want to
see it."

His only explanation, again, is that such people have a childlike mentality, a traditional one that does not look for change. This mentality also
impinges on those who have tried to leave the barrio, undermining their
ability to succeed in the "real" world, the Anglo one.

You gotta keep on trying, man! See, I grew up there and just because I
grew up there doesn't mean I was gonna stay there! And I'm twenty-eight
years old and it doesn't mean I'm gonna stay at this level either all my
life! I'm not gonna stop trying! But I know I'm gonna have to work harder than somebody else to get that opportunity. And more importantly,
because I can relate to this too . . . in those instances when we got an
opportunity, being referred to as a Hispanic . . . the two times I saw somebody get an opportunity, they both failed, they both came back home. And
that goes back to our upbringing. Where we didn't want to leave or didn't
. . . we were intimidated.

Hence, Albert thinks that there is something in Mexican American culture that plays against Hispanics when they attempt to escape the ethnic enclave to venture into the "real" world. Here we finally encounter the hidden side of the melting pot ideology so well-learned by Albert: successful adjustment to U.S. society is presumed to necessitate complete disassociation from Mexican American culture because the origin of Mexican Americans' problems lies in the culture itself. Thus, Albert, who not by chance refers to himself as Hispanic, having embraced the acculturation-assimilation discourse, signaled the Chicanos as the Other, because Chicanos are precisely those who reject the assimilationist discourse and advance another possible explanation of the problems Mexican Americans face in U.S. society: discrimination.[11]

A similar argument was advanced by Domingo. He is in his forties and was born in Juárez but has always lived in El Paso. He used to be a white-collar worker but was unemployed at the time of the interview.

> Chicano . . . brown power means you are prejudiced, you tend to be with your own kind. You see an Anglo, you see a black, you kinda say you're not part of the group. What would they call it before? . . . brown berets, I think. . . . What was his name? . . . César Chávez . . . he used to organize the unions, down in California.

Domingo accuses Chicanos of being as prejudiced as the Anglos they attack for supposedly having prejudices against people of Mexican descent. In addition, the connotation Domingo places upon the word "Chicano" makes an analogy among militants, violence, and gangs, things that, of course, he dislikes:

> The word "Chicano" reminds me of the Second Ward.[12] . . . It's becoming too militant . . . like these people that walk down the streets . . . the blue angels . . . the brown berets. . . . It's becoming too dangerous . . . drive-by shootings and you've gotta belong to a gang. That's what that world reminds me of . . . the little emblem there . . . like brown power.

In a very interesting interpretation of the word "Chicano," Domingo makes a parallel between the ethnic segregationist rhetoric used by the Chicano movement during the 1960s and the territorial segregationism that characterizes present-day gangs in the Second Ward: "They're forming their own little groups down there, whether it's gangs, whether it's unions. The older generation's saying, 'Hey, we've had enough . . . this is our own little group.' It's just groups of people trying to protect each other."

Here again, it is not by chance that in addition to looking at Chicanos as the Others, Domingo referred to himself as Hispanic. What Domingo said appeared repeatedly in my interviews: many people established an equivalence between Chicanos and gangs, most of the time referring to a particular kind of Mexican American gang: *cholos.* This sentiment was reflected in the comments by Mike, a man we interviewed with a group of first-generation Mexican Americans (i.e., U.S.-born children of immigrants) who worked in a variety of manual and semi-skilled occupations: "If I hear somebody say, like, 'Hey, here come some Chicanos,' I'm gonna think about like people that are in gangs . . . *cholos.* . . . That's the way I've always heard the word being used." Something similar was expressed in an interview I conducted with an Anglo middle-class couple:

> Joe: Me growing up here . . . the Chicano word meant, something negative like, you know . . . like a gang . . . ummm, those are Chicanos! [laughs] you know. . . . And then you see it . . . I see on people's resumes, you know, "Chicano Society, [laughs] from the University of Illinois" or something [laughs]. Okay, [laughs] you know.
>
> Theresa: It's not as bad as you thought.
> Joe: But, but that's slang, you know.

Moreover, according to other interviewees, not only would people refer to Chicanos as *cholos,* but *cholos* themselves would be among the few people in El Paso who would identify themselves as Chicanos. This relationship between the words *cholo* and "Chicano" introduces us to a related meaning the "Chicano" label has in El Paso: the parallelism many people establish between the label "Chicano" and poor Mexican Americans.

> Susie: The label doesn't make the race stand up . . . I don't think it does. . . . Why do we have to call ourselves Chicanos if . . . you know, we're Mexican Americans, we have to be proud of our race and Chicanos all are doing is like putting it down. I think, because mainly . . . the lower people, the lower-class people are the Mexicans who name themselves Chicanos.
>
> Author: And what do you think about that word?
> Tom: I have never liked it either. To tell you the truth I don't know, because I have never liked the sound of the word.
> Author: And what do you think about the word?
> Arturo: It is ugly, it sounds sort of lower class, it sounds to me. . . . It sounds like a bad word . . . Chicano, . . . people from . . .
> Cristi: Lower class.
> Arturo: Yes, yes . . . (author's translation of original Spanish)

Thus, we see that *many* interviewees do not like the word "Chicano" for several reasons. Some of them feel it is too militant, whereas others perceive it as referring to *cholos* or a lower-class kind of people they want to avoid. Nevertheless, most of them recognize that the label is somehow related to a particular struggle to preserve Mexican heritage in the United States. Other interviewees, however, do not like the word because they consider Chicanos to be precisely those people who, for different reasons, do not preserve the Mexican heritage! This was quite prominent in our interviews with Mexican immigrants living in El Paso, like Encarnación:

> When I lived in Mexico I didn't understand what Chicano meant. . . . I didn't know . . . but now I know it's a sort of Mexican culture, with our roots. It's an honor for Hispanic people to say: "I am Chicano." But they still don't know what it is . . . they don't relate. . . . They don't even know how to start, do you understand? (author's translation of original Spanish)

According to Encarnación, Chicanos are those Mexicans living in the United States who struggle to retain a similar Mexican culture but nevertheless are totally unsuccessful in their attempts. Ruth, another lower-middle-class first-generation interviewee, was even more critical regarding the relationship between Chicanos and Mexican heritage:

> But they say that those people changed, that they only wanted to be American, that they didn't want to know anything about their Mexican roots. . . . Because even the word . . . the word itself is Mexican, is a Spanish word, Chicano, and supposedly these people . . . they don't want to know anything about their Mexican heritage . . . (author's translation of original Spanish)

As we can see, the "Chicano" label exhibits a continuum of meanings in El Paso. At one extreme, it refers to those who struggle for the maintenance of Mexican-ness in the United States. At the other, it refers to persons of Mexican descent who are no longer "truly" Mexican.

Conclusion

Based on a long history of conquest and immigration, the use of multiple ethnic labels has been pervasive among people of Mexican descent living in the United States. Because this population is heterogeneous in terms of national origin, ethnicity, region (both in Mexico and the United States), class, and time of migration, it is not by chance that people of Mexican descent use so many ethnic identifiers to frame their experience.

The close relationship between class and ethnicity and its impact on

Mexican labeling has been well documented in the literature (Acuña 1988; Barrera 1979; Gonzáles 1989; Montejano 1987; Oboler 1995). At the end of the nineteenth century, sectors of New Mexico's elites began increasingly to refer to themselves as Hispanos or Spanish-Americans, stressing their supposedly "pure" Spanish origin and separating themselves from the supposedly racially miscegenational and mestizo "Mexicans."

> By the early part of this century, prejudice and discrimination against Mexicans had increased such that the term "Spanish-American" had become widely used among the Spanish-speaking elites in the United States, particularly by the New Mexican *ricos* . . . insofar as they were rich and considered themselves to be white, by the early twentieth century the *ricos* had adopted it to distinguish themselves in the context of Anglo society from the *mexicanos pobres:* "You don't like Mexicans, and we don't like them either, but we are Spanish-Americans, not Mexicans." (Oboler 1995: 25)

People of Mexican descent in Texas favored the label "Latino" in the first part of this century for similar reasons. Since then, several labels have been developed by the people themselves or imposed by the state in order to categorize people of Mexican descent living in the United States. Nowadays, different people prefer different labels to refer to themselves, and each label relates to Mexican heritage differently. In this situation, "Mexican American" (with or without hyphenation) seems to be a "neutral" term. It does not deny Mexican heritage, but it adds the American component of that heritage.[13] "American of Mexican descent" seems to stress the American part of the identity more than the Mexican one, but the word "Mexican" is still present on the label. It is not present in either "Hispanic" or "Latino" and is one of the reasons Mexican Americans complain about the latter terms. "Mexican" or *mexicano,* the label most people prefer to use in El Paso, on the contrary, completely avoids any reference to "American," strongly stressing the Mexican origin and heritage of those who prefer to use it. In spite of all these different meanings, one thing that distinguishes the label "Chicano" from the others mentioned above is its polysemous character. There is no other label in El Paso that has so many different meanings, not only for different people, but also for the same person at different times and under different circumstances.

Obviously, the preferred usage of the label "Mexican" in El Paso does not imply in itself a homogeneous relationship either to Mexico, Mexican nationals, or Mexican culture. In another article (Vila 1997), I have proposed how the label "Mexican" operates differently depending upon how it is incorporated into the different narrative identities of people of Mexican descent in El Paso. Diverse individuals, playing with the various meanings the word "Mexican" takes on the border (where it refers to both a nationali-

ty and an ethnicity), use the label differently to construct the Other, sometimes in a very negative way. Nonetheless, it is quite clear that the use of
the "Mexican"/*mexicano* label is very popular in El Paso, something that is
not the case with the "Chicano" label.

What we have in El Paso is a hotly contested symbolic struggle over
the meaning of being a person of Mexican descent living on the U.S. side
of the U.S.-Mexico border. On the one hand, we have several labels competing with each other to address this experience, each with its own set of
connotations. On the other hand, we have the particular label advanced by
the most important Mexican American social movement, "Chicano," which
has several contradictory connotations. As Angie Chabram-Dernersesian
(1993: 38) points out:

> The term *Chicana* itself is a field for multiple cultural critiques (inside
> and outside the Chicano community) that unsettle previously conferred
> identities: Anglo, Hispanic, Pocho, Mexican American, Spanish, and
> Chicano. As Norma Alarcón suggests, the story of Chicanas/os has not
> turned out to be definitive; for, as she elaborates, even the term *Chicana/o*
> has become a critical site of political, ideological and discursive struggle.

Thus, we discover not only that different people use the label differently,
but also that the same person can utilize the label differently, depending
upon the kind of narrative she or he is developing. Nevertheless, not only
does the label "Chicano" seem to be barely used in El Paso, but even when
it is used, it usually takes on negative connotations, ranging from people of
lower-class background to *cholos* and from separatist militants who do not
want to assimilate to U.S. society to "cultural traitors" who supposedly
want to abandon any kind of relationship with their Mexican heritage. As
we can see, this is a very difficult situation within which the Chicano
movement must attempt to advance its preferred meaning for the label: a
Chicano as someone who not only defends Mexican-ness and is proud of
her or his Indian past but also as someone who struggles against discrimination in the United States.

Notes

I want to thank the following programs and institutions for supporting my research:
Rockefeller Foundation; Social Science Research Council; Seminario de Estudios
de la Cultura; Population Research Center (University of Texas–Austin); Center for
Inter-American and Border Studies, University Research Institute, Liberal Arts
Faculty Development Grant, and Sociology and Anthropology Department (all at
the University of Texas–El Paso [UTEP]); and El Colegio de la Frontera Norte. I am
also indebted to Yvonne Montejano, Teresa Hughes, Angela Escajeda, Abigaíl
García, Pablo Luna, and Araceli Arceo for their outsanding research assistance. As

usual, Howard Campbell and, especially, Dennis Bíxler-Márquez made some insightful comments for which I am greatly appreciative.

1. A note on terminology is appropriate here. I use the term "Mexican origin" to refer to any person of Mexican descent (immigrants and U.S.-born alike) living in the United States. I use the term "Mexican American" for those who were born in the United States, whereas I reserve "Chicano" exclusively for those who identify themselves as such.

2. Kathy Staudt, personal communication, November 14, 1995. According to Dennis Bíxler-Márquez, director of the Chicano Program at UTEP (personal communication, November 22, 1995), the result may have been influenced by geographical location, that is, their interviewees may have been recent immigrants who identify themselves as *mexicanos*. The interviews were done in a "core" downtown neighborhood, an old periphery neighborhood, and a new periphery *colonia*. Staudt mentioned to me that they have a little more representation of people born outside the United States than did the 1990 census.

3. Dennis Bíxler-Márquez (personal communication, November 22, 1995) claims that one of the reasons for the low percentage of people of Mexican descent who identify themselves as Chicanos in El Paso is the absence of Chicano studies courses in the local high schools. According to him, "In Texas, high school curriculum reform in the 1980s . . . spelled the demise of Chicano or other ethnic studies courses. In El Paso, it has only been in the last two years that we have re-activated the Chicano Studies curriculum in five local high schools. . . . Thus, the number of politicized young Chicanos coming to UTEP is small but growing."

4. The term *cholo* is used to refer to members of a working-class youth subculture that spans the U.S.-Mexico border. Because of their distinctive slang and appearance, *cholos* are often presumed to be gang members, though this is not necessarily the case. For a pathbreaking study of *cholo* culture, see Valenzuela (1988).

5. Translation: "It begins to suit me that they call me 'Chicano,' man; it's like it makes you something, not just some greaser or *pocho*."

6. In CARA, the very important exhibit of Chicano culture that toured nationally in 1992, the exhibit book addressed two aspects of Chicano identity: (1) Chicanos as a politicized group, the political cognoscenti, those aware of their political, cultural, and economic status who are also engaged in bringing about change through various means; and (2) Chicanos as mestizos, who identify overwhelmingly with the Indian component of their cultural and racial heritage (Dennis Bíxler-Márquez, personal communication, November 22, 1995).

7. According to Dennis Bíxler-Márquez (personal communication, November 22, 1995), "the civil rights movements and its Chicano offshoot, the Chicano movement, is at a juncture where the term, as you note, is appropriated and politicized—as in the CARA definition . . . the Movimiento ideologues in the 1960s and 1970s [declared] that Chicano should refer to individuals of Mexican ancestry who acknowledge with pride their Mexican heritage, particularly the Indian component, while acknowledging also that they live in the U.S. and/or are American citizens, and that American Culture and the English language also form part of their cultural identity. Thus, a Chicano is the result of positive synthesis of Mexican and American, in an acculturationist and additive way, which can be found projected in literary works like *The Autobiography of a Brown Buffalo,* as the resolution of a cultural identity crisis, as opposed to the assimilationist biography of Richard Rodríguez, *Hunger of Memory.*" Thus, for instance, Norma Alarcón (1990: 250) claims that "the name Chicana, in the present, is the name of resistance that enables cultural and political points of departure and thinking through the multiple migra-

tions and dislocations of women of 'Mexican' descent. The name Chicana, is not a name that women (or men) are born to or with, as is often the case with 'Mexican,' but rather it is consciously and critically assumed and serves as point of re-departure for dismantling historical conjunctures of crisis, confusion, political and ideological conflict and contradictions of the simultaneous effects of having 'no names,' having 'many names,' not 'know(ing) her names,' and being someone else's 'dreamwork.'"

8. Dennis Bíxler-Márquez (personal communication, November 22, 1995) comments: "The Chicano movement, while wanting to expand usage and acceptability of the term, at times constrained its spread when some of its leaders declared that Chicanos also have to be knowledgeable of their political and socioeconomic condition and be proactive in its improvement, often via radical means."

9. Of course, we have to know the particular performance or language game that was under way when the labels were being employed because, in some circumstances, the label "Hispanic" can be used to make a political statement. As Dennis Bíxler-Márquez (personal communication, November 22, 1995) points out: "Rudy de la Garza reports how Hispanic students at U.T.-Austin in the 1980s voiced a similar militant rhetoric and political concern to Chicanos in the 1960s, but identified themselves as Hispanics, because they were brought up when the hegemonic Hispanic label was widely in use, while 'Chicano' seemed to them to belong to an older generation of 'activistas.' . . . Thus, their identity is comparable in terms of politics and different only in label."

10. According to Dennis Bíxler-Márquez (personal communication, November 22, 1995), "There are . . . geographic factors that may affect the use of Chicano. In academic circles, El Paso is located between two regions that use different ethnic labels, with some overlap. Texas typically has used Mexican American. Look at its universities, and you'll find only El Paso has Chicano Studies. Even U.T.-Arlington, with José Angel Gutiérrez, former head of the Raza Unida Party, has a Mexican American Studies program. California has Chicano or Raza Studies. The Rocky Mountain corridor's large cities use Chicano Studies: Metro State at Denver, UNM in Albuquerque, UTEP, and UNAM in Mexico City. I believe the latter to be the result of California not Rocky Mountain institutions' influence. These institutions tend to influence the students that attend them. The stronger the curriculum program the stronger its influence on students, many of whom do not adopt (or reject) an ethnic identity label until they take Chicano Studies courses."

11. In this regard, Dennis Bíxler-Márquez (personal communication, November 22, 1995) makes the following observation: "Albert's situation in a maquila probably forces upon him to some degree the rejection of Chicanos, as he probably works for Anglo bosses, with and for Mexicano bosses, over and with Mexicanos. His rejection may stem from being the odd man out with ethnic groups that in a variety of ways 'demand' that he display a 'correct' ethnic and national identification. He's likely been asked, 'in case of war between Mexico and the U.S., on which side would you fight?' Chicano, Mexican American, Hispanic, et cetera, do not satisfy that acid test [for Mexicans], since these labels imply national allegiance to the U.S., not Mexico." The question about the imaginary war between Mexico and the United States was very prominent in many of my interviews in Juárez.

12. The Second Ward (which most people refer to as *Segundo Barrio*) is the oldest Mexican barrio in town. All across the city it is regarded as the epitome of Mexican poverty.

13. According to Dennis Bíxler-Márquez (personal communication, November 22, 1995), this "neutrality" was precisely the reason the Chicano movement rejected the term in the 1960s: "Chicano ideology in the 1960s and 1970s rejected the term Mexican-American as assimilationist and contributing to the notion of not being Mexican or American. The first step toward rejection was the abolition of the hyphen. The cultural and political transformation of 'Chicano' as a replacement for Mexican American came next."

References

Acuña, Rodolfo. 1988. *Occupied América: A History of Chicanos.* New York: Harper and Row.

Alarcón, Norma. 1990. "Chicana Feminism: In the Tracks of 'the' Native Woman." *Cultural Studies* 4, no. 3: 248–256.

Althusser, Louis.1971. *Lenin and Philosophy and Other Essays.* London: New Left Books.

Barrera, Mario. 1979. *Race and Class in the Southwest: A Theory of Racial Inequality.* Notre Dame: University of Notre Dame Press.

Brah, Avtar. 1992. "Difference, Diversity and Differentiation." In *Race, Culture and Difference,* James Donald and Ali Rattansi, eds. London: Sage Publications, 126–145.

Chabram-Dernersesian, Angie. 1993. "And, Yes . . . the Earth Did Part: On the Splitting of Chicana/o Subjectivity." In *Building with Our Hands: New Directions in Chicana Studies,* Adela de la Torre and Beatríz M. Pesquera, eds. Berkeley: University of California Press, 34–56.

Foucault, Michel. 1970. *The Order of Things: An Archaeology of the Human Sciences.* New York: Vintage Books.

Gonzáles, Manuel G. 1989. *The Hispanic Elite of the Southwest.* Southwestern Studies no. 86. El Paso: Texas Western Press.

Gramsci, Antonio. 1971. *Selections from the Prison Notebooks.* Quintin Hoare and Geoffrey Nowell-Smith, trans. and eds. London: Lawrence and Wishart.

———. 1975. *Quaderni del carcere.* Turin: Valentino Gerratana.

Hurtado, Aída, and Carlos H. Arce. 1986. "Mexicans, Chicanos, Mexican Americans, or Pochos . . . ¿Qué somos? The Impact of Nativity on Ethnic Labeling." *Aztlan* 17, no. 1: 103–130.

Laclau, Ernesto. 1991. *New Reflections on the Revolution of Our Time.* London: Verso.

Laclau, Ernesto, and Chantal Mouffe. 1985. *Hegemony and Socialist Strategy: Towards a Radical Democractic Politics.* London: Verso.

———. 1987. "Post-Marxism Without Apologies." *New Left Review* 166: 79–106.

Limón, José. 1981. "The Folk Performance of 'Chicano' and the Cultural Limits of Political Ideology." In Richard Bauman, *"And Other Neighborly Names": Social Process and Cultural Image.* Austin: University of Austin Press, 197–225.

Montejano, David. 1987. *Anglos and Mexicans in the Making of Texas, 1836–1986.* Austin: University of Texas Press.

Mouffe, Chantal. 1985. "Hegemony and Ideology in Gramsci." In *Culture, Ideology and Social Process: A Reader,* Tony Bennett et al., eds. London: Open University Press, 219–234.

Oboler, Suzanne. 1995. *Ethnic Labels, Latino Lives: Identity and the Politics of (Re)Presentation in the United States.* Minneapolis: University of Minnesota Press.

Parker, Ian. 1989. "Discourse and Power." In *Texts of Identity,* John Shotter and Kenneth J. Gergen, eds. London: Sage Publications, 56–69.

Staudt, Kathleen. 1998. *Free Trade? Informal Economies at the U.S.-Mexico Border.* Philadelphia: Temple University Press.

Valenzuela, José Manuel. 1988. *¡A la brava ese!* Tijuana: Colegio de la Frontera Norte.

Vila, Pablo. 1997. "Narrative Identities: The Emplotment of the Mexican on the U.S.-Mexican Border." *Sociological Quarterly* 38, no. 1: 147–183.

Volosinov, V. N. 1973. *Marxism and the Philosophy of Language.* New York: Seminar Press.

Weedon, Chris. 1989. *Feminist Practice and Poststructuralist Theory.* Oxford: Basil Blackwell.

Part 4

Debordering and Rebordering

10

New Relationships Between Territory and State: The U.S.-Mexico Border in Perspective

Mathias Albert and Lothar Brock

The formation of sharply defined, mutually exclusive territories is one of the fundamental features of the modern, state-based world. More than anything else, a change in the territorial order would challenge the modern international political order.

The language analyzing this change is dazzling. Friedrich Kratochwil (1986) and John Ruggie (1993) see the increasing number of transborder phenomena as an "unbundling" of the territorial state. Ivo Duchacek, Daniel Latouche, and Garth Stevenson (1988) talk of "perforated sovereignty." Peter Taylor (1995) seeks to describe the state as a holed container. States as spheres of power are coming under strain, and their ability to regulate economic and societal developments in the framework of fixed territorial boundaries is waning. The diminishing regulatory competence translates into a loss of social competence and cohesion. In the face of ongoing transnationalization of social relations, the problem is aggravated by mounting difficulties in regulating the relationship between citizen and state via the instrument of citizenship in its prevalent form.

We propose to analyze these developments as an expression of debordering processes in the world of states, by which we mean an increasing permeability of borders together with a decreasing ability of states to counter this trend by fortifying border controls. However, new political spaces are emerging that transcend territorially defined spaces without leading to new territorial demarcations (i.e., to simple shifts in borderlines). In this sense, traces of a debordering of the world of states may be found in the institutionalization of "governance without government" (Rosenau 1992) or the creation of multilevel systems of governance consisting of transgovernmental and transstate networks that link parts of governments and substate actors across borders.

In referring to (incipient) debordering processes, we do not speak of the disintegration but rather of the modification of the territorial bases of politics. Furthermore, this modification does not progress in a continuous and ubiquitous fashion. Our analytical approach remains open to countervailing trends manifesting themselves in new militant fights over borderlines and new border demarcations. To be more precise: we regard the simultaneous occurrence of debordering processes and new demarcations as one of the core issues. We refuse to elevate this simultaneity of contradictory tendencies to the rank of a universal dialectic. Yet we realize that the factual debordering processes in the world of states do proceed as a diffusion of patterns of collective orientation, which may bring about a new spirit of an open, more cosmopolitan communality but also the desire for new rigidities of intercommunal demarcations.

To what extent can a dominant trend be identified among the broad mass of contradictory developments? To what extent, given their mutual dependence, can the processes of debordering and demarcation under discussion be understood in terms of an evolution of world society? We analyze these questions in two ways: first, through conceptual discussions of debordering in economy, state, and society; and second, through illustrations of this phenomenon, primarily in North America and Europe.

Democratization and Debordering: Historical Perspectives

The formation of the modern system of states can be understood as the gradual enforcement of the principle of territoriality. This view implies that territorial amalgamation and demarcation do not fulfill the same function at all times and have not always had the same significance as far as the organization of public life is concerned.

The multifarious border demarcations in history and the diversity of concepts of territoriality can scarcely be overlooked. The borders of the Roman empire and of ancient China, despite their solid physical markers (limes, walls), did not in practice constitute hard-and-fast demarcations but rather zones of transition between the empire and the surrounding world. In contrast, the borders of modern states are divisions between political entities of equal legal status. The borders themselves are regarded as inviolable.

The feudal system of medieval Europe was founded not on a territorial but on a functional partition of political space. There emerged a complex division of labor between secular power and papacy, between feudal lord and peasant, and in the transition to the modern era, between city and country. In the Middle Ages, kings, dukes, archbishops, and bishops could all render feudal service to one and the same person. A patchwork of interwoven, overlapping, redundant areas of power emerged, involving varying and sometimes conflicting relations of loyalty.

In contrast, a central aspect of the formation of the modern system of states was the gradual establishment of the territorial contiguity and equal legal status of each of the respective spheres of power, with central control of internal territorial affairs and unambiguous requirements in terms of loyalty. The Peace of Westphalia (1648) marks the transition to this modern system of political rule—a system that, at the time, already carried within itself the germ of its eventual spread across the whole world. The Holy Roman Empire of the German nation was nothing but a veil that wafted across from the previous age into the modern era. It could not mask Europe's new image for very long, even if, in Germany and Italy, territorial contiguity of political space was not achieved until the nineteenth century.

One looks back into the past to envisage alternatives to the present system. But where should the path out of the modern era and into the postmodern era take us? One possible vista opens up if a more precise definition is given of territoriality. Territoriality is, as Robert Sack observes, "the geographical expression of social power" (1986: 5). The aim is to control people and resources by demarcating a particular area—in other words, curtailing free access. Territoriality is also aimed at ensuring the security and well-being of those who live in the territory, preserving communities, and strengthening the ability of the latter to assert themselves in the international or global competition for scarce resources.

Space is a general referential system for ordering our thoughts, our perceptions, our feelings. Territoriality, a particular way of arranging social relations, has become dominant in the modern age. It has acquired a ubiquitous influence on the options that are available in the modern era for endowing meaning, for attaining self-assurance, for shaping identity, and also for being able to exist in society. Demarcation vis-à-vis the Other becomes an important element in the constitution of a self or, to put it generally, of a modern subjectivity. In so doing it converts a striving for security into ownership-based thinking. Territoriality not only transforms power spaces into territorial states by means of abstract, spatial lines; through the necessary regulation of ownership claims in the form of abstract property rights, it also reaches right into the structure of social relations within these borders.

Under the pressure of debordering processes within the world of states, territorial determinants of social life and the political process are beginning to break down. They are being represented in other forms, which in their turn are beginning to allow new combinations. In terms of an ideal type in the Weberian sense, this re-combination could mean that the public tasks with which every society is faced would come to be viewed in state-transcendent and functional rather than territorial terms. Economic and political regions would take shape whose essence lies not in a national border (understood as a physical line persisting in space) but in the growth of communication, transportation, and economic activity along purely abstract lines tracing transaction flows instead of delineating territories. Areas of joint responsibility would emerge, taking the place of territorial spheres of influence. Transnational coalitions, in which state and nonstate actors collaborate in varying constellations, would take shape around particular issues or public concerns. The spatial differentiation of states would also change internally. Still speaking in terms of an ideal type, all this would take place not in the form of intensified provincialism or local patriotism but as a functional decentralization of social practice and as the restoration of public spaces. In order to understand this incipient change, we discuss three dimensions of debordering processes in what follows: economy, multiple states, and society.

Debordering the Economy

Although the world economy and the world system of states evolved together, there is a tension between the two that became particularly marked in the forms of protectionism and trade wars in periods of crisis like the 1930s and 1980s. In the context of increased globalization, that tension is growing even more acute as a result of the rigidity of national borders. The function of these, in this chapter's context, is to mobilize and safeguard economic potential. Yet by virtue of what is in economic terms arbitrary territorial demarcation, the rigidity of national borders blocks the full realization of economic potential. It raises the transaction costs of international economic relations.

Reactions to these problems are multiple. One method is to internationalize production. Another is to institute globally agreed-upon reductions in trade restrictions. A third is to conclude regional agreements instituting free trade areas such as the North American Free Trade Agreement (NAFTA), or, as in the case of the European Union (EU), economic integration. With approaches such as these, borders are circumvented, obstacles resulting from the existence of borders are reduced, or borders are shifted from the internal relations between the states in a particular group to the external relations between these states and third countries. In this latter case, an economic debordering takes place in the internal relations of the states concerned.

A general debordering of what were formerly known as "national economies" is taking place as a result of the globalization of economic activities and the formation of new international economic centers at local (subnational) and regional (transnational) levels. By globalization, we mean the transition from the internationalization of production to global sourcing; the incorporation of all economic activities into a global relationship of competition, with increased capital concentration and partial cooperation between major rivals associated in strategic alliances; the formation of a worldwide financial market combined with a revaluation of invisible trade; and a resultant pressure on all states to adjust their own economic structures to the worldwide economic situation. Multinational corporations and financial institutions should not be regarded as stateless bodies, given that they are still subject to the control of the states within which they operate or of their home countries. In this sense, the world economy does not theoretically have any "offshore" zone in the strict sense of the word, lying entirely outside the borders of existing national economies. However, the transnational activities of large global players do effectively invalidate state controls. Even more important, the national provenance of multinationally operating firms ceases to have any bearing on their strategic planning and, above all, on taxation.

Globalization is not happening evenly all over the world as a result of the emergence of dynamic centers of international economic development at the sub- and transnational levels. The territorially segmented world economy is being transformed into a functionally partitioned space with globalized locations (world cities) and transnationalized regions (Sassen 1991).

Debordering is here viewed as a reflection of the uneven distribution of locational factors, combined with a revaluation of the locational issue in the wake of stiffer competition on the world market. It is true that one of the driving forces of globalization consists precisely in the efforts of businesses to reduce their dependence on factors that they cannot control: in other words, to ensure they can act globally. Global action always has a local dimension, however, and businesses cannot just choose as they please in this matter. They have only a limited capacity to play economic locations and their political representation against one another because they themselves are interested in operating in particular regions. Business does not simply gain in scope what the state loses through the material erosion of its sovereignty. In fact, the ability even of the major global players to act autonomously or to exert a controlling influence on the conditions governing the development of the world economy is limited, despite international concentration of capital and the formation of strategic alliances. The new forms of cooperation and communication at the global level are better described as networks and "flattened hierarchies" than as a centralized command economy operated by a handful of strategic groups. Only from this standpoint can one explain the genuine scope that exists for local and regional politics.

Debordering States

In his well-known article, Kenichi Ohmae asserts that, in a borderless world, "the nation-state has become an unnatural and dysfunctional unit for organizing human activity" (1993: 78). In Europe, North America, and the Middle East as well as Southeast Asia, he claims, intranational and transnational zones of economic growth and technological innovation are emerging that break the bounds of the international territorial-state order. For Ohmae, therefore, the task of states is to create the legal, social, and infrastructural conditions that will ensure that these economic zones achieve their full potential and to refrain from any other kind of intervention. In Ohmae's vision, the world of states is transformed into a world of marketplaces that is no longer steered by political ideas and interests but by the desire of customers to secure their needs. This, in Ohmae's world, can only occur through the interactive communication of all market participants. The retreat of the state, not its transformation, is the message. The citizen turns into a consumer.

Arguing from the perspective of political geography, Taylor puts forward a thesis more akin to the idea of new political spaces. He claims there are signs of a long-term transition from interstate to transstate relations. Such a transition would involve the convergence of two differing trends: on the one hand, the formation of capital control centers that transcend state economies and create a world network of flows in which political boundaries count for little; and on the other, the growth of new social movements operating on a global scale. The activities of these groupings, says Taylor (1995: 13), are examples of the increasing "evasions of sovereignty" and the emergence of "global political agendas in which the states are not central players." In Taylor's view (he here bases himself on Hopkins 1990), U.S. hegemony has played a decisive role in fostering those forces, which he contends are now transforming the world of states. What Taylor postulates is not the retreat of the state as envisaged in Ohmae's liberal strategy but a marginalization of interstate relations as a determinant of social life because of the actions of nonstate actors (social movements, major urban centers).

Some worry, as does Ralf Dahrendorf (1994), that this new localism and regionalism will lead to nothing more than a fragmentation of the world of states, multiplication of conflicts, and decreased willingness to seek ordered compromise and assume social responsibility. Ours is a different view. What is involved is the transformation of that world by means of a tempering of territoriality as an organizational principle. The decisive factor, in our view, is not how far intrastate competences between territorially distinct entities are preserved or newly distributed but how new forms of reciprocal action emerge between economy, politics, and society, which are shaped more by functional needs and less by territorially determined notions of identity and difference. Commenting on the new regionalism, James Rosenau (1995: 27) says:

> It seems clear . . . that cities and microregions are likely to be major control mechanisms in the global politics of the twenty-first century. Even if the various expectations that they replace states as centers of power prove to be exaggerated, they seem destined to emerge as either partners or adversaries of states as their crucial role becomes more widely recognized and they thereby move from an objective to an intersubjective existence.

States, hardly fixed entities, do change. A relevant case in point is Mexico's evolving definition of economic nationalism. Another is the EU, which is now accepting the spread of a transnational regionalism following an initial period of reluctance. However, although the changes to the German constitution (Basic Law) necessitated by the Maastricht Treaty resulted in a considerable increase in the say that the *Länder* (states) have in the federal government's Europe-related decisions, those original centralized state competences that are associated with the claim to sovereignty continue to exist.

Debordering Society: Transnational Communities and Coalitions

According to estimates produced by the International Labour Organisation in 1992, about 100 million people were living outside their native countries at the beginning of the 1990s. Their number could rise to 500 million early in the next century. Compared to world population, these are not particularly impressive figures. What makes them significant, however, is that migration, like globalization, is not taking place evenly but is concentrated in particular places and societies. Here, transnational communities are being formed that occupy, not territorially but culturally or ethnically, delimited spaces.

> Transmigrants . . . develop and maintain multiple relations, familial, economic, social, organizational, religious, and political, that span borders. . . . Transmigrants take actions, make decisions, and feel concerns within a field of social relations that links together their country of origin and their country or countries of settlement. (Glick Schiller, Basch, and Blanc-Szanton 1992: ix)

Transnational communities exist in, and at the same time beyond, the world of states. They transcend the classical categorizations of population and territory and thus escape the application of the instrument by which that categorization is achieved—citizenship. As far as the world of states as a system of theoretically equal and sovereign political entities is concerned, the granting of citizenship is a constitutive element. It aids external demarcation in its usefulness for the internal functioning of the state, that is, for the maintenance of public order. That is why one of the essential features of citizenship is that its award is not arbitrary but selective. To what extent should the role and award of citizenship be adapted to the emergence of transnational communities? Recently, publications have burgeoned on this topic, with the reflections on citizenship being embedded in the current debates about nationalism, culture, identity, gender, and ethnicity (see Chapters 3 and 6 in this volume).

The reason for the growing interest in citizenship is seen not simply in the spread of transnational communities per se but also in the changes that have taken place in the global context within which that spread is occurring. Besides those who migrate, globalization affects also those who are left behind and those whose societies become the object of major immigration. Under the pressure of international competition, social cleavages within states deepen. Beyond those cleavages, immigration puts further strain on social budgets, infrastructures, and value orientations. Thus, multicultural pressures on the existing, if imagined, social identities of immigrant societies and the intranational repercussions of the tightening international competition for foreign markets and capital work hand-in-hand to discard the idea of social equity across intrastate classes and regions. While immigrant societies continue to view themselves as communities of interests, values, and cultural habits distinct from others, the sociocultural and economic basis of this identity erodes. As a result, the states' internal social equilibrium is threatened.

In addition, the national community of interests, values, and cultural habits is being pervaded by a new universalism in consumption, involving globally standardized world goods and world news (CNN) and the propagation of a unitary *Weltlebensgefühl,* or worldwide sense of life (music and dance as delivered by MTV). Furthermore, there is the confrontation with new threats to individual prospects of well-being (environmental destruction, internationalized crime, new diseases, new fundamentalisms). In sum, even in the economically dominant countries, people experience the emergence of a unified world order that runs counter to the narrative constructions by means of which the nation-state, national economy, and national society present themselves as the (almost) holy trinity on which life is founded.

Sections of national societies are reacting to globalization and its challenges by organizing themselves to act as champions of global causes such as the safeguarding of human rights, democratization, equality, and the preservation of an environment that is conducive to the preservation of life. In these domains, new forms of cooperation are emerging, sometimes through interaction with governmental associations, conferences, and negotiating processes. Thus, transnational coalitions that present a new challenge to politics in the world of states, if not to the world of states as such, are appearing alongside transnational communities. Transnational communities derive their identity not so much from their national origins as from the fact that they suffer collective homelessness. Their "ethnicity" is not simply a throwback to premodern times; it can be interpreted as an attempt to gain a foothold in the new society without necessarily aspiring to becoming a lifelong member of it. Global sourcing increasingly refers not only to capital movement but also to the movement of labor in search for jobs. In this way, transnational societies are also transitory societies. As such they may have a deeply disturbing effect on the established members of the immigrant societies. Chauvinism and political separatism feed on this disturbance.

In addition to the spread of transnational societies, transnational coalitions and networks form that aim at getting the world of states to adjust to new problems and challenges. These transnational communities ideally converge in promoting both internal differentiation and a tempering of external demarcation, thus creating new spaces in which meaning, self-localization, and public commitment take shape.

As a parallel to multiple statehood, one could speak here of multiple identities of the individual and of social groups. The alternative would be to look not for a spread of multiple identities but for the formation of ever more complex identities that would enable the individual to withstand ambivalence and to transform contradictory experiences into learning processes (see Chapters 8 and 9 in this volume). We shall not opt for one or the other view here, but we do wish to point out that debordering, understood as the dissolution of clear territorial demarcations during the period of radical change at the end of the modern era, extends to configurations that, like the territorial state, can also be regarded as building blocks of the modern world order. One such configuration is the construction of a unitary, unfragmented subjectivity.

The creation of new public spaces that use up less energy on demarcation and thus open up more opportunities for organizing communal life is a utopian project on which far-reaching, concrete expectations hang. In Chapter 6 of this volume, Kathleen Staudt, Angélica Holguín, and Magda Alarcón analyze community renewal among Mexican-heritage borderlander residents, not all of whom are citizens. Elizabeth Meehan (1993: 1), talking about the EU, says:

> My thesis is . . . that a new kind of citizenship is emerging that is neither national nor cosmopolitan but that is multiple in the sense that the identities, rights and obligations, associated . . . with citizenship, are expressed

through an increasingly complex configuration of common community institutions, states, national and transnational voluntary associations, regions and alliances of regions.

Debordering and demarcation processes set stages for new activities at borders, some promising and far-reaching, but simultaneously other contradictory trends undermine them, as we see in the next section.

New Roles for Borders

The above observations regarding economic, political, and social debordering point to a change in the function of borders. In the new scheme, borders would cease to act as separators and transit zones but would change into spaces of economic cooperation, political-cum-institutional innovation, and transnational communication. We see this change documented in the relevant literature focusing on the Americas. Lawrence Herzog, for example, perceives a sea change in the development of border regions. The time of the Maginot and Siegfried lines, he says, is over: "The most obvious change has been the shift from boundaries that are heavily protected and militarized to those that are more porous, permitting cross-border social and economic interaction" (1992: 5). Border regions have, says Herzog, changed from being peripheral areas to being the focus of new expectations in regard to growth:

> Where once boundaries were seen as marginal spaces in a world that was largely organized around centrist nation-states, the late twentieth century has seen the old system fade away; in the new global territorial order, boundary regions may become centers of production and urban life. Thus a new form of city has evolved: the international border—or transfrontier metropolis. (1991: 520)

Drawing on Saskia Sassen, Kathleen Staudt discusses the former Paso del Norte (Juárez–El Paso) as an "aspiring global city" (1998). Similarly, the European Commission (1992), in *Europe 2000,* sees increased evidence that cities and regions are linking up in new networks in order to strengthen their position within the world economic system networks, which cut through or overarch traditional political borders.

Various transborder economic regions have emerged, the most noteworthy being Mexico's export-processing zone in 1965 and NAFTA in 1994 (although NAFTA does not stipulate proximity to the border as a condition of trading privileges for multinational companies). In this volume, Chapters 5 and 6 unearth the complex layers of interaction between the two sides, elucidating the broader dimensions of U.S.-Mexico cross-border interaction.

In the case of (Western) Europe, the increased regard for and promotion of the regions, and consequently also the promotion of transborder cooperation between substate actors, has been included in the policy of European integration since the end of the 1980s. At the same time, the number of transnational link-ups at the regional level has risen significantly.

The efforts, notably of the German *Länder,* to counter political centralization in the EU member-states in the wake of further integration have strengthened interests in the other EU countries to decentralize political systems. With the aid of the Committee of the Regions, different subdivisions of states will be able to work together to extend their scope of action in relation to central governments and to improve their access to the new central bodies in Brussels. The heterogeneous nature of the committee will not necessarily be a hindrance in this regard. It may rather be seen as an advantage because the multilayered nature of the interests represented in the committee and the way in which they are represented makes it more adaptable in its dealings with the commission and Council of Ministers. There is a redundancy of options for action, allowing problems to be tackled in a variety of ways.

In 1990, the Linkage Assistance and Co-operation for the European Border Regions (LACE) was created. It is administered by the Association of European Border Regions (formed in 1971), which has thereby won EU "recognition" and acquired an enhanced status. LACE represents the kind of link-up and reciprocal interpenetration of public and nonpublic levels of action that is here interpreted as a debordering of the state, in the sense of a breaking down of existing rigidities. Local authorities, chambers of commerce, trade unions, and all other institutions and initiatives wishing to promote transborder cooperation may take part in LACE.

In 1990, the INTERREG program was launched as well; it provides funds for structural adjustment and development in border regions. These funds may be applied for by the various associations of border regions that currently exist across the whole integrated area and also in the areas adjoining some external borders. Allen J. Scott (1988:13) sees in this development a change of paradigm in the European policy of integration toward border regions. In our view, it signals an erosion of territoriality as a device for ordering social relations.

In North America, too, the activities of substate actors in the domains of foreign policy and foreign trade are on the increase. New institutions and new patterns of communication are being created that simultaneously bridge two sets of dividing-lines, those between states and those between public and private institutions and groupings. This trend is more advanced on the U.S.-Canada border than on the U.S.-Mexico border, with the drifting apart of the peripheral regions of Canada lending particular weight to the north-south linkage between the east (Quebec), the center, and the west (British Columbia) (Duchacek, Latouche, and Stevenson, 1988).

Conceptually, the most fascinating entity here is undoubtedly Cascadia, the West Coast region. It stretches from Alaska down to and including Oregon, which also has affinities with northern California, where the southern part of the state, on account of its proximity to Mexico and Central America, is regarded as the source of all evils. Up to now, Cascadia has taken the form of a number of mixed organizations and initiatives. These include the Pacific Northwest Economic Region, an association comprising the governments of the participating U.S. states and Canadian provinces; the Pacific Corridor Enterprise Council, a private-sector regional organization; and the Cascadia Transportation/Trade Task Force, a strategic alliance of urban centers in the south of the region. The International Center for Sustainable Cities is also involved at the Cascadia level. The perceived challenge is to strengthen Cascadia's position on the world market while respecting the precepts of ecological sustainability, which in turn is seen as a means to improve or maintain the attractiveness of the area for local and external investors.

Ecological issues also play an important role on the U.S.-Mexico border, but more in terms of disaster prevention than of creating an actual utopia. The maquiladora program of industrialization launched in 1965 not only boosted economic growth, chiefly on the Mexican side of the border, but also it resulted in an enormous increase in environmental problems. This was one of the reasons for the creation of a Border Environmental Cooperation Commission (BECC) in 1994, in accordance with an agreement concluded by the United States and Mexico within the framework of the NAFTA negotiations. The activities of the BECC, which is based in Ciudad Juárez, are financed by the North American Development Bank (NAD Bank), which was also set up as part of NAFTA. The composition of BECC's executive committee once again conveys the now-familiar picture of the linking of the state with the nonstate and of the national or international with the local levels of action. The board of directors includes representatives of the International Boundary and Water Commission (a binational U.S.-Mexico organization set up in 1944), the border states, the border districts, and the inhabitants of the border areas. The board meets quarterly and is required to hold public meetings at similar intervals, in order to ensure the public of its representation in BECC's work.

The inclusion of environmental issues (and issues concerning working conditions) in the NAFTA negotiations is due to the formation of a transnational alliance of nongovernmental organizations, individual specialists, and ad hoc local authorities, among others. They secured a voice in the NAFTA negotiations through trinational public relations work and the systematic lobbying of the relevant governments. This instance of influence on interstate negotiations is undoubtedly one of the most important examples of the significance that the formation of transnational alliances can have in shaping interstate politics.

As far as the activities of the U.S. states in the domains of foreign politics and foreign trade are concerned, there are signs, as in Europe, that such substate entities are gaining in self-confidence as international actors. This trend was set in motion by, among others, the Kennedy administration, which sought to involve the resources of the U.S. states and of its North Atlantic Treaty Organization (NATO) partners in international development cooperation. As at the *Land* level in Germany, what has resulted is a carefully targeted policy of safeguarding and promoting industrial locations in the context of harsher competition on the world market. Although the process of transborder political innovation in North America does lag behind developments in Europe, we can generally agree with Daniel Elazar (1984: xix) that "the transformation of the international system from one in which politically sovereign states under international law were the only legitimate actors to one in which other entities, particularly the constituent states of federal systems, are also involved is one of the major developments of the post–World War II period."

Countertendencies

Change is not quite as clear-cut as may appear in view of the previous observations. Countertendencies exist, a few of which are mentioned here. First of all, we should remind ourselves that globalization proceeds hand-in-hand with a new protectionism and new strategic trade policies aimed at shielding the national economy from outside competition and at fostering national competitiveness in world markets by political means. In this respect, economic debordering in the world of states seems to work against a debordering of the world of states. This observation is only partly modified by the new (globally oriented) regionalism: the "local content" provisions through which Mexico sought to expand its industrial production before liberalization reappear in the framework of NAFTA. The formation of transborder economic spaces between Mexico, the United States, and Canada is being promoted, but this happens by way of creating common external borders designed to attract foreign capital and at the same time to shield parts of the regional economies against global competition.

It is also untrue that globalization leads to straightforward political innovation. The political process follows its own specific dictates in relative autonomy vis-à-vis the development of the world economy. The believers in transborder cooperation can only dream of seeing the measures they consider necessary (like joint regional planning) translated into reality. As in other domains, the actual course things take depends to a not inconsiderable extent on the people involved. These people involve mayors, or sometimes a single person who is responsible for the city's economic relations with a whole region. Monetary devaluations, such as the Mexican peso crisis that surfaced in January 1995, also wreak damage on regional interchange. And then, of course, there is the intensification of border controls that began at the U.S.-Mexico border in 1993.

Empirical studies conducted on the "narrative identities" of U.S.-Mexico border residents show that the self-images, political attitudes, and behavioral patterns of the transnational communities mentioned previously cannot simply be inferred from their ethnic origins. In fact, those who have "made it" by migration tend to distance themselves from those who may follow, rather than to show solidarity toward them (Vila 1994). There seems to be ample evidence that the much-discussed phenomenon of ethnicity is a means not of essential but of instrumental demarcation from the immigrant society. The purpose of such instrumental demarcation may well be to achieve integration by way of self-assertion. In this case there could be no talk of Mexamerica as a "nation" (Garreau 1981).

Recently, Mexico has authorized dual nationality for emigrants to the United States. It seems that this way Mexican emigrants are to be encouraged to become U.S. citizens by offering them the possibility of retaining all the rights of a Mexican citizen, excluding the right to political participation. As citizens of the United States, the emigrants would then be able to look after their interests better than they could as aliens, and they would have a better chance to improve their economic status. They would also have an incentive to pass more of their economic prosperity back to Mexico. Viewed this way, the formation of transnational communities would become a tool in Mexico's promotion of its own interests!

Such migration problems not only occur on the U.S.-Mexico border but are also to be found in the avant-garde area of radical change, namely, the EU. Examples here are the Schengen Agreement and the recently instituted entry restrictions introduced by the individual states (asylum regulations). The arguments about these regulations show that borders have by no means become obsolete as a result of globalization. Borders are still embattled not only in Bosnia or East Timor, in the Peruvian/Ecuadorian rain forest or the steppe and mountain areas of the former Soviet Union, but also at Frankfurt airport and other centers of the world economy, which are both levers and social flashpoints of postindustrial development. Although universalistic-minded "regionalists" such as Ohmae (1993) and Darrel Delamaide (1995) present us with amazing maps of a poststate era, national thinking, following the end of the East-West conflict, has once again become a subject of discussion in places where it was considered to have been largely resolved.

It follows that debordering clearly cannot be understood as a straightforward linear process. It is accompanied by demarcatory processes that may be regarded as regressive phenomena (in the sense of the aftereffects of a long history of territoriality) but also as consequences of debordering and as functional adjustment to it.

The World of States and World Society

We suggested earlier that globalization, while fostering debordering processes in the world of states, may also lead to debordering of the world of states, thus providing starting points from which to structure the question of continuity and change in international relations. Three dimensions of debordering were distinguished: the economic, the political, and the social. We also cautioned, with illustrations, that developments are not proceeding in a straightforward manner and that debordering is accompanied by demarcation. How do these countervailing trends relate to one another?

We distinguish three structural elements of international relations, or of what has up to now been vaguely termed the world of states: the international system, the society of states, and world society. The international system is currently characterized by complex interdependence and the society of states by anarchy kept in check by a process of regime formation. The "world society" element, on the other hand, relates to the nature of international relations as a multilayered network. We here see the network as a metaphor for the reciprocal interpenetration of territorially and functionally defined spaces and for a mixing of interstate and transstate patterns of interaction. The intention here is not only to highlight the fact that in any analysis of the external behavior of states, account must also be taken of internal factors. Our prime object, rather, is to make sure that the indistinct nature of the divisions between state and nonstate levels of activity and between the political, economic, and social-cultural spheres (which should also be regarded as enjoying relative autonomy) is taken into consideration. Networks do not render the question of the control of economic and political power invalid, but rather they make new forms of control necessary, as we illustrated earlier. This has to be taken into account when it comes to network design. Our concept of "world society" is intended to draw attention to just these aspects of the new developments (see, for example, Albert, Brock, and Wolf forthcoming).

Within both the society of states and world society, a process of community formation occurs on the level of state and nonstate entities and is

characterized by the claim of particular historical, cultural, ethnic, or ideological affinities. Communities are always particularist; the formation of a
global "international community" should therefore be viewed as unlikely, if
not impossible. This is another reason why we talk of "world society." The
strengthening of the "world society" element may cause the demarcatory
tendencies between different state or nonstate communities to increase, as
seems to be the case when one looks at relations between the great cultures
of the world (the Islamic world, the Christian world). The theses advanced
by Samuel Huntington (1993) in this regard cannot simply be dismissed as
enlisting religion for political purposes. However, demarcation can mean
many different things. In its mildest variant, it would mean "only" a more
pronounced awareness of one's own cultural traits; in the worst case, it
would mean attempts at mutual repression and annihilation.

Our structural scheme is also a developmental model to the extent that
we assume that, as globalization proceeds, interdependence will grow deeper, regime formation will continue, and the blurred area between state and
transstate levels of activity, between state, economy, and society, will grow.
Here, new areas of public life will emerge in which the identity of the
actors and their behavior will become in part interchangeable: states will
behave like businesses, businesses like states; communities will mask as
societies and societies as communities (both in the Weberian sense).

It is not at all our intention to neglect the various processes of transnational community formation. They are indeed an integral part of world society formation. We do, however, counsel against idealizing everything nongovernmental and transnational in terms of a positively weighted concept
of community. There are transnational communities that promote their
interests through sociocultural demarcation and transnational alliances that
come together in order to defend or promote universalist values (peace,
democracy, human rights, the environment). Both, however, are not per se
"good." Transnational communities can be just as blinkered as national
ones, and many universalist alliances also serve special interests.
Furthermore, the growing competence and political weight of international
nongovernmental organizations also increase the vested interests in these
organizations. Therefore, we do not regard it as sensible to juxtapose governmental and nongovernmental organizations on normative grounds.

We see tendencies toward the formation of world society at those
points where state freedom and ability to subject the whole of international
relations to its control are declining and territoriality is losing its centrality
as a controlling device. We work on the assumption that the evolving soci-
etization of the international system will reduce the likelihood of interstate
wars because of the increasing fuzziness of borders and the decreasing danger of an interstate polarization of interests. However, this is not a foregone
conclusion because when the borders between inside and outside are indis-

tinct, people find it difficult to orient themselves, and new efforts at demarcation result, expressing an existential yearning for sharp distinctions and a clear view of a muddled situation.

Yet the simultaneous occurrence of debordering and demarcation does not in itself signal a zero-sum game. We view the processes of demarcation described previously as social phenomena within the framework of an overall debordering of the world of states that is prompted by the globalization of the economy, communications, transportation, consumer expectations, and attitudes about life. One can go a step further and describe the demarcation phenomenon as a specific reaction to the debordering processes that are actually taking place. Tightened border control stems illegal crossings in monitored border space, but crossing increases elsewhere. Viewed in this light, demarcation would be, first and foremost, a way of regulating the process of transformation, not of arresting it.

Borders are lines of encounter rather than of isolation. They are a way of regulating proximity, not distance. In the debordering process, we must ask: what new forms of social regulation are coming into being to replace the old ones? Multiple interests in dynamic power relations are the stakes we need to examine.

Note

We would like to thank Kathy Staudt for her substantial editorial revisions to this chapter.

References

Albert, Mathias, Lothar Brock, and Klaus-Dieter Wolf, eds. Forthcoming. *Reconfiguring World Society.*

Ashley, Richard K. 1989. "Living on Border Lines: Man, Poststructuralism and War," In *International/Intertextual Relations: Postmodern Readings of World Politics,* James Der Derian and Michael Shapiro, eds. Lexington, Mass.: Jossey-Bass.

Czempiel, Ernst-Otto. 1991. *Weltpolitik im Umbruch.* Munich: IAFA.

Dahrendorf, Ralf. 1994. "Europe der Regionen." *Merkur* 45, no. 8 (August): 703–708.

Delamaide, Darrel. 1995. *The New Superregions of Europe.* New York: NAL-Dutton.

Duchacek, Ivo D., Daviel Latouche, and Garth Stevenson, eds. 1988. *Perforated Sovereignties and International Relations: Trans-Sovereign Contacts of Subnational Governments.* New York: Greenwood.

Elazar, Daniel J. 1984. "Introduction." *Publius* 14: 1–4.

European Commission (EC). 1992. *Europe 2000: Outlook for the Development of Europe's Territories.* Brussels: EC Directorate General for Regional Policy.

Garreau, Joel. 1981. *The Nine Nations of North America*. Boston: Houghton Mifflin.

Glick Schiller, Nina, Linda Basch, and Cristina Blanc-Szanton, eds. 1992. *Towards a Transnational Perspective on Migration*. New York: Annals of the New York Academy of Sciences.

Herz, John. 1957. "Rise and Demise of the Territorial State." *World Politics* 9, no. 4: 473–479.

———. 1968. "The Territorial State Revisited." *Polity* 1: 11–34.

———. 1976. *The Nation-State and the Crisis of World Politics*. New York: D. McKay.

Herzog, Lawrence A. 1991. "Cross-National Urban Structure in the Era of Global Cities: The U.S.-Mexico Transfrontier Metropolis." *Urban Studies* 28, no. 4: 519–533.

———. 1992. "Changing Boundaries in the Americas: An Overview." In *Changing Boundaries in the Americas,* Lawrence Herzog, ed. San Diego: UCSD and Center for U.S.-Mexican Studies, 3–24.

Holm, Hans Henrik, and Georg Sorensen, eds. 1995. *Whose World Order? Uneven Globalization and the End of the Cold War*. Boulder: Westview.

Hopkins, T. K. 1990. "Note on the Concept of Hegemony." *Review* 13: 409–411.

Huntington, Samuel. 1993. "The Clash of Civilizations?" *Foreign Affairs* (summer): 22–49.

Krasner, Stephen. 1994. "International Political Economy: Abiding Discord." *Review of International Political Economy* 1, no. 1: 13–19.

Kratochwil, Friedrich. 1986. "Of Systems, Boundaries, and Territoriality." *World Politics* 39, no. 1: 32–37.

Meehan, Elizabeth. 1993. *Citizenship and the European Community*. London: Sage.

Ohmae, Kenichi. 1993. "The Rise of the Region State." *Foreign Affairs* (spring): 78–87.

Rosenau, James. 1995. "Governance in the Twenty-First Century." *Global Governance* 1: 13–34.

Rosenau, James, and Ernst-Otto Czempiel, eds. 1992. *Governance Without Government*. Cambridge: Cambridge University Press.

Ruggie, John Gerard. 1993. "Territoriality and Beyond: Problematizing Modernity in International Relations." *International Organization* 47, no. 1: 174.

Sack, Robert D. 1986. *Human Territoriality: Its Theory and History*. Cambridge: Cambridge University Press.

Sassen, Saskia, 1991. *The Global City*. Princeton: Princeton University Press.

Scott, Allen John. 1988. *New Industrial Spaces: Flexible Production Organization and Regional Development in North America and Western Europe*. London: Pion.

Staudt, Kathleen. 1998. *Free Trade? Informal Economies at the U.S.-Mexico Border*. Philadelphia: Temple University Press.

Taylor, Peter J. 1995. "Beyond Containers: Internationality, Inter-stateness, Interterritoriality." *Progress in Human Geography* 19, no. 1: 1–15.

Vila, Pablo. 1994. "The Construction of Social Identities in the Border: Some Case Studies in Ciudad Juárez/El Paso." In *Sociological Explorations: Focus on the Southwest*, Howard Daudistel and Cheryl Howard, eds. Minneapolis: West, 51–64.

11

Conclusion: Rebordering

David Spener and Kathleen Staudt

The fall of 1993 was an auspicious moment for Mexico, the United States, and the border between them. The North American Free Trade Agreement (NAFTA) had been signed by Presidents George Bush and Carlos Salinas de Gortari, as well as Canadian prime minister Brian Mulroney. The U.S. Congress was in the middle of a rancorous debate over whether to ratify the agreement, and the result was in doubt. Local political leaders and businesspeople in the border region voiced their support for the agreement; in the preceding years they had already begun to reach across the border to their counterparts on the other side to promote binational commerce and cooperation. Mexican American businesspeople, in particular, believed that their cultural and social connections across the border presented them with unique opportunities to prosper with the advent of free trade (Spener 1995, 1996). Leaders of pairs of U.S.-Mexican cities along the international line regarded their metropolitan areas as the crucible for North American economic integration and had come to accept and even celebrate the social integration that accompanied close economic ties.

In El Paso–Ciudad Juárez, for example, civic leaders planned a series of cultural and artistic events under the rubric "We Are All *Fronterizos*," which was to culminate in a "Day of Unity" on October 10 when both mayors would sign a "good neighbors" convention on the international line marked on the "Free Bridge" connecting Mexico and the United States (Bean et al. 1994).[1] In many ways, the border was arguably "open" to all who wished to cross it in El Paso del Norte. As was the rule elsewhere, Mexican authorities routinely admitted southbound entrants from the United States with no inspection of citizenship or immigration documents. Many long-term residents of Ciudad Juárez were either U.S. citizens or

233

U.S. legal permanent residents or possessed a border-crossing card that permitted them to travel up to 25 miles into the United States on an as-desired basis.

People from Juárez who lacked entry documents for the United States could cross an essentially unguarded border: every morning beneath the Santa Fe international bridge, a "water taxi," consisting of an old rowboat and oarsman, ferried Mexican passengers across the Río Bravo del Norte/Río Grande into downtown El Paso for a small sum. Many of the passengers using this service were women on their way to work as domestic help in the middle-class neighborhoods of the Texas city (see Quintanilla and Copeland 1996; Nathan 1987; and Romero 1992 for a description of Mexican commuter maids in El Paso). For those who were even less fearful of detection by the U.S. authorities, it was often possible to walk north across one of the international bridges on the wrong side (i.e., against the flow of southbound pedestrian traffic) and thus avoid the immigration checkpoint (Bean et al. 1994). The U.S. Border Patrol *was* present and active in the area but spent most of its time chasing down suspected unauthorized entrants around the neighborhoods and outskirts of El Paso. Considered a largely ineffectual and, at times, rogue force by many in the community, its intimidation and harassment of Mexican American residents had been the subject of a successful lawsuit brought by students of one of the local high schools (Bean et al 1994; Staudt 1998: 96–97).

Operation Blockade: A Watershed Moment in the History of the Mexico-U.S. Border

The apparent nonexistence of the border came to an abrupt end on the morning of September 19, 1993, when Silvestre Reyes, recently appointed chief patrol agent for the El Paso sector of the U.S. Border Patrol, ordered the launching of Operation Blockade.[2] This operation sought to put an end to unauthorized border crossings by Mexicans in the urbanized portions of the El Paso sector by stationing hundreds of agents and vehicles along 20 miles of the international line itself. Reyes and the Border Patrol launched the operation without consulting local officials and took residents of both cities by surprise. Highly effective, the operation dramatically reduced unauthorized border crossings into the city of El Paso. Greeted with dismay by Mexican officials, both local and national, and with howls of protest by Juárez residents, the blockade appeared to be immensely popular in El Paso, where many Anglos and U.S.-born Mexican Americans applauded bringing the border back "under control."[3]

Soon it was discovered, however, that the blockade was leading the undocumented to cross the border around the ends of the blockade, particularly at Puerto Anapra, Chihuahua and Sunland Park, New Mexico, and over Monte Cristo Rey, a mountain that straddled the border. These spots were located to the west of El Paso, past where the Río Grande turned north and the international boundary was little more than a line in the sand. In order to stem the flow of undocumented persons through this area, on October 10, 1993, the Border Patrol proposed building a 2.8-kilometer steel wall on the slopes of Monte Cristo Rey in the vicinity of Puerto Anapra. Reaction to this proposal was swift and largely negative on both sides of the border. The Mexican consul general in El Paso called it "an unjustifiable aggression." The Mexican press dubbed it as a proposal for "the border's own Berlin wall." On the U.S. side, the governor of New Mexico, El Paso's congressional representative, and a variety of business and other nongovernmental organizations condemned the proposal as sending "the wrong message" to Mexico on the eve of NAFTA. The "Day of Unity" signing ceremony, which, coincidentally, had been scheduled for October 10, was cancelled. The mayors of both El Paso and Ciudad Juárez issued official statements opposing the idea of building any new walls along the border (Bean et al. 1994: 10–11).[4]

Although no one may have realized it at the time, in retrospect Operation Blockade seems to have been as much of a watershed event in the history of the U.S.-Mexico border as the creation of the North American Free Trade Area. It has, after all, been generalized all along the border, in the form of Operations Río Grande and Gatekeeper, the building of a wall between *ambos* (both) Nogales, and the use of military troops to halt cross-border drug traffic. In the interior of the United States, the blockade has been transmogrified into California's Proposition 187 and the 1996 federal welfare reform law. That the creation of the free trade area and the blockade took place almost simultaneously constituted an irony that was not missed by human rights activists concerned with the treatment of Mexican migrants: wasn't it a contradiction—and an unjust one at that—to be opening the border to the movement of goods and services but not to people? Didn't economic integration also imply important social integration? Or, as some left activists were quick to point out, wasn't all this open border talk just an ideological veil being lowered over the eyes of the working classes on both sides—a border open to capital but closed to workers? In this sense, the arrival of NAFTA and the accompanying clampdown on the border were quite explicable: before free trade, U.S. capitalists did not have unfettered access to cheap Mexican workers. It was necessary, therefore, to "import" Mexican workers into the United States. Now, with the Mexican state opening its territory to unfettered foreign investment, U.S. capital had a greater interest in keeping Mexican workers in Mexico, which constituted something of a low-wage labor reserve for manufacturing. In fact, at the time of the blockade, some cynics speculated that the Border Patrol was actually in cahoots with the operators of maquiladoras in Ciudad Juárez, who complained that they were faced with a shortage of assembly workers at the going rate of pay.[5] Perhaps if *juarenses* were kept from working in El Paso, they would have no alternative but to accept maquiladora employment. Other commentators of a different ideological persuasion insisted that because of their tremendously different levels of income and development, it was simply inconceivable to have a social as well as an economic union between the United States and Mexico—this was not Europe, after all (Weintraub 1992).

The Dialectic of the Border

In Chapter 10, Mathias Albert and Lothar Brock introduced the notion of "debordering" with regard to the "world of states," where debordering refers to "an increasing permeability of borders together with a decreasing ability of states to counter this trend by fortifying border controls." Although they recognize that "militant fights over borderlines and new border demarcations" accompany debordering processes, Albert and Brock decline to elevate such struggles to "a universal dialectic." In this concluding chapter, however, we take up the present transformations of the U.S.-Mexico border as an example of such a dialectic and push their line of analysis a step further toward universality.

In Chapter 1, we argued that borders in their various territorial and social manifestations are a fundamental aspect of the human condition and are simultaneously the object and product of sociopolitical struggle. Here we continue that line of argument by introducing the term *rebordering* to denote the countertendencies to debordering identified by Albert and Brock (using the term *demarcation*). By rebordering, we mean processes that involve the reassertion or rearticulation of socially constructed boundaries, both territorial and nonterritorial. The dialectical cycle the debordering-rebordering antimony implies is one in which an existing boundary is challenged and penetrated (debordered), only to be reestablished, repositioned, or reconfigured in a new guise in response to a competing set of interests (rebordered).[6] Viewed in this way, borders are never "finished"; rather, they are inherently processual, that is, in a constant state of becoming. In this light, events such as Operation Blockade can be seen as a specific moment in a dynamic historical process.

In addition, by using the term *rebordering,* we strive to emphasize the multidimensionality of boundaries. In our formulation, boundaries are not so much made more permeable, rendered less relevant, or done away with altogether so much as their position, function, and differential permeability in one or more of their dimensions are rearticulated as the outcome of contestation. In fact, the notion of the dialectic may be too limiting to accommodate our vision of rebordering, if we think of the dialectic strictly as the relationship between only two polar opposites, between thesis and antithesis: contestation may actually be considerably more complex, involving multiple contradictions among several groups of opposing interests, each with its own vantage point, agenda, and amount of power relative to other groups. Thus, for example, creation of the North American Free Trade Area may imply freer transborder movement of money and some (but not all) types of products, as well as of investors, businesspeople, and certain types of employees, while at the same time tighter controls are placed on the cross-border movement of other products and persons, such as Asian consumer goods and working-class Mexican migrants.

In the remainder of this chapter we will further examine debordering and rebordering processes as they relate to the international boundary between Mexico and the United States. In the interest of brevity and simplicity of presentation, we limit our discussion to the social realm and more specifically to the question of bordering-rebordering as it relates to the movement and status of Mexican nationals on either side of the international line, although examples could just as well be drawn from economic, political, and cultural developments in the region. A considerable amount of new evidence about both processes has emerged in the last year or so, particularly with regard to efforts by the U.S. government to reassert control over its southern border. Much of the evidence we present is drawn from newspaper accounts, since relatively few academic studies to date have been able to provide more detailed accounts of recent developments along the border.

Debordering

The evidence with regard to Mexico and the United States seems to point overwhelmingly to the force of this process. In many ways, the border is a case of "imagine no line" instead of "a Maginot line" separating the two countries (Avalos and Welchman 1996). The movement of people across the border has been and remains breathtaking. In 1996, 280 million legal land crossings were made from Mexico into the United States, making this border one of the busiest in the world (Spener 1997b). Cross-border commuting in the binational twin cities—to work, shop, use services, or socialize—was routine and large-scale and was facilitated by the possession of a U.S.-issued border-crossing card by more than 5 million Mexican residents (U.S. Information Agency 1997). In addition to border-crossing cards, U.S. consulates in Mexico issued 508,400 temporary, "nonimmigrant" visas to Mexican nationals in fiscal year 1996, which further facilitated cross-border movement of persons (Spener 1997b). Around 40,000 residents of

Tijuana alone worked routinely in San Diego County, California (*San Diego Dialogue,* cited in O'Connor 1997b), and hundreds of managers of U.S.-owned maquiladoras lived in the U.S. border cities across the border from the plants whose operations they supervised. As many as 400,000 U.S. nationals resided in Mexico at least part of the year by 1997, with many of them retirees—more U.S. Social Security recipients reside in Mexico than any other foreign country (Emling 1997). In addition, many "Mexican" residents of Mexican border cities are U.S. citizens by birth, having been born to Mexican mothers in hospitals or midwiferies on the U.S. side. Others have become U.S. citizens by marriage or have inherited U.S. citizenship from a parent or even a grandparent.[7]

Néstor Rodríguez (1996: 23) argues that Mexican migration to the United States has built "transnational structures" that function "as if the border did not exist," and his position is illustrated by recently published reports. The number of Mexican-born persons residing in the United States has increased phenomenally over the past twenty-five years: in 1970, 760,000 Mexican nationals resided north of the border; by 1980, the number had risen to 2.2 million; by 1990, it had nearly doubled to 4.3 million; and by 1996 it was estimated that between 7.0 and 7.3 million Mexican immigrants were living in *el norte* (Spener 1997b; Gelbard and Carter 1997).[8] Although in 1990 the great majority of Mexican immigrants (85 percent) still lived in just four states—Arizona, California, Illinois, and Texas—during the present decade Mexican immigrants have fanned out to the farthest reaches of the United States, including Alaska, Arkansas, Florida, Georgia, Iowa, Maine, Maryland, Nevada, New Jersey, New York, and even Hawaii (Spener 1997b; Cooper 1997; Gelbard and Carter 1997; McDonnell 1998). They found work in agriculture, construction, the meat-packing industry, labor-intensive manufacturing, and personal services. Many were recruited by representatives of agricultural and manufacturing companies at the border, and others were successfully smuggled across the border by organized rings, sometimes at the behest of employers (Spener 1997b; Cooper 1997; Marks 1997; "Border Patrol" 1998; Wilgoren 1997).

The presence of several million Mexican nationals working in the United States has given rise to many businesses that facilitate cross-border travel and communications. An example is found in Houston's Magnolia section, the site of one of the city's oldest Mexican communities, where a major boulevard is lined with the terminals of Mexican bus companies that link migrants via direct connections to points all over Mexico as well as to cities throughout the United States, including such "new" destinations as Atlanta, Georgia, and Raleigh-Durham, North Carolina. According to one published report, "the demand for bus seats across the border has reached an estimated four million annually, growing by about 20 percent a year"

(Myerson 1997). Greyhound, the dominant interstate bus carrier in the United States, is now seeking to enter the "transborder" market: the company's chief executive officer recently led his board on a tour of the Mexican terminals of Houston and is attempting to develop a partnership with at least one of the cross-border carriers (Myerson 1997). Wire-transfer companies are located in areas of Mexican settlement in the United States and facilitate remittances to Mexico that totaled U.S.$2.5–$3.9 billion in 1995, an amount equivalent to over half the foreign exchange earned by Mexico through direct foreign investment during that same year (Spener 1997b). Mexicans residing in the United States can communicate with friends and family still "on the other side" by telephone and fax and can listen to Mexican megawattage radio stations and watch their favorite Mexican television shows on Spanish-language networks (Rodríguez 1995). Some are long-distance commuters, who live in the United States for a week, two weeks, or a month at a time and return home to their families in Monterrey, Hermosillo, or Tijuana at regular intervals (see Myerson 1997, for example). Others, such as the *poblanos* living in New York City, the *zacatecanos* in Los Angeles, or the *coahuilenses*, *guanajuatenses*, and *potosinos* in San Antonio, remain active in their communities on both sides of the border (Silva 1997; Smith 1992, 1998; these identities refer to Mexican states of origin). And, of course, many Mexicans, especially young men, sojourn as workers in the United States on a periodic basis without ever establishing permanent residence north of the border.

Should we assume that this transborder social integration results mainly from "cracks" in U.S. border enforcement? Like Rodríguez (1996) and others, Carlos Vélez-Ibáñez warns that we should not:

> This point of view . . . places too much power in the dominating group and not enough in those being affected; it licenses without intent an idea that somehow domination "slips" and allows cracks so that those dominated have the opportunity to invent alternate options and histories that act in opposition. This idea eliminates agency from those dominated and induces a kind of victimization that may provide a morally superior position to those dominated but allows them no agency. Agency is allowed only by the fissures in the "dominating" process and not by the conscious organizational and mobilizing ability of cultural creators. (1996: 271–272)

Migrants and informal workers "counter" the hegemonies of nation-states, but their strategies to counter the petty hegemonic state regulations may very well feed other grand global hegemonies (Staudt 1998: 12–15, also chap. 8). It can be effectively argued that in many senses the state itself grants "agency" to Mexican *transmigrantes* through its policies with regard to migration and citizenship. We must remember a very large proportion, if not the majority, of the Mexicans who reside in the United States do so *legally*. From 1981 through 1995, over 3 million Mexicans were admitted to the United States as legal immigrants (around 2 million of these legalized their status as part of the amnesty program of the Immigration Reform and Control Act of 1986) (Gelbard and Carter 1997); 233,000 Mexican immigrants became naturalized U.S. citizens in 1996, shattering the previous single-nation annual record of 106,626 set by Italy in 1944 (Spener 1997b; McDonnell 1998). The Mexican government, in recognition of the reality that between 5 and 10 percent of its citizens reside permanently outside national territory, has recently amended its constitution to allow Mexicans abroad to keep their Mexican citizenship even after becoming citizens of other countries (Spener 1997b; McDonnell 1997; "Mexico Passes Law" 1996). Increasingly, Mexican politicians and the Mexican government have begun to pay attention to the needs of their constituents-citizens residing north of the border (Smith 1998). Thus, to a large extent, the "cracks" in the structure of domination may not be cracks at all, but rather state-sanctioned channels for transborder intercourse and integration.

Rebordering

Operation Blockade proved to be the avatar of a wave of rebordering between Mexico and the United States. That this rebordering has been imposed mainly by the United States or U.S. nationals is a reflection of the "asymmetry of power" between the two nations discussed by Jorge Bustamante (1989), who noted that with regard to border processes, those emanating from the United States tend to be predominantly proactive, whereas those emanating from Mexico are typically reactive. As is the case with regard to debordering, multiple instances of rebordering are present in current events. In this section we will discuss a few of these that have made the news, as well as others, drawn from our own research, that have not been highlighted in the press.

The most obvious indicators of rebordering involve the United States' efforts to exert a physical control over its southern border that has heretofore not been attempted. Although Timothy Dunn's (1996) pioneering work on the militarization of the U.S.-Mexico border shows how this "project" has antecedents that go back as many as twenty years or more, his account ends in 1992, a year before the project entered the new phase inaugurated with Operation Blockade. Still, his framework for analyzing border militarization as the U.S. government's attempt to control an insurgent subject population—Mexican migrants—remains quite apt. Autonomous transnational migrants, to use Rodríguez's term, "deborder" U.S. territory when they make unauthorized crossings of the international line and commune in unauthorized ways once inside the country. The state responds by attempting to reassert its sovereign right to exclude unauthorized migrants physically—either by arresting and forcibly returning them to Mexico (1.3 million in 1995 alone) (Spener 1997b) or by fortifying the international line with walls, fences, helicopters, floodlights, land vehicles, and additional Border Patrol agents, as in the case of Operations Blockade, Gatekeeper, Safeguard, and Río Grande (Bean et al. 1994; Haynes 1997; Immigration and Naturalization Service 1997; MacCormack 1997; O'Connor 1997a; Verhovek 1997b).[9] In the last five years, the U.S. Border Patrol has added 5,000 agents to its force (giving a total of 6,500) and the INS budget has doubled to $3.8 billion, most of which goes to its enforcement activities (Bettelheim 1997; Branigan 1997b). As this book goes to press, the Clinton administration has called for the hiring of 1,000 additional Border Patrol agents and for increasing the INS budget to a record $4.2 billion for the coming fiscal year (Copley News Service, February 3, 1998).

This "material" rebordering has not altogether halted unauthorized cross-border movements, but it has certainly made them far more difficult and expensive for undocumented migrants, who must make their crossings in more remote areas at greater physical risk and pay increasingly exorbitant rates to the *coyotes* who smuggle them (Bean et al. 1994; Eschbach, Hagan, and Rodríguez 1997; Haynes 1997; O'Connor 1997c; Reza 1998). In addition, the latest counterinsurgency efforts of the Border Patrol have been accompanied by the initiation of drug-interdiction operations at the border on the part of the U.S. military, with sometimes deadly consequences for members of the local population (see Herrick 1997b and Verhovek 1997a on two incidents involving troops firing on civilians, one of which resulted in the death of a young goatherd near Redford, Texas).[10] The United States' heightened commitment to halting the flow of illegal narcotics from Mexico has led it to embark on a new five-year plan to use high-tech X-rays and fences to keep drug shipments from entering Texas, Arizona, and California (Matthis 1997). The increased enforcement capacity of the Border Patrol has also made itself felt in locations in the U.S. interior, where roundups of undocumented Mexicans have occurred as far away from the border and from traditional areas of Mexican immigrant settlement as Colorado, Iowa, and Georgia (Callahan 1997; Bendavid 1997; Cooper 1997; Graham 1997). The Border Patrol's enforcement efforts have been bolstered not only by added resources and assistance from the military but by occasional vigilante action as well (see, for example, Herrick 1997a).

Rebordering has also taken the form of legislation designed to deny immigrants many of the social rights guaranteed to U.S. citizens, some of which they had previously enjoyed. The most prominent recent examples are California's Proposition 187, passed by voters in November 1994, and the federal welfare reform legislation enacted into law in 1996. The federal legislation made noncitizen immigrants ineligible to receive public welfare benefits such as food stamps, Supplemental Security Income, Medicaid, and the like. Proposition 187 was more far-reaching and barred undocumented youth from attending public schools in California, although enforcement of this provision has been blocked in the courts thus far (Armbruster, Geron, and Bonacich 1995). Also in 1996, the Illegal Immigration Reform and Immigrant Responsibility Act was signed into law. This act expedited the deportation without hearing or judicial review of most unauthorized migrants who had been apprehended by the INS, increased the criminal penalties applied to illegal migration, and raised the standards for suspension of deportation based on "extreme hardship" (Spener 1997b). Ten years earlier, the Immigration Reform and Control Act (IRCA) had for the first time established borders throughout the United States at the point of employment. Key IRCA provisions made it illegal for employers to knowingly hire immigrants who lacked proper work authorization and required all workers to present documents demonstrating their legal right to work as a condition of their employment.

There has been political resistance to rebordering in both the United States and Mexico. The Mexican government has objected to the new U.S. attitude and policies but has had little leverage to exercise on this matter, given its heightened economic dependence on its northern neighbor since the peso crash of 1994. Following the launching of Operation Blockade in El Paso–Ciudad Juárez, there were protests on the Mexican side and calls for boycotts of U.S. goods and businesses (Bean et al. 1994). In Mexico City, a McDonald's restaurant was vandalized by protesters enraged by the likely passage of California's Proposition 187 (Carroll 1994). In the United States, political resistance has shown its face in a number of forms. Latino high school students in California staged walkouts to protest Proposition 187's provisions denying public education to the undocumented. A massive march against the proposition, peopled mainly by Latinos, was held through downtown Los Angeles. Lawsuits were filed against its implementation (Armbruster, Geron, and Bonacich 1995; Smith and Tarallo 1995). Recently, when Governor Pete Wilson ordered prenatal healthcare benefits to be cut off for 70,000 undocumented women as part of Proposition 187's implementation, the California Primary Care Association (CPCA) directed its 250 member clinics to continue to provide care for all women, regardless of legal status (PR Newswire, January 29, 1998).[11] Since enactment of the federal welfare reform law in 1996, advocates for the poor and immigrant rights have lobbied for a restoration of food stamp benefits to legal immigrants (implementation of the law resulted in 935,000 immigrants losing their food stamps) (Dao 1998).[12] Recently, Latino residents of Chandler, Arizona, filed two separate lawsuits against the city government seeking a total of nearly $44 million for being "unlawfully stopped, arrested, interrogated, detained, searched, beaten, and/or deported" during a roundup of 432 undocumented Mexicans carried out in July 1997 in a joint operation by Chandler police and the Border Patrol (Magruder 1998). The Mexican American Legal Defense and Education Fund has filed a lawsuit to stop the Joint Task Force 6 project of the military and the Border Patrol to build 240 miles of roadway, twelve helicopter launch pads, and fifty high-tech lights along the border near Laredo, Texas, because the organization fears it could lead to increased illegal search and seizure of Mexican Americans in the area, as well as damage the environment they depend on (Schiller 1998).

In spite of this resistance, rebordering seems to be enjoying widespread support among the voting public in the United States; Silvestre Reyes, the chief patrol agent in El Paso and leader of Operation Blockade, was elected to Congress in 1996 on the wave of popularity he enjoyed in its aftermath; California voters passed Proposition 187 by a 3 to 2 margin; in Texas, a recent poll showed that 61 percent of respondents thought that the federal government was not doing enough to stop "illegal immigration" and that 86 percent of Anglos and 69 percent of Latinos thought illegal immigration was a "serious problem" (Herrick 1997c).[13]

The Deterritorialization of the Border

The presence of many thousands of Mexican migrants in communities in the U.S. heartland, the laws that have been enacted to exclude immigrants from the social rights of U.S. citizenship, and the enhanced ability of the INS to engage in surveillance and physical control of this population have combined to substantially deterritorialize the Mexico-U.S. border in ways that are as much material as they are metaphorical (see Chapter 8 in this volume, for metaphorical examples). The border is no longer located *only* on the international boundary, but anyplace and everyplace where Mexicans confront barriers to their full participation in U.S. social, economic, and political life.

Roger Rouse's (1991) comment that in the postmodern period we are witnessing the eruption of multiple "border zones" inscribed in U.S. social space presaged developments in the 1990s. Propelled by the strength of their historically developed transborder social networks (Massey et al. 1987; Massey and García-España 1987) and in response to deepening economic and political crises in Mexico and growing demand for their services on the part of employers in the United States, Mexican migrants have extended the geographic range of their communities and increased their numbers rapidly and massively in the United States. In so doing, they have prompted an intense reaction on the part of the U.S. government, whose traditionally ambivalent attitude toward Mexican *workers* has been overcome by a decidedly negative attitude toward Mexican *residents,* especially the Mexican poor who may impose a burden on the public budget at a time when the social welfare benefits to U.S. citizens themselves are being rescinded in the name of fiscal responsibility.

Indeed, an important piece of the puzzle in understanding the rebordering directed by the U.S. government toward Mexicans is to understand its leadership of the debordering of social citizenship (on citizenship conceptions, see Chapters 3 and 6 in this volume). As long as the government protected U.S. citizens and legal residents from the unrestrained operation of the marketplace—through food stamps, Aid to Families with Dependent Children, generous unemployment insurance, support of labor unions, subsidized housing, public works programs, Supplemental Security Income, and strong enforcement of workplace health and safety regulations and minimum wage laws—the citizens and residents thus protected might rationally choose to reject many jobs where the pay was too low or the working conditions too poor or both. This form of bordered "protectionism" practiced by the welfare state created a "need" for unprotected (i.e., "debordered") labor willing to pick crops, tend babies, wash dishes, and push wheelbarrows for a pittance. Under welfare state conditions, this unprotected labor had to be "imported," and Mexican workers willingly supplied it. In so doing, they arguably subsidized the affluent lifestyles of U.S. consumers.[14] Now, with the welfare state being rolled back to a startling extent, to the point where workers have no alternative but to accept whatever work they can in order to subsist, the special need for unprotected labor can be expected to decline (other things being equal). In fact, a recent General Accounting Office report considered the possibility that in the future growers in need of farm labor should hire U.S. citizens cut from the welfare rolls rather than continue to rely on immigrant workers, 40 percent of whom are undocumented (General Accounting Office 1997a; Simon 1998). In this way we can better comprehend the anti-immigrant politics embodied in the thunderous right-wing populism of a Pat Buchanan—no more welfare, no more immigrants, and especially no more welfare for immigrants.

The debordering of many of the economic relationships between Mexico and the United States, as exemplified in the provisions of NAFTA, also redounds in unforeseen ways on the status of Mexican immigrants in the United States. The garment industry provides an interesting case in point because it traditionally has recruited a female, largely immigrant workforce. Since the 1970s, international trade in garments has been governed by the Multifiber Agreement (MFA). The MFA strictly regulated where and with what tariff and quota implications different aspects of the binational production of garments could take place in the United States and Mexico (where it occurred largely under the auspices of the maquiladora program). Under MFA regulations, garment districts in the southwestern United States, such as the one in El Paso, were major producers of men's clothing, especially blue denim jeans. NAFTA substantially altered the quota and tariff arrangements governing the cutting, sewing, and finishing of these garments such that places like El Paso could no longer compete effectively with Mexican producers of the same garments in an increasingly price-sensitive market.[15] The result has been massive loss of garment jobs in recent years, with 5,000 or more lost in El Paso alone since the end of 1993 (Spener 1997a; Staudt 1998). At the same time, the growth of garment maquiladora employment in Mexico has been substantial, with nearly 54,000 net jobs added since the creation of NAFTA (CIEMEX-WEFA 1996).

Tragically, most of the workers losing their jobs in El Paso are middle-aged Mexican immigrant women, few of whom speak English well or have completed high school and most of whom are not U.S. citizens and thus are no longer eligible for most welfare assistance.[16] Ironically, many of these women previously labored in the garment maquiladoras before finding work in the United States, and some of them continue to reside in Ciudad Juárez, commuting across the international line to their jobs on a daily basis (Spener 1997a). Indeed, the U.S. industries where workers are most likely to lose their jobs to free trade (e.g., garments and electronics) typically feature low-paying, labor-intensive assembly in which immigrant workers are disproportionately concentrated. This places an ironic twist on Ross Perot's comment that NAFTA would create a "giant sucking sound" of "American" jobs heading south of the border.

Migrant Agency in the Face of Rebordering

In spite of the massive buildup of Border Patrol agents, high-tech infrastructure, and military force along the border, a 1997 General Accounting Office report stated that it was as yet impossible to determine whether the billions of dollars spent in this effort in recent years had actually reduced the flow of undocumented Mexicans into the United States (Branigan 1997a; General Accounting Office 1997b). Although it seems clear that rebordering has made unauthorized border crossing more difficult, it is also indubitable that Mexican migrants continue to live out their "crossover dreams" in massive numbers regardless of the deterrents placed in their way. That they persist in doing so is a testament both to the disparity in incomes and standards of living between the United States and Mexico and to the strength of migrant networks that span the border.

The continued flow of migrants is also a testament to the human smuggling and false documents industry, which has grown apace with U.S. rebordering efforts. There has long been a resale market for documents such as residency cards, birth certificates, and Social Security cards, a market that grew substantially after IRCA required employers to require job applicants to present work eligibility verification. Now, however, with the tightening of physical control over the border, we are witnessing a boom in the sophisticated manufacture of counterfeit or altered documents, including U.S. passports and visas. Although high-quality documents can cost thousands of dollars, there may be economies of scale to be gained in their manufacture that are bringing their price down. In Ciudad Juárez, for example, Mexican authorities recently raided the installations of a company that specialized in forging U.S. passports and other documents. This small operation did a U.S.$10,000 per week business selling counterfeit passports for the bargain rate of $70 each (Bizar 1998a). A woman interviewed by David Spener in 1997 confirmed the ready availability of such documents at a low price; she was in deportation proceedings in an immigration court and stood little chance of being allowed to remain in the United States. When asked what she planned to do if she was forcibly returned to Mexico, the woman—who came from a poor family and had little in the way of savings to show for her many years of working in the United States—said she would visit her family for a month or so and then return, stopping off to see her "cousin" in Monterrey who sold visas and passports.

The U.S. State Department and the INS are aware of the false documents challenge and are taking measures to curb their use by adding biometrics to border-crossing cards, making visas and passports harder to forge, and developing databases to monitor their use to enter and leave the country (see Martin 1997 for INS plans to monitor document use and U.S. entry/exit by Mexican nationals at the border crossing in Eagle Pass, Texas; see Bizar 1998b and U.S. Information Agency 1997 for introduction of the laser visa replacement of the traditional border-crossing card). This may not solve the problem, however, since the United States issues entry documents, including the widely held border-crossing card, based in large measure on applicants' presentation of *Mexican* documents that demonstrate their eligibility for the U.S. entry permit. These documents include birth certificates, diplomas, rent receipts, paycheck stubs, and letters from employers. While investigating the effects of Operation Blockade, for example, Spener came across informants who spoke of border-crossing cards that were issued after applicants purchased letters of employment, pay stubs, and so on from a petty official in the personnel office of a Juárez maquiladora. In this way, the U.S. document itself would be legitimate (Bean et al. 1994; U.S. concern with this issue was confirmed by a personal communication with Spener from David Hobbs, coordinator, Border

Biometrics Program, Bureau of Consular Affairs, U.S. Department of State, February 13, 1998).

Coyotes, the smugglers of human contraband, have become part of the folklore of the U.S.-Mexico border. In the past, they mainly aided unauthorized migrants in getting through the immediate border region in highly patrolled areas such as Tijuana–San Diego. Now, however, immigrant smuggling rings have become highly sophisticated operations that not only provide assistance in getting through the defenses of the Border Patrol at the international line but also transport migrants to cities and sometimes to jobs in the U.S. interior. In January 1998, for example, Border Patrol agents stopped three semitrucks in Imperial County, California. The trucks were carrying 417 unauthorized migrants bound for Los Angeles (Reza 1998). The owner of a Georgia t-shirt factory was indicted for smuggling Mexicans to work in his plant. The investigation of this smuggling ring began after Border Patrol officials stopped a van across the country in Hatch, New Mexico (Bendavid 1997). Of course, the most famous case of the smuggling of migrants to date involves the exploitation of deaf Mexicans as street peddlers in New York City, which involved a ring that linked points as distant as Mexico City, Los Angeles, New York, Chicago, and the small town of Sanford, North Carolina (McDonnell and Tobar 1997; Sexton 1997). Thus, we see how state-led rebordering begets another round of debordering efforts on the part of migrants and their hired service providers (or exploiters, as the case may be).

Of course, not all new debordering efforts on the part of migrants involve activities that are illegal in the United States. As noted above, Mexican immigrants have been legalizing their status and taking the oath of U.S. citizenship in record numbers. This may in part be due to worries about being cut off from state-provided income and services that have been a feature of internal rebordering in the United States. By becoming U.S. citizens, immigrants repenetrate the border separating them from the benefits of social citizenship and fell the border between themselves and full U.S. political participation as well. Already we may have seen some concrete political change as a result of this, as conservative (and anti-immigrant) Republican Robert Dornan lost his seat in Congress representing Orange County, California, to Democrat Loretta Sánchez, who rode the crest of a wave of new Latino votes in the district.

The Transnational Mexican Community: A Border Runs Through It

The presence of Mexico in the United States in the form of millions of Mexican migrants and their offspring seems as irreversible as the economic interdependence of the two countries, which features an enormous presence of U.S. companies and their personnel in Mexico.[17] Many Mexicans do indeed run their lives almost as if the border did not exist, and many more surely will in the future. At the same time, the border is a harsh reality that cuts through the Mexican community in a most intimate way, creating divisions that determine behaviors and identities. Indeed, the border is the defining feature of Mexican transnational communities, for the border is what makes them transnational, in effect. Four examples from our own research are illustrative.[18]

Example 1

In the spring of 1994, a Mexican man and woman from Durango lived in El Paso with their U.S.-born daughter and son. Both the man and woman moved to El Paso as unauthorized migrants in the late 1970s. They were poor in El Paso but much better off than they would be had they stayed in Durango. After IRCA, both applied for legalization, but an incompetent lawyer filed their application incorrectly so that only the husband was able to obtain his legal residency permit (they were still trying for the wife's permit, but it had not yet been approved, and they were short of money to pay a new lawyer to press their case). The family made visits to the woman's relatives in Durango at regular intervals, driving back and forth in their old station wagon. Because the wife/mother did not have legal papers to enter the United States, the rest of the family would drop her off on the bank of the Río Bravo in Juárez, drive across the international bridge into El Paso, and pick her up on the other side after she had waded or gotten a "water taxi" ride across. Since Operation Blockade was launched, family trips to Durango had ended, for it would be impossible for the woman to return to El Paso. Recent news reports confirm that tighter control of the border can actually work to "trap" Mexican migrant workers in the United States (Schodolski 1997). A study of Mexican migration conducted jointly by U.S. and Mexican researchers has concluded that cyclical migration between the two countries is on the wane, and that intensified patrolling of the border may be part of the reason (Spener 1997b).

Example 2

A woman from Tamaulipas who has been residing in Houston for over ten years is in danger of having the eldest two of her four children deported. She herself is a legal permanent resident of the United States. Her youngest two children are U.S. citizens, having been born in Houston while she was married to her second husband, from whom she has since separated. The older two, who are now teenagers and have spent little time in Mexico, were born in Tamaulipas and are the children of her first husband. Immigration attorneys whom we have interviewed tell us that half or more of the deportation cases they handle involve families in which some members are U.S. citizens or legal permanent residents.

Example 3

A family from rural Michoacán has its members split between Mexico City, a major Texas city, and their small hometown. The mother lives in a tiny shack without indoor plumbing on a *rancho* not far from Morelia. She has never been to the United States and has no papers that would allow her to enter the country legally. With her live several grandchildren, a grown daughter, and her youngest son, who is around eighteen years old. A grown son lives in Texas and is married to a Mexican American woman; he is a U.S. legal permanent resident who owns his own business and has children who are U.S. citizens. His sister and another of his brothers also live in Texas but have been picked up by the INS and are in deportation proceedings. The sister is married to a legal permanent resident from the state of Nuevo León, whose own father was the son of migrant workers and was born in Texas. This couple has a young daughter who is a U.S. citizen. The sister has not been back "home" in nearly fifteen years. Her younger brother—the eighteen-year-old who is living on the *rancho*—had come to live with them in Texas after crossing the border illegally. She had not seen him since he was a toddler. In Texas, he met many of his childhood friends who were now working and living there. Because he did not have working papers, however, he found it difficult to find steady employment and eventually returned to Michoacán.

Example 4

Various commentators have noted that distinctions in migration/citizenship status have created important social, cultural, and political divisions among the Mexican-origin population in the United States (Gutiérrez 1995; Vélez-Ibáñez 1996; Vila forthcoming; Villar 1994; and Chapters 5 and 9 in this volume). State-led rebordering may have the effect of intensifying these divisions among U.S. Mexicans, as illustrated by a January 1998 exchange of messages between subscribers to an electronic mail list server concerned with Latino issues in the United States. One Mexican-born subscriber posted a message expressing his displeasure with a public service announcement for a University of Utah Hispanic scholarship fund broadcast recently on a public television affiliate. According to his posting, the advertisement featured a young Mexican American (i.e., a U.S.-born person of Mexican ancestry) telling viewers he wanted them to know that not all Mexicans in the United States were troublemakers or "wetbacks." The subscriber, who was a graduate student at the University of Utah, reported that he had contacted university administrators to protest the use of the derogatory term "wetback" in the advertisement. He also urged all subscribers to the list server to contact the University of Utah and ask that the offending advertisement be taken off the air. Another subscriber to the list server, who was a Mexican American from South Texas, argued that although the use of "wetback" was unfortunate, it was quite understandable given the reality she encountered along the border:

> I am surprised that you would be offended by the commercial. What the student was explaining to the public is true. Not everybody is a wetback or a troublemaker. I do believe that the student could have used a better choice of synonyms. Down south close to the border in Río Grande City, Laredo, McAllen, Brownsville, Texas these are the exact words that are used to describe or refer to an individual that is in this country illegally. The other word that is used is "mocho." I have come to learn the reason these words are used. They are often used when referring to certain individuals due to the attitude that these individuals possess. For example, I know of a particular situation that is occurring at this moment in Laredo. The mother of a four year old child was put on a waiting list for over a year until there would be room for her child to be admitted in to the Head Start children's program. There were only five children that were born here in the U.S. that were enrolled in the program. The rest of the thirty-five were illegal aliens. On the weekends these families go back across the border to spend whatever monies or sell whatever products that were acquired through the government programs. This other woman whose child is still on the waiting list pays property taxes on a run down home, her husband is unemployed and is seeking employment, does not qualify for food stamps or AFDC because she owns a ratty old car. This is the reason for the name calling. . . . I get offended myself when someone tries to compare me with a individual from Mexico because right away I state we are not the same and we will never be the same.[19]

These words were written very close to the sesquicentennial of the signing of the Treaty of Guadalupe Hidalgo on February 2, 1848, the act that created the present border between Mexico and the United States. They were written by a woman who is the descendant either of at least one Mexican who crossed the border before the latest attempts to close it or a *tejano/a* (Texan of Mexican heritage) whose presence in the United States antedated the current border. We cannot and should not take her words as representative of the majority of the Mexican American community, for transcendance of the border *is* a reality for many of its members. At the same time, her sentiments and the untold number of Mexican migrants who have died attempting to cross the border demonstrate how this contested frontier exercises considerable force over the inhabitants of the space it divides. It most likely will continue to do so for the foreseeable future.

A Final Comment

Throughout Chapter 1 and now in this conclusion we have attempted to bridge the gap between material and metaphorical discourses on borders by pointing out the operation of border making and unmaking processes in varying aspects of social life. In doing so, we have also repeatedly emphasized the intrinsically conflictive nature of borders in general and of the U.S.-Mexico border in particular. In closing, we note that there is always a temptation to retreat from conflict, especially the kind of conflict that arises in encountering an intimate other. "I kiss good-bye the howling beast on the borderline that separated you from me," sang Bob Dylan in the aftermath of a failed love affair. About fifteen years ago, journalist Alan Riding wrote about the United States and Mexico as "distant neighbors." Although much distance remains between the two countries, there can be no doubt today that the fates of people residing on opposite sides of the international boundary are inextricably intertwined. Mexico and the United States are locked in a territorial embrace that precludes disengagement, no matter how much conflict arises in the relationship. Their shared border divides them but is also the ineluctable seam that binds them together. We conclude with the words of Carlos Fuentes (1997: 266), the great Mexican novelist, who at the end of his novel *The Crystal Frontier* reminds us that although the border marks the limits of commonality, it bespeaks a common destiny as well:

> to the north of the río grande
> to the south of the río bravo
> let the words fly
> poor México
> poor United States
> so far from God,
> so near to each other.

Notes

1. A similar type of event had taken place every February in Laredo/Nuevo Laredo for many years. Traditionally, the border separating the two towns had been opened for a joint festival on the occasion of Washington's birthday.

2. In response to objections from the local community, the name of the operation was subsequently softened to "Hold the Line."

3. Support for the blockade was far from universal in El Paso, however. As described by Staudt (1998: 163), when the U.S. Commission on Immigration Reform held hearings in El Paso in early 1994, a number of community leaders, including the Catholic bishop and officials of the local chambers of commerce,

expressed "grave concerns about the Blockade's impact on poverty, family interaction, and commercial exchange in the highly integrated twin cities of El Paso and Juárez." Spener also interviewed businesspeople, unionists, social workers, and community activists who opposed the blockade (Bean et al. 1994).

4. A fence has subsequently been built in this location.

5. The growing scarcity of young women willing to work in the maquiladoras has been documented by Brannon and Lucker (1989).

6. Víctor Zúñiga's account of the relation between a nation-state's internal and external borders (see Chapter 2) can be thought of as a manifestation of debordering-rebordering: in the process of constituting itself, the nation must at once eliminate internal boundaries that prevent the construction of a homogeneous national identity (a debordering task) and establish external boundaries that distinguish its territory and people from other nations (a rebordering task).

7. Immigration attorneys we have interviewed relate how they occasionally are able to save a Mexican client from deportation because he or she is a U.S. citizen but did not know it. These cases typically involve children or grandchildren of Mexican American citizens, that is, U.S. citizens by birth, but Mexicans by residence, language, and ethnicity.

8. The figures given by the 1970, 1980, and 1990 censuses may considerably understate the true number of Mexican immigrants residing in the United States at those times. For example, Jeffrey S. Passel (1985), found that between 20 and 40 percent of undocumented immigrants went uncounted by the 1980 census (cited in Woodrow and Passel 1990: 65). Even taking this cautionary note into account, the growth of the Mexican population in the United States has been extraordinary.

9. Of course, the buildup of force at the border itself reduces unauthorized entries by migrants, thus lowering the number of apprehensions and deportations.

10. These armed patrols by the military were halted in July 1997 following the fatal shooting of Ezequiel Hernández of Redford, Texas. Recent news stories have reported that the Pentagon plans to scrap armed patrols, although it will continue to engage in construction projects and reconnaissance missions along the border (Scripps Howard News Service, January 14, 1998).

11. According to the newswire report, "CPCA is a statewide association representing approximately 250 nonprofit community clinics, health centers and regional clinic consortia, including urban and rural clinics, migrant health centers and free clinics . . . [which serve] more than 1.3 million people."

12. In his most recent budget, President Clinton proposed to spend $2.5 billion over the next five years to provide food stamps to legal immigrants who were cut from the rolls by the 1996 law—though key Republican leaders in Congress opposed any such restoration (Dao 1998). As we go to press, the Republican majority in Congress has relented and many immigrants have had their access to food stamps restored.

13. That Texas has not followed California's example and enacted its own state anti-immigrant measures is a reflection of Texas' greater economic dependence on trade with Mexico. Texas trades with Mexico more than any other state in the United States, and the state's governing elite has been hesitant to promote measures that might jeopardize economic relations with its neighbor across the Río Grande.

14. Although it was not limited to Mexican immigrants, a 1994 study conducted by the Urban Institute, for example, found that "annual taxes paid by immigrants to all levels of government more than offset the costs of services received, generating a net annual surplus of $25 billion to $30 billion" (Fix and Passel 1994: 6).

15. Increased competition from Mexico was not the only consequence of NAFTA. The massive devaluation of the Mexican peso at the end of 1994 played a large role in tipping the scales toward increased garment production in maquiladoras. Currency devaluation, whether intentional or the result of economic mismanagement, can itself be seen as a debordering/rebordering process. When the peso takes on a high value relative to the dollar, Mexico's borders are more "open" to the entry of U.S. goods; when its currency is worth less relative to the dollar, Mexican goods more effectively penetrate the U.S. border. The substantial integration of the U.S. and Mexican economies along with their shared territorial boundary obliged the United States to intervene to shore up the value of the peso at a level that avoided destabilization of both countries' economies.

16. Immigrant garment workers who have been employed in informal sweatshops may be especially vulnerable when laid off. However hardworking those who work informally may be, new laws create the need for new documentation to verify that labor. In interviews Staudt conducted in 1998 for the University of Houston Center for Immigration Research's statewide study of the effects of the 1996 federal welfare reform, community leaders cited people's difficulties documenting their eligibility for Supplemental Security Income (SSI) (to be eligible for this benefit, immigrants must demonstrate forty quarters of employment in the United States). The employers who have hired immigrants to work for them as maids, gardeners, or agricultural laborers have been reluctant to provide their former employees with the documentation they need to demonstrate their eligibility for SSI. They fear that they may be prosecuted for nonpayment of Social Security taxes or minimum wages. (See also Staudt [1998: 74] for the usually minimal burdens that the privileged bear in the employer-employee relationship.)

17. In 1995, U.S. companies had 823 affiliates in Mexico, with total assets of over $59 billion and approximately 744,000 employees (U.S. Bureau of Economic Analysis, February 3, 1993, http://www.bea.doc.giv/bea/di/usdia-d.htm#usdia-2). By 1996, trade between the two countries had reached $131.1 billion annually, having more than doubled since the beginning of the decade (U.S. Bureau of the Census, January 31, 1998, http://www.census.gov/foreign-trade/sitc1/1996/c2010.htm#YTD).

18. Some of the details of these cases have been altered to protect the anonymity of the persons involved.

19. This posting was made in January 1998 on the list server "La Red Latina" at http://www.inconnect.com/~rvazquez/sowest.html. We contacted the writer of this message and received her permission to reproduce it here.

References

Armbruster, Ralph, Kim Geron, and Edna Bonacich. 1995. "The Assault on California's Latino Immigrants: The Politics of Proposition 187." *International Journal of Urban and Regional Research* 19, no. 4.

Avalos, David, and John C. Welchman. 1996. "Response to the Philosophical Brothel." In *Rethinking Borders,* John C. Welchman, ed. Minneapolis: University of Minnesota Press, 187–199.

Bean, Frank D., et al. 1994. *Illegal Mexican Migration and the United States/Mexico Border: The Effects of Operation Hold the Line on El Paso/Juárez.* Washington, D.C.: U.S. Commission on Immigration Reform.

Bendavid, Naftali. 1997. "INS Ties Mexican Smuggling Ring to Georgia Factory." *Chicago Tribune,* December 23, p. 1.

Bettelheim, Adriel. 1997. "Immigration Divides Nation: Issue Sparks Debate over Priorities, Money." *Denver Post,* December 21, p. A1.

Bizar, Jodi. 1998a. "Mexico Arrests 12 in Bogus Documents Raid." *San Antonio Express-News,* January 17, p. 19A.

———. 1998b. "Laser Visas Could Chafe Border." *San Antonio Express-News,* February 10, p. 1B.

"Border Patrol Breaks Up Immigrant-Smuggling Ring in Waco Raid." 1998. *San Antonio Express-News,* February 14, p. 13A.

Branigan, William. 1997a. "Border Control Strategy Difficult to Assess." *Washington Post,* December 15, p. A25.

———. 1997b. "INS Recruits Military Leader to Oversee Field Operations." *Washington Post,* December 31, p. A19.

Brannon, Jeffery T., and G. William Lucker. 1989. "The Impact of Mexico's Economic Crisis on the Demographic Composition of the Maquiladora Labor Force." *Journal of Borderlands Studies* 4: 39–70.

Bustamante, Jorge A. 1989. "Frontera México–Estados Unidos: Reflexiones para un marco teórico." *Frontera Norte* 1, no. 1: 7–24.

Callahan, Patricia. 1997. "INS Raid at Worksite Nets 58." *Denver Post,* May 13, p. B1.

Carroll, Paul B. 1994. "A McDonald's in Mexico City Is Trashed in Protest Against California Proposition." *Wall Street Journal,* November 9, p. A19.

CIEMEX-WEFA. 1996. *Maquiladora Industry Analysis.* Eddystone, Pa.: CIEMEX-WEFA.

Congress of the United States. 1986. *Immigration Reform and Control Act.* Washington, D.C.: U.S. Government Printing Office.

———. 1996. *The Personal Responsibility and Work Opportunity Reconciliation Act of 1996.* Washington, D.C.: U.S. Government Printing Office.

Cooper, Marc. 1997. "The Heartland's Raw Deal: How Meatpacking Is Creating a New Immigrant Underclass." *The Nation* (February 3): 11–17.

Dao, James. 1998. "Aliens Would Get Food Stamps Back in Clinton Budget." *New York Times* (electronic edition), February 2.

Dunn, Timothy J. 1996. *The Militarization of the U.S.-Mexico Border, 1978–1992: Low-Intensity Conflict Doctrine Comes Home.* Austin: Center for Mexican American Studies, University of Texas.

Emling, Shelley. 1997. "Americans Making Run for Border: Mexico Mania: From a Relaxed Atmosphere to a Lower Cost of Living, U.S. Citizens Are Finding Reasons to Relocate." *Atlanta Constitution,* May 7, p. A4.

Eschbach, Karl, Jacqueline Hagan, and Néstor Rodríguez. 1997. "Death at the Border." Working Paper WPS 97-2. Houston, Tex.: Center for Immigration Research.

Fix, Michael, and Jeffrey S. Passel. 1994. *Immigration and Immigrants: Setting the Record Straight.* Washington, D.C.: Urban Institute.

Fuentes, Carlos. 1997. *The Crystal Frontier: A Novel in Nine Stories.* New York: Farrar, Straus, and Giroux.

Gelbard, Alene H., and Marion Carter. 1997. "Mexican Immigration and the U.S. Population." In *At the Crossroads: Mexico and U.S. Immigration Policy,* Frank D. Bean, Rodolfo O. de la Garza, Bryan R. Roberts, and Sidney Weintraub, eds. Lanham, Md.: Rowman and Littlefield, 117–144.

General Accounting Office (GAO). 1997a. *H-2A Agricultural Guestworker Program: Changes Could Improve Services to Employers and Better Protect Workers.* Washington, D.C.: GAO.

————. 1997b. *Illegal Immigration: Southwest Border Strategy Results.* Washington, D.C.: GAO.

Graham, Steven. 1997. "INS Deports 500 Undocumented Immigrants in Sting." *Denver Post,* April 26, p. B4.

Gutiérrez, David. 1995. *Walls and Mirrors: Mexican Americans, Mexican Immigrants, and the Politics of Ethnicity.* Berkeley: University of California Press.

Haynes, V. Dion. 1997. "Increased Border Patrols Raise Risks for Migrants: Mexicans Take Dangerous Routes to Avoid Detection." *Chicago Tribune,* August 17, p. 3.

Herrick, Thaddeus. 1997a. "Armed on the Border: Ranchers Along Río Grande Take on Illegal Intruders Themselves." *Houston Chronicle,* November 2, p. A1.

————. 1997b. "Borderline Shootings: Two Cases This Year Raise Questions About Military's Role on Rio Grande." *Houston Chronicle,* June 22, p. A1.

————. 1997c. "Poll Finds Many Texans Want Troops on Border." *Houston Chronicle,* November 17, p. A1.

Immigration and Naturalization Service. 1997. "Fact Sheet: Operation Gatekeeper: Three Years of Results at a Glance." Press release, October 7.

MacCormack, John. 1997. "Patrols Beefed Up on Texas Border." *San Antonio Express-News,* August 26, p. A1.

Magruder, Janie. 1998. "Chandler Faces $8.7 Million in Claims Related to Roundup." *Arizona Republic* (electronic archive edition), January 24.

Marks, Alexandra. 1997. "Tight Border Aids People-Smuggling: Case in New York Shows How a Tighter Mexican Border May Lead to Exploitation." *Christian Science Monitor,* July 24, p. 1.

Massey, Douglas, et al. 1987. *Return to Aztlán: The Social Process of International Migration from Western Mexico.* Berkeley: University of California Press.

Massey, Douglas, and Felipe García España. 1987. "The Social Process of International Migration." *Science* 237: 733–738.

Martin, Gary. 1997. "INS to Test Tracking Program at Eagle Pass Border Crossing." *San Antonio Express-News,* December 5, p. 23A.

Matthis, Nancy. 1997. "High-Tech Plan to Zap Drugs: X-rays, Sensors to Be Set on Border with Mexico." *Houston Chronicle,* December 12, p. A4.

McDonnell, Patrick J. 1997. "Mexico Delays Dual-Nationality Plan 1 Year." *Los Angeles Times,* March 6, p. A3.

————. 1998. "Mexican Arrivals Seek New Frontiers: Far-flung Regions like Maine and Alaska Join in Witnessing Largest Sustained Mass Migration to U.S. of Any Group." *Los Angeles Times,* January 4, p. A1.

McDonnell, Patrick J., and Hector Tobar. 1997. "Mexicans Link L.A. to N.Y. Ring: Group Peddling Trinkets Smuggled Deaf Recruits into Southland and Sent Them East, Investigators Say." *Los Angeles Times,* July 23, p. B3.

"Mexico Passes Law on Dual Citizenship." 1996. *New York Times,* December 12, p. A8.

Myerson, Allen R. 1997. "Success of Mexican Bus Companies Eludes Greyhound." *New York Times,* December 18, p. D1.

Nathan, Debbie. 1987. *Women and Other Aliens: Essays from the U.S.-Mexico Border.* El Paso: Cinco Puntos Press.

O'Connor, Anne-Marie. 1997a. "INS Crackdown Expands into Imperial Valley." *Los Angeles Times,* October 8, p. A3.

————. 1997b. "On the Border: The Best of Both Worlds." *Los Angeles Times,* June 25, p. A3.

———. 1997c. "Thwarted Border Crossers Fill Tijuana." *Los Angeles Times,* January 17, p. A3.

Passel, Jeffrey S. 1985. "Undocumented Immigrants: How Many?" In *Proceedings of the Social Statistics Section of the American Statistical Association 1985.* Washington, D.C.: American Statistical Association, 65–71.

Quintanilla, Michael, and Peter Copeland. 1996. "Mexican Maids: El Paso's Worst-Kept Secret." In *U.S.-Mexico Borderlands: Historical and Contemporary Perspectives,* Oscar J. Martínez, ed. Wilmington, Del.: Scholarly Resources, 213–221.

Reza, H. G. 1998. "Border Patrol Seizes Undocumented in Big Rigs." *Los Angeles Times* (electronic edition), January 31.

Rodríguez, Néstor. 1995. "Lessons on Survival from Latin America." *Forum for Applied Research and Public Policy* (fall): 90–93.

———. 1996. "The Battle for the Border: Notes on Autonomous Migration, Transnational Communities, and the State." *Social Justice* 23, no. 3: 21–37.

Romero, Mary. 1992. *Maid in the U.S.A.* New York: Routledge.

Rouse, Roger. 1991. "Mexican Migration and the Social Space of Postmodernism." *Diaspora* 1, no. 1: 8–23.

Schiller, Dane. 1998. "Army, MALDEF Set for Court Fight." *San Antonio Express-News Online,* February 4.

Schodolski, Vincent J. 1997. "Migrants Feel Trapped in U.S.: Easy Border Crossings Impossible." *Chicago Tribune,* November 2, p. 3.

Sexton, Joe. 1997. "More Deaf Mexicans Are Found 'in Bondage' in North Carolina Raids." *New York Times* (electronic edition), July 26.

Silva, Elda. 1997. "Immigrants Organize to Help Less Fortunate Back Home." *San Antonio Express-News,* November 23, p. 12A.

Simon, Stephanie. 1998. "Growers Say U.S. Wrong, Labor Is in Short Supply." *Los Angeles Times,* January 5, p. A3.

Smith, Michael Peter, and Bernadette Tarallo. 1995. "Proposition 187: Global Trend or Local Narrative? Explaining Anti-Immigrant Politics in California, Arizona and Texas." *International Journal of Urban and Regional Research* 19: 664–676.

Smith, Robert C. 1992. *Los ausentes siempre presentes: The Imagining, Making, and Politics of a Transnational Community Between New York City and Ticuaní, Puebla.* Ph.D. diss., Columbia University, New York.

———. 1996. "Diasporic Politics at Home, Domestic Politics Abroad: Chicano-Mexican Relations and Transnationalism." Paper presented at the 91st Annual Meeting of the American Sociological Association, New York, August 20.

———. 1998 (forthcoming). "Transnational Localities: Community, Technology, and the Politics of Membership Within the Context of Mexican and U.S. Migration." In *Transnationalism from Below,* Michael Peter Smith and Luís Eduardo Guarnizo, eds. New Brunswick, N.J.: Transaction Publishers, 196–238.

Spener, David. 1995. *Entrepreneurship and Small-Scale Enterprise in the Texas Border Region: A Sociocultural Perspective.* Ph.D. diss., Department of Sociology, University of Texas at Austin.

———. 1996. "Small Firms, Social Capital, and Global Commodity Chains: Some Lessons from the Tex-Mex Border in the Era of Free Trade." In *Latin America in the World Economy,* Roberto Patricio Korzneiewicz and William C. Smith, eds. Westport, Conn.: Praeger, 77–100.

————. 1997a. "The Unraveling Seam: NAFTA and the Decline of the Apparel Industry in El Paso, Texas, U.S.A." Presented at the meeting titled "Global Production, Regional Responses, and Local Jobs: Challenges and Opportunities in the North American Apparel Industry," arranged by the North American Studies Program and the Department of Sociology, Duke University, Durham, N.C., November 7.

————. 1997b. *Migration Between Mexico and the United States.* Binational Study on Migration. Washington, D.C.: U.S. Commission on Immigration Reform.

Staudt, Kathleen. 1998. *Free Trade? Informal Economies at the U.S.-Mexico Border.* Philadelphia: Temple University Press.

U.S. Information Agency (USIA). 1997. "Briefing Paper: Mexican Border Crossing Cards." October 9. Washington, D.C.: USIA.

Vélez-Ibáñez, Carlos, 1996. *Border Visions: Mexican Cultures of the Southwest United States.* Tucson: University of Arizona Press.

Verhovek, Sam Howe. 1997a. "After Marine on Patrol Kills a Teen-ager, a Texas Border Village Wonders Why." *New York Times,* June 29, p. A16.

————. 1997b. "Tiny Stretch of Border, Big Test for a Wall." *New York Times,* December 8, p. A1.

Vila, Pablo. Forthcoming. *Everyday Life, Culture and Identity on the Mexican-American Border: The Ciudad Juárez Case.* Austin: University of Texas Press.

Villar, María de Lourdes. 1994. "Hindrances to the Development of an Ethnic Economy Among Mexican Migrants." *Human Organization* 53, no. 3: 263–268.

Weintraub, Sidney. 1992. "North American Free Trade and the European Situation Compared." *International Migration Review* 26: 506–524.

Wilgoren, Jodi. 1997. "Company, 9 People Indicted in Alleged Immigrant Ring." *Los Angeles Times,* December 23, p. A4.

Woodrow, Karen A., and Jeffrey S. Passel. 1990. "Post-IRCA Undocumented Immigration to the United States: An Assessment Based on the June 1988 CPS." In *Undocumented Migration to the United States: IRCA and the Experience of the 1980s,* Frank D. Bean, Barry Edmunston, and Jeffrey S. Passel, eds. Washington, D.C.: Urban Institute Press, 33–72.

About the Contributors

Mathias Albert is a research associate in the World Society Research Group at the University of Frankfurt/Main. His current research interests are in the field of international relations theory, particularly international sociology. He has recently worked on the U.S.-Mexico border.

Lothar Brock is chair of international relations at the University of Frankfurt/Main. In addition to his interests in general international relations, he has published extensively on Latin American politics and development theory.

Julie Murphy Erfani is associate professor of politics in the Interdisciplinary Department of Social and Behavioral Sciences at Arizona State University West. She is author of *The Paradox of the Mexican State: Rereading Sovereignty from Independence to NAFTA* (Lynne Rienner 1995). Her forthcoming book on globalization, urban architecture, and power in Buenos Aires, Mexico City, Santiago, and São Paulo will be published by Duke University Press in 2000.

Bradley J. Macdonald teaches political theory in the Department of Political Science at Colorado State University. He is co-founder and co-editor of the interdisciplinary journal *Strategies: A Journal of Theory, Culture, and Politics*. He has published essays on the tradition of Western Marxism, cultural politics, and contemporary political theory, and is currently working on a genealogy of post-Marxism.

Bryan R. Roberts holds the C. B. Smith, Sr., Centennial Chair in U.S.-Mexico Relations and is professor of sociology at the University of Texas at Austin. After completing his doctorate at the University of Chicago in 1964, he returned to the United Kingdom and taught at the University of Manchester for twenty-two years until 1986. His research concentrates on social and economic development, primarily in Latin America, but also including Europe and the border region of the United States.

Olivia Ruiz, a cultural anthropologist, works at El Colegio de la Frontera Norte in Tijuana, Baja California, where she carries out research on ethnicity, migration, family, and gender along the U.S.-Mexico border. She is the co-editor of *Mujeres, Migración y Maquilas en la Frontera Norte* (Colegio de la Frontera Norte 1995) and *Reflexiones sobre la Identidad de los Pueblos* (Colegio de la Frontera Norte 1996).

Michelle A. Saint-Germain is associate professor at the Graduate Center for Public Policy and Administration at California State University, Long Beach. She is also director of the Bureau of Government Research and Service. Her research involves comparing public management practices of U.S. and Mexican municipal administrators.

David Spener is assistant professor of sociology at Trinity University in San Antonio, Texas. He has written several articles and book chapters on cultural, economic, and migration issues along the U.S.-Mexico border.

Kathleen Staudt is professor of political science at the University of Texas at El Paso. She has published more than fifty academic articles and ten books, the most recent of which are *Free Trade? Informal Economies at the U.S.-Mexico Border* and *Women, International Development and Politics: The Bureaucratic Mire* (Temple University Press 1998). She works with a variety of regional and community organizations at the U.S.-Mexico border. Her next book, with Susan Rippberger, examines education and nationalism in public schools on both sides of the border.

Pablo Vila is assistant professor of sociology at the University of Texas, San Antonio. He has published several essays on identity issues in the *Sociological Quarterly, Studies in Latin American Popular Culture, Popular Music, Latin American Music Review, Transcultural Music Review,* and *Frontera Norte.* Currently, he is completing two book projects: an ethnograpy on narrative identities on the U.S.-Mexico border and an edited volume on migration, culture, and identity in Ciudad Juárez–El Paso.

Víctor Zúñiga is professor of sociology at the Universidad de Monterrey and a member of the doctoral committee for the social sciences at the Universidad Autónoma de Nuevo León.

Index

African American, 12, 172–173, 184.
  See also ethnicity
Alegría, Tito, 40, 108
Anderson, Benedict, 18
Anglo, 156, 186, 195, 197, 198. *See
  also* ethnicity
anthropology, 20, 22, 148, 173
Anzaldúa, Gloria, 6, 15–16, 169
apartheid, 18
architecture, 150–166
Aristide, Jean-Bertrand, 23
art, 176, 178, 182
Association for Borderlands Scholars,
  27n.12

Baja California. *See* Tijuana
Bhabha, Homi, 6, 44–45
Border Patrol, 234–235, 241, 243, 245,
  247
border(s), 5, 14–17, 84; conceptualized
  as spaces, 4–5, 144, 150, 227; constructions of, 37–38, 46, 145,
  216–231; crossers, 27n.2, 94, 97,
  101n.12, 105–119, 149, 225, 233,
  235, 237–238, 245; diversity along,
  72, 83–100, 217, 235; exceptionalism, 87; internal, 40–44, 83, 149,
  225, 252n.6; materialist views, 6,
  14–15, 251; metaphors, 6, 14–17,
  19, 144–166, 169–182, 251; public-
  private, 11–12, 19, 148, 226; statistics, 4, 16, 21, 60; typologies, 15, 38,
  66–67; urban, 143. *See also* debordering; geography; immigration;

rebordering; U.S.-Mexico border;
  and specific cities
boundary, international, 4, 7, 35, 144,
  216–231. *See also* border(s)
bureaucracy, 10–11; surveillance of,
  23–24, 36. *See also* public officials
business, 83–98, 233, 242. *See also*
  NAFTA

California, 125, 232, 241–242. *See also*
  specific cities
Canada, 226, 227
Catholic church, 37, 134
Chicano, 185–210. *See also* ethnicity
citizenship, 19, 22, 122–124, 136,
  221–222, 228, 239, 240, 243, 244,
  247, 252n.7
Ciudad Juárez, 5, 60, 64–78, 83–98,
  122–136, 144–145, 201, 233,
  245–246
class, economic, 14, 18, 20, 154
Colegio de la Frontera Norte (COLEF),
  83, 93, 111, 127
colonias, 121–122, 125
culture, 3, 14–22, 23, 106–107,
  118–119, 170–172, 177–178, 188,
  190, 203, 205, 223; civic, 121–122,
  129, 136

debordering, 215–231, 236, 237–240
de Certeau, Michael, 170, 174, 175,
  181
democracy, 48–51. *See also* culture,
  civic

261

disciplines, 3, 6, 15, 17–18, 22, 24, 145
Durkheim, Emile, 9–10

education, 75, 112, 197, 208n.3,
    209n.10, 242
El Paso, 5, 60, 64–78, 83–98, 122–136,
    144–145, 185–210, 223, 245, 248
El Paso Interreligious Sponsoring
    Organization (EPISO), 125, 134
empires, 37
employment, 242, 253n.16. *See also*
    labor
environment, 69, 71, 226
EPISO. *See* El Paso Interreligions
    Sponsoring Organization
ethnicity, 19, 40–41, 46–47, 90, 105,
    118–119, 185–210, 223. *See also*
    African American; Anglo; Chicano;
    Latino; Mexican American
Europe, 37, 39, 47, 50–52, 216, 218,
    220–221, 223–225, 227–228, 236

federalism, 71, 127, 133
feminist, 15, 18–19, 143–150, 156
Foucault, Michel, 27n.3, 190–191
Foucher, Michel, 36, 39

gender, 14, 15, 18, 45, 145, 154
geography, 15, 39, 46, 51, 144, 217,
    235; cultural, 45, 149
geo-politics, defined, 145
globalization, 3, 22, 143–144, 147–149,
    154, 157, 173, 222, 227, 231; cities
    in, 23, 219, 224
graffiti, 143, 171–182
Gramsci, Antonio, 19, 27n.3, 189, 190
Guadalupe Hidalgo, Treaty of, 38, 250
Guatemala, 14

health, public, 112–113, 119, 129, 136,
    136n.4, 242, 244
Houston, 47–48, 238; University of,
    27n.2, 248, 253n.16

identity, 169–182, 186–210, 222, 228,
    239–240, 244
immigration, 4, 12–13, 23, 24, 47,
    122–125, 173, 221–222, 234, 238,
    242, 248–250
indigenous people, 25, 36–43, 45–46,

50–51, 52n.3, 52n.4. *See also* ethnic-
    ity; Mesoamerican
interdisciplinary, 3. *See also* disciplines
international relations, 3, 20, 144,
    215–231

Juárez. *See* Ciudad Juárez

King Jr., Martin Luther, 12

labor, 23, 85, 235, 244, 245; division of,
    7–9, 23; global, 10, 15, 18, 173;
    informal, 23, 93, 122, 159–165;
    253n.16; reserves, 24, 85; unions,
    68, 244. *See also* class; globalization
language, 7–9, 23, 27n.4, 107, 112, 127,
    133, 180, 189, 190–191, 209n.9
Latino, 170, 206, 242–243, 249. *See
    also* ethnicity
liberalism, 41–42, 48–50; trade, 84–85,
    87, 99, 150–155, 161, 164, 218–220,
    227, 245. *See also* maquiladoras;
    NAFTA
Los Angeles, 46, 47, 108, 143, 169–182,
    242, 247

mapping, 6, 22–23, 52, 149, 228. *See
    also* borders
maquiladoras, 4, 15, 64, 83, 85, 86, 88,
    128, 201, 226, 236, 245–246
Marx, Karl, 9–10, 27n.3, 27n.8
media, 122, 132–134
men, 121, 129
Mesoamerican, 143, 148, 149–150, 157,
    160
mestizaje, 41–43
Mexican American, 85–98, 110–119,
    185–210. *See also* ethnicity; social
    capital
Mexico, 14, 36, 40–52, 143–166,
    227–228, 246; internal borders in,
    40–43; people of, 110, 124,
    185–210, 237–240, 243–244,
    249–250. *See also* U.S.-Mexico bor-
    der
Mexico City, 143–166
Mexico-U.S. border. *See* U.S.-Mexico
    border
military. *See* security
migration. *See* immigration

modernity, 35, 42–45, 48–50
Monterrey, 48, 98, 126

NAFTA. *See* North American Free
  Trade Agreement
nation-state, 3, 17–21, 144, 155, 164,
  215–231; boundaries thereof, 13–14,
  35–52; welfare from, 112, 117, 235,
  242, 244
North American Free Trade Agreement
  (NAFTA), 15, 23, 74–75, 78, 83,
  85–87, 151, 226–227, 233, 244,
  247n.12, 247n.14, 252; community
  of, 136; explained, 63–64, 68–69,
  85–87; pre-NAFTA, 91, 97, 235

organizations, collective, 11–12,
  122–136, 192; global movements,
  220–224

police, 172–174, 182, 243
political machinery, 18, 124, 129
political parties, 125–126, 130, 209n.10
political science, 20
Portes, Alejandro, 12–13, 90, 124
poverty, 112, 172, 206
public interest, 59–78
public officials, 17, 44, 51, 59–75,
  151–152, 164, 234–235; services,
  126–127, 129, 136

race, 12, 154
racism, 172
rebordering, 236, 237, 240–245, 249
religion, 134–135, 230

Rodríguez, Néstor, 24, 238, 240
Rosaldo, Renato, 16–17, 22
Rouse, Roger, 4, 243

San Antonio, 94–96
San Diego, 5, 39, 106–119, 247
schools. *See* education
security, national, 23, 61, 217, 240
social capital, 80, 92, 93, 98–99, 101n.9
space, 4–5, 101–109, 114, 117–118,
  122; urban, 144–149, 155, 161,
  171–175, 180–181
state. *See* nation-state

Tijuana, 5, 39, 106–119, 161, 172, 238,
  247
Tocqueville, Alexis de, 123–124
trade. *See* business; labor; liberalism;
  NAFTA
transnational communities, 23,
  148–149, 150–151, 153, 157, 230.
  See also organizations
Treaty of Guadalupe Hidalgo, 38, 250
Turner, Frederick Jackson, 15

United States, 37. *See also* Border
  Patrol; public officials; *specific
  cities*
U.S.-Mexico border, 3–6, 15, 23, 25,
  35–36, 39–40, 51, 144, 161, 207. *See
  also* border(s), crossers

Weber, Max, 9–11, 18, 217, 230
women, 111–112, 117, 123, 124, 129,
  134, 135, 136n.6, 209n.7, 242, 245

About the Book

Exploring the construction of spatial lines and zones in physical, social, and academic terms, this volume presents the U.S.-Mexico border as a site from which to survey both the social and economic networks and the issues of identity and symbolism that surround borders.

The editors provide a theoretical introduction to the intrinsic nature of borders, as well as an overview of current trends in borderlands studies, to serve as a framework for the contributors' case studies. A concluding section examines the implications of transcending traditional borders.

David Spener is assistant professor of sociology at Trinity University. **Kathleen Staudt** is professor of political science at the University of Texas at El Paso. Her most recent publications include *Free Trade? Informal Economies at the U.S.-Mexico Border* and *Women, International Development and Politics: The Bureaucratic Mire.*

the outside; they commit suicide." Without love, we will all rot from within—individuals, nations and civilizations.

Christianity preaches the love of God and the brotherhood of man. If it can win significant converts to express this love in action, Christianity will emerge as the outstanding world religion, which will involve an understanding and tolerance of different cultures and varying concepts of the universe.

The Christian philosophy that apathy and laziness get us nowhere and its insistence that we must use our talents lest we lose them, has evolved a progressive civilization. The philosophies of Eastern religions state that each individual is responsible only for himself and this has led to acceptance of the *status quo,* rather than to progress. In being passive rather than aggressive, however, they do not attack Christianity or any other religion or ideology and thus are not inclined to wage war.

Communism is a third and powerful force, but it accepts neither God nor immortality. Its Utopia of universal liberty and equality may be reached by barbaric means. As Adlai Stevenson put it, "Communism resolves no anxieties. It multiplies them. It organizes terror. It is without spiritual content or comfort. It provides no basic security."

Russia is already discovering that her Utopia does not work. Suspicion of the motives of others and hatred of success elsewhere may still cause communistic leadership to do a great deal of harm. Moreover, communism cannot provide the inspiration necessary for a progressive psychosocial evolution. Our only hope for progress lies in a revitalized and unified Christianity.

THE PHYSICAL UNIVERSE

In the preceding chapter I stated that there is a polarity between spirit and matter. It seems foolish to ignore either the one or the other in our search for the meaning of eternal life. We have noted how the ancient Greeks acquired mistaken notions of certainty because of their misconceptions regarding the nature of the universe. It seems pertinent, therefore, to inject here the recent views of physicists and astronomers regarding the physical cosmos.

To understand the immortality of the sidereal requires a vivid imagination. There are from 100- to 200-billion stars in our galaxy, which is known as the Milky Way. And the Milky Way is only one of billions of galaxies.

Astronomers have not yet agreed on how the universe began. The Bible says: "In the beginning God created the heaven and the earth" (Genesis 1:1). Professor F. Hoyle of Cambridge University claims that the universe is everlasting, without a beginning or an end, and that matter is continuously being created somewhere. But others say that the universe began with a "big bang" explosion of a giant atom and this happened some fifteen billion years ago.

At this writing, great excitement is stirring astronomers because of the discoveries made by Dr. Allen R. Sandage of the Mt. Wilson and Palomar observatories. Dr. Sandage discovered a novel class of distant blue celestial objects, that does not emit radio signals. These new quasi-stellar blue galaxies were discovered unexpectedly while he was looking for quasi-stellar radio sources (QSRS). The distance of these quasi-stellar blue galaxies (QSBG) from the earth is so great that, as we observe their light, we are looking at a part of the universe as it was before our sun and earth were formed.

From the preliminary evidence provided by his observation of nine QSRSs and three QSBGs, Dr. Sandage has drawn the following conclusions: the universe is a closed, finite, and pulsating universe in which the expansion is gradually slowing down. In part he has estimated that the life of the universe takes 40 billion years to expand and 40 billion years to contract. Fifteen billion years ago our present universe began with a big bang explosion. Accordingly, if Dr. Sandage's conclusion is correct, we have another 25 billion years left for expansion, and another 40 billion years before we return to the giant egg.

In other words, one universe succeeds another in endless life cycles of about 80 billion years—an explosion causing an expansion followed by an inevitable contraction, which condenses the energy within the universe into an unimaginable concentration of power. Presumably this increased power explodes at a given point and a new universe is born.

Thus, modern astronomers agree with the Hindus who stated long ago that one universe follows another in endless succession. If this theory is true, energy or matter is immortal: it merely expands and contracts.

But, if the universe is basically and eternally indestructible, it is not explained how this colossal amount of energy came into being. The only statement that can be made about it is that it always was and always will be.

A VIEW OF IMMORTALITY

Modern theologians do not concern themselves with cosmology. In view of the size of the sidereal it makes sense to leave astronomy to the astronomers. Would it not be wise to leave energy to the physicists?

In one way, yes; in another, no. We do not know yet what energy is, but we should give physicists all our support in their continued research. There are now two recognized forms of energy: matter and antimatter, which are "allergic" to each other. That much we know.

A century ago, the belief that someday we might prove the existence of antimatter might have been ridiculed. Today, we are skeptical about the existence of consciousness apart from the physical body. But if antimatter exists independently of matter, is it foolish to visualize the existence of a world of active consciousnesses—which for lack of a better word we call a spirit world—independent of the body?

Naturalists take the view that consciousness is a by-product of the physical universe, never that the physical universe is a product of consciousness. This is in direct opposition to the Christian belief that God, the great consciousness, created all there is. Can man (whose mind has performed wonders on this earth in an incredibly short period of time), in looking at the majestic complexity of the universe, not visualize a consciousness far superior to his own?

It would be absurd to assume that in the vast stellar regions the increasing consciousness of our human species is preeminent. We should think of ourselves as just one of the numerous units of consciousness which are gradually graduating into the "unobstructed" universe—where we will use our supraconsciousness in useful creativity. Time and space are the essential measurements of the physical universe. Consciousness, however, cannot be so measured. Consciousness moves in any direction or, rather, it is pres-

ent anywhere at the command of the will. As such it anni-
hilates space; it is timeless: the past, present, and future
are its trinity.

So why should we not take the view that the basic energy (as Pierre Teilhard suggested) is psychic energy and
that the material universe serves consciousness because
the Great Creative Source *is* consciousness and his universe exists *by* and *for* consciousness?

Then, we may think of matter as a form of condensed or
primitive energy, which serves as the essential polarity to
spirit. Whatever the final explanation may be, we cannot
escape the fact that polarity is manifested throughout the
universe.

It seems to me that unless theologians accept this view
of the cosmos, they cannot present the foundation on
which the claim of Christian immortality must rest.

We may hold as many tentative views about the ultimate nature of energy and the cosmos as we wish, as long
as our faith in the creativity of God is as solid as rock.

I have tried to show that a supercivilization is only a
preview of immortal life. Uncivilized as well as civilized
life, however, is a phase of immortality. But, when the consciousness rises to the state of pure spirit, its procedure
changes: the soul must be a self-starter, it must be morally
incorrupt; *it must find joy in work.*

The old concept of a tribal God holding court in His
family palace is no longer serviceable. The human mind
can discard old myths but can it live without new ones?

We may hold a tentative view concerning the truth or
reality of a theory, but in the mainstream of life we need
commitments to basic values. In the realm of morals, humanism or an ethical society may provide us with the necessary supplies for commitment. But Christianity goes far

271

beyond that. Christianity must stand or fall on the basis of personal immortality. Without personal immortality, Christianity loses its vitality, its very reason for being. (Witness the overflow attendance at Easter services.) Christianity, with a conviction of immortality which does not defy reason but is in accord with the highest knowledge and assumptions of man, will become the most vitalizing religion in the world.

How can we visualize immortality as a process?

First of all, evolution is the process by which God arranges the ascent of consciousness; the highest development of consciousness is its creativity.

Creativity is a process; creativity is love in action, love in and for whatever we are doing. Our immortality can be in that process only.

When we have mastered the process of creativity through physical experience and we no longer live in physical planes but live and move and have our being in the realm of the spirit, what—as youngsters on earth so frequently ask—what is there to do?

The answer is not as difficult as it may seem. Those who have already acquired the ability to engage in scientific research know the challenge and excitement found in such work. The more one discovers the more one becomes convinced of the *inexhaustibility* of research.

Creativity is a process that extends eternally into the infinite. Perhaps we may rest occasionally, as God is said to have rested on the seventh day from His labor of creation. But work—as Jesus so clearly stated—is the primary occupation of God and His children. *And any labor done in love is creative.*

Jesus also said: "In my Father's house are many mansions . . ." (John 14:2). Could not this mean that we shall

272

live and work together in groups with congenial interest? Also, such groups may combine in the performance of greater tasks. Why should we assume that cooperation is limited to earth?

As we grow through billions of years of knowledge and the power of creativity, we may perform tasks far beyond our present imaginations. We may witness the formation of new planets and we may, together with other groups, be given the task to undertake the development of life and the ascent of consciousness on one of these newly formed planets.

In spite of the little we know, man's creative imagination has accomplished much on this earth already, and this should strengthen our faith in the vision of untold wonders yet to come. Jesus expressed His belief in the progress of man when he said, ". . . He that believeth on me, the works that I do shall he do also; and greater works than these shall he do . . ." (John 14:12).

Our life on earth has been enriched by the workers in conscious creativity. The blind have been made to see; the lame to walk. Now, man can fly and his creative imagination has reached the moon and aims for the stars. But all this is only a clue to what the creative consciousness of man may accomplish in the future. How truly exciting are the prospects of man's creativity *in heaven* as well as on earth!

OUR RESPONSE TO THE UNKNOWN

If religion is our response to the unknown, then its focal point is: *how* do we respond?

We may respond with doubt and timidity, with fear and

trembling, or with indifference. On the other hand, we may respond with faith and courage, with hope and enthusiasm, with love and determination. There is no escape from responding in some way.

Perhaps not in an earthshaking fashion, but nevertheless in a realistic sense, every tomorrow is an unknown event. Religion as our response to these unknown events is an integral part of our reactions to daily life. Or we may say that religion has become "blessedly" secularized, for our response to the unknown is positive.

If what has been said here about immortality is true, it must be clear that the Christian can only respond with all his heart and mind, with all his strength and love, for he knows that he is traveling in God's universe, in which the search eternal reveals progressively God's wonders. In our creative endeavors, we all are seeking after God.

Our response to the unknown must be twofold: individual and collective. Because we cannot separate ourselves from our own culture, we must not only be concerned with the factors determining our psychosocial evolution, our response must also be a positive one—translated into action.

Each search discussed in this book (and others could be added) exemplifies an area in our personal and social lives which challenges a specific response. But all of these searches—and all of their challenges—melt into one search eternal.

Our search for existence on earth is an integral part of our search for heaven. We must constantly seek answers to new and perplexing questions. We must ever search for more knowledge. We must commit ourselves to justice in the search for law and values. Wisdom crowns the union of knowledge and understanding; it blends goodness with truth. The search for wisdom is basic to personal and so-

cial development. Our search for happiness finds fulfillment in loving others as ourselves and presupposes that we
already have learned to love ourselves suitably and sufficiently. Our searches for Utopias require careful scrutiny
lest they lead us astray; the energy of these searches
should be channeled into workable ideals.

The search for God is basic in the understanding of our
role in the universe. Our search for God and our response
to the unknown are never ending. Our God is not a static
entity but a living God whose creation was not a one time
affair and whose creativity is never ceasing. In evolution
we see the eternally creative search at work. In the vast-
ness of the stars and the complexity of the microscopic elements of life our scientists are only beginning to see the
wonders of divine intelligence.

In our response to the unknown, in our search after
God, we are building the stairway to our own immortality.
The only immortality that exists in the universe is realized
in the eternally creative search. Contrary to Buddhistic
teachings we must not eradicate desire, we must encourage
it and *direct* it into the proper channels. Desire *is the life-
blood of all progress, whether in the flesh or in spirit.* God's
desire to create includes this or any other universe. Creativity is the replenishment of the self. When we are fulfilled
with the accomplishment of one creative act, the restless
urge of the search eternal inspires, prods, and moves us on
to the next endeavor.

Certainty is the opposite of doubt, and doubt we must if
we are to find certainty. In the struggle between doubt and
certainty, we must find our own assurance.

The search for self should convince us of the truth that
the happiness and security within the individual is not
found in existential feelings of loneliness and misery, but

275

in a reflection of the individual's interest in and concern for others, and in the pouring of his energies into creative activities, which means that he *enlarges his capacity to imbue all his endeavors with love.*

Finally we arrive at our search for the mystery of life. What is the basis of the universal energy which seemingly supports the universe? Here we have accepted Pierre Teilhard's assumption that all energy is basically psychic energy, and his statement that "Contrary to the appearance still admitted by physics the great stability is not at the bottom in the infra-elementary sphere but at the top in the ultra-synthetic sphere." [55]

Thus we have found our stability in the ultrasynthesis of the divine Consciousness and our concept of the universe must start with the power from on high which is the Great Creative Source we call God. Since it is God's nature to work and to be creative, our being in the image of God must not be thought of as an anthropomorphic reflection, but as an image of His consciousness. It is in this consciousness that we must rise and glorify our Father.

Consciousness is the final reality of the universe. But since there are degrees of consciousness there are also degrees of reality. Consciousness is not static; neither is reality. Motion and change are inseparable parts of the cosmos. For, if everything were endlessly fixed there would be no progress, no change, no life, no creativity of any kind. We must no longer think of ourselves as fixed, unchanging entities in the center of the universe, we must think of ourselves as part of a ceaseless creative process eternally in motion.

"The more man becomes," said Pierre Teilhard, "the less will he be prepared to move except toward that which is *interminably* and indestructibly new." [56]

The concept of the search eternal is not put forth merely to destroy the naïve belief in eternal bliss in a static heaven but to present a challenge worthy of our highest aspirations.

Naturally, our concept of God must exceed our concept of the sidereal, enormous as that concept is. In view of the majesty of the universe, an attempt by the leaders of the Christian church to make us more comfortable is long overdue. If such an attempt is not made, Christianity will lose its vitality, and it will become, primarily, a social organization emphasizing moral conduct. The church cannot ignore the cosmos and if the church continues to do so, increasing numbers of Christians will not.

The search eternal is basic in the architecture of the universe, because it expresses the nature of God and those created in His image.

The moral values contained in modern humanism are largely those of secularized religion, and while this is by no means to be deplored, the vision of the Christian must extend far beyond the dream of a supercivilization. We can work hand in hand with humanism to create a better world, but this is only a part of the greater vision for the Christian.

The search eternal is a never ending process operating between eternity and infinity. This never ending process is our chief concern, and our greatest need is to comprehend it more adequately.

In order to assume the responsibilities we have for ourselves and for society, more readily and cheerfully, we must accept the search eternal, which, rooted in eternal creativity, is the glory of God and the meaning of life.

The search for meaning is the search for self.

MARCUS BACH

The search for self
    is the search for life
                and
The search for life
    is the search for God;
The search for God
    is the search for His continuous creativity
                and
The search for God's continuous creativity
    is THE SEARCH ETERNAL,
In which we live, move and have our being.

SOURCE NOTES

PART I

1. Pierre Teilhard de Chardin, *The Phenomenon of Man* (New York, Harper & Brothers, 1959), p. 257.
2. Edmund W. Sinnoth, *Matter, Mind and Man* (New York, Harper & Brothers, 1957), p. 85.
3. Bertrand Russell, *Human Knowledge, Its Scopes and Limits* (New York, Simon and Schuster, Inc., 1962), p. 158.
4. Lyman Bryson, *An Outline of Man's Knowledge of the Modern World* (New York, McGraw-Hill Book Co., Inc., 1960), p. 2.
5. Russell, *op. cit.*, pp. v, 6.
6. *Loyola Digest,* June, 1962.
7. *Ibid.*
8. *Ibid.*
9. Lewis Mumford, "Irrational Elements in Art and Politics," *New Republic,* April 5 & 12, 1954.
10. *The Humanist Frame,* ed. Julian Huxley (New York, Harper & Brothers, 1961), p. 6.
11. *Ibid.*
12. *Ibid.,* pp. 277–8.
13. *Ibid.,* p. 272.
14. *Ibid.,* p. 7.

PART II

15. Paul Tillich, *Dynamics of Faith,* (New York, Harper & Brothers, 1957), p. 52.

16. *The Humanist Frame,* p. 402.

17. *The Philosophy of Alfred North Whitehead,* ed. Paul Arthur Schilpp (New York, Tudor Publishing Company, 1941).

18. Lincoln Barnett, *The Universe and Dr. Einstein* (New York, William Sloane Associates, Inc., rev. ed.), p. 109.

19. Paul Tillich, *The Shaking of the Foundations* (New York, Charles Scribner's Sons, 1948), pp. 180–81, paperback.

20. Tillich, *The Dynamics of Faith* (New York, Harper & Brothers, 1957), p. 61.

21. *Ibid.*

22. *Ibid.,* p. 62–63.

23. Tillich, *The Shaking of the Foundations* (New York, Charles Scribner's Sons, 1948), p. 59.

24. John A. T. Robinson, *Honest to God* (Philadelphia, The Westminster Press, 1963), p. 125, paperback.

25. Burnett Hillman Streeter, *Reality: A New Correlation of Science and Religion* (New York, the Macmillan Company, 1926), p. 129.

26. *Reincarnation, An East-West Anthology,* comps. & eds. Joseph Head and S. L. Cranston (New York, The Julian Press, Inc., 1961), pp. 302–3.

27. Barnett, *op. cit.,* p. 108.

28. Teilhard de Chardin, *op. cit.,* p. 258.

29. John Dewey, *The Quest for Certainty* (Gifford Lectures, New York, G. P. Putnam's Sons, 1929), p. 312.

30. *Ibid.,* p. 312.

31. Erich Fromm, *Man for Himself* (New York, Holt, Rinehart and Winston, Inc., 1961), p. 6.

32. Viktor E. Frankl, *Man's Search for Meaning* (Boston, Beacon Press, 1959), p. 108.

33. *Ibid.,* p. 106.
34. *Ibid.,* p. 120.
35. Henry Sloane Coffin, *The Meaning of the Cross* (New York, Charles Scribner's Sons, 1931), pp. 138–39.
36. Frankl, *op. cit.,* p. 104.
37. *The Humanist Frame,* p. 43.
38. *Space Age Christianity,* ed. Stephen F. Boyne, Jr. (New York, Morehouse-Barlow Co., Inc., 1963), p. 37.
39. Teilhard de Chardin, *The Phenomenon of Man,* pp. 267–68.
40. *Ibid.,* p. 281.
41. *Ibid.,* p. 59.
42. *Ibid.,* p. 62.
43. *Ibid.,* p. 63.
44. *Ibid.,* p. 64.
45. *Ibid.,* p. 271.
46. *Ibid.,* p. 60.
47. *Ibid.,* p. 258.
48. *Ibid.,* p. 251.
49. Sigmund Freud, *A General Introduction to Psychoanalysis* (New York, Liveright Publishing Corp., 1935), pp. 22–23.
50. Teilhard de Chardin, *op. cit.,* p. 275.
51. Alan W. Watts, *The Two Hands of God* (New York, George Braziller, Inc., 1963), p. 17.
52. *Ibid.,* p. 49.
53. Teilhard de Chardin, *The Phenomenon of Man,* p. 272.
54. *Ibid.,* p. 307.
55. *Ibid.,* p. 271.
56. *Ibid.,* p. 230.

GLOSSARY

ANTIMATTER—The antideuteron is the first complex atomic nucleus of antimatter known to exist. Its negative nuclei are surrounded by positive electrons. Antimatter is the reverse, or mirror-image, of matter as we know it. When bits of matter and antimatter meet, they annihilate each other, turning into light and heat.

ANTHROPOGENESIS—The evolution of man from his primitive beginning to his highest potential.

ASCENT OF CONSCIOUSNESS—The hypothesis that the goal of evolution is toward ever increasing consciousness.

COMPLEXIFICATION—A term used by Pierre Teilhard de Chardin, meaning: The Genesis of increasingly elaborate organization during cosmogenesis, as manifested in the passage from subatomic units to atoms, from atoms to inorganic and later to organic molecules, and then to cells, to multicellular individuals, to cephalized metazoa with brains, to primitive man, and now to civilized societies.

CONSCIOUSNESS—1.) Mind: present in all matter and living things, rising to self-awareness in man, reaching beyond man to the Great Consciousness-Operator of the universe. 2.) The basic reality of the universe. The degree of consciousness determines the degree of reality.

COSMIC POLARITY—The basic polarity of the universe on which all other polarities depend. Primarily it conveys the polarity of matter and spirit; matter serving for increased consciousness and supra-consciousness producing and manipulating matter, thus balancing the eternally creative evolution of the cosmos.

COSMOGENESIS—The creative process or evolution of the inorganic, organic, and spiritual aspects of the universe.

ENERGY—The basic "stuff" of the universe which comprises all manifestations of both the seen and the unseen realities of the cosmos. It has two major aspects: physical and psychic. The dominance of convergence over divergence is prominent in all areas of energy.

EVOLUTION—Five phases: 1) inorganic; 2) organic; 3) psychosocial; 4) purposive; 5) spiritual. The first two are accepted in accordance with present scientific knowledge and theory, except that in the biological development of homo sapiens, man may not have reached his highest form. The brain of man may, possibly, increase in size as well as in quality.

3.) The psychosocial evolution—a term used by Julian Huxley to denote Pierre Teilhard's concept of hominisation: All the processes and events which followed the appearance of man in our world and led to the socialization, intermingling, and interrelating of all mankind at the natural level. The process by which the original proto-human stock became, and is still becoming, more truly human. The process by which potential man realizes more and more of his capabilities.

4.) The purposive evolution—a higher phase of man's development, when he will be consciously directing the progress of the human race on a global scale, far beyond the present one. This would include setting goals for worldwide control

286

of population, eugenics, education, food and fresh water supplies, clean air, and, in general, applying scientific principles to improve the quality of the physical and mental aspects of man. Such progress is possible only after war—a barbarian instrument for settling disputes—is outdated.

5.) Spiritual evolution—is closely interwoven with both the psychosocial and purposive evolutions. Its goal is the progressive and spontaneous creativity of man. The full humanization of man will bring deeper spiritual insights. When man's spiritual evolution gains ascendance, new attitudes and behaviour produce a rise in consciousness and spiritual power, allowing man to become more fully and spontaneously creative. Since the consciousness or spirit-soul of man is indestructible, his spiritual evolution will continue, far beyond earthly time and space, in other areas of the cosmos.

HOMINISATION—Same as progressive psychosocial evolution.

INTELLECTRONICS—The extension of the mind by electronics.

INVOLUTION—Rolling up or folding in upon itself. (An irregular piece of steel, which was placed recently in a vacuum in outer space, rolled up and became a round ball. What science will learn from this spheric phenomenon is not yet known.)

LOVE—Cosmic affinity expressed through cosmic energy which is inherent in all that exists, from the inorganic to man. From the obvious differences in degree of affinity emerge new forms or kinds of love leading eventually to cosmic love. "Love the Lord thy God with all thy heart, and with all thy soul, and with all thy mind" (Matthew 12:37).

NOOSPHERE—Another word coined by Teilhard: The realm of the mind or reflective thought, the layer of thinking creatures—humans—who spread gradually over the surface of the earth. The sphere of mind superimposed on the biosphere and acting as a transforming agency which promotes hominisation.

SOUL—Soul and Spirit are frequently used interchangeably. But spirit comes first, then soul. (See Spirit.)

SPIRIT—An indestructible, immortal, and individualized part of the Great Spirit we call God. We are parts of God's spirit, as grains of sand are part of the beach. To better understand our individualized spirits, we may visualize them as viruses which we cannot see, feel, or weigh, but whose existence is nevertheless real. When spirit enters the human body the proper name for its life is soul, for soul changes the individualized life of body and being of spirit into a personalized entity. Spirit, soul and body form a trinity of being, desire and energy. The being, nature, and essence of our spirits never change; only our souls change and develop. Spirit as being is not subject to time and space, spirit as soul is. However, its temporary confinement in space-time enables it to grow in self-awareness. Spirit-soul, in occupying the body, becomes one with it. In their higher form within the process of cosmic polarity, the functions of matter and spirit are far beyond the comprehension of modern science and philosophy. We are only beginning to visualize some of the potentials. The realization that matter is as essential to spirit as spirit is to matter is important; they are the two basic elements in the eternal evolution of the Cosmic Organism.

SPIRIT OF THE EARTH—The electromagnetic atmosphere of psychic energy or mind surrounding the earth.

VASTY DEEP—A mystical term coined by Aldous Huxley meaning the inner core of reality.